GA

Why Catholic Bibles Are Bigger

Revised Second Edition

Published by Catholic Answers, Inc.
2020 Gillespie Way
El Cajon, California 92020
1-888-291-8000 orders
619-387-0042 fax
catholic.com

Printed in the United States of America

Cover design by Theodore Schluenderfritz
Interior design by Sherry Russell

978-1-68357-051-6
978-1-68357-052-3 Kindle
978-1-68357-053-0 ePub

Contents

Preface to the Second Edition 7
Acknowledgements 11
Introduction 13
Abbreviations 16

1. Was the Old Testament Closed Before Christ? 17
2. The Deuterocanon and the New Testament 49
3. The Closing of the Rabbinic Bible 71
4. The Bible of the Earliest Christians 83
5. When Contents Became Canon 117
6. Crossing the "Apocrypha" Line 145
7. The Age of Preservation 167
8. "As Jerome Saith . . ." 195
9. Florence, Trent, and the Renaissance 215
10. Why Protestant Bibles Are Smaller 237
11. The Deuterocanon in Exile 277
12. Answering the Ultimate Question 293

Appendix 1
Sola Scriptura and the Problem of the Canon............. 303
Appendix 2
The Deuterocanon and Biblical Inerrancy............... 311
Appendix 3
Esdras, Carthage, and Trent 317
Endnotes 325
Index 377

PREFACE TO THE SECOND EDITION

The first edition of *Why Catholic Bibles Are Bigger* was certainly a success by anyone's standard, especially in light of the limited resources available to produce and promote the book. It was the first book-length Catholic defense of the deuterocanon since A.E. Breen wrote his *General and Critical Introduction to the Sacred Scripture* back in 1897, and even Breen only dedicated about half of his pages to the topic. Needless to say, much of the material Breen offered in his book is now out of date (although a good portion of it is still serviceable), and apologetics on the deuterocanon was sorely in need of an update. More specifically, there needed to be a work that specifically tackled one of the questions most frequently asked by Protestants and Catholics: did the Council of Trent add books to Old Testament Scripture or did Protestantism remove them?

The question is easy to ask, but a good answer requires an enormous amount of research. The original manuscript for *Why Catholic Bibles Are Bigger* was well over a thousand pages, and it looked like, at one point, that it would come out as a two-volume set, far too long for a popular work on the subject.

In 2006, the mammoth task of editing began. Much of the book was left on the proverbial cutting room floor. While trying to trim down this unwieldy manuscript, the complexity of the subject made even the simplest edit difficult. Even citing a source correctly is not easy since different sources use different versification. As a result, the first edition was a solid work, but it did have its share of problems, such as typos and versification errors. Whatever its faults, though, reception of the first edition was very positive.

My attention was then drawn to other areas of apologetics. However, the deuterocanon remained one topic that I could never totally avoid. Over the past ten years, my research continued. I couldn't help but gather more data on the subject. Items that I decided not to include in the first edition because I felt I couldn't adequately substantiate the point became solidified. The years after the first edition also allowed me to get a better overall picture of the subject and see connections that I missed while working out the details. Along with my continuing research in the area of the deuterocanon, I also received some very good constructive criticism. Despite my best efforts, *Why Catholic Bibles Are Bigger* wasn't the easiest book to read for someone not already familiar with the topic. It didn't have an introduction. Some people expected *Why Catholic Bibles Are Bigger* to give a positive case for the deuterocanon being inspired Scripture, instead of focusing on the question of whether Protestantism or Catholicism changed the Old Testament canon. To meet the need for a positive case for the deuterocanon, I wrote my second book on the topic, *The Case for the Deuterocanon: Evidence and Arguments* (Nikaria Press, 2015).

The publication of that book helped bring into better focus what exactly *Why Catholic Bibles Are Bigger* needed to address. There were places where the first edition spent too little time looking at important issues and too much time looking at secondary issues. With more data to bring to the discussion and better appreciation of the overall subject, the time had come for a new edition.

Readers familiar with the first edition will notice several changes. The most glaring is disappearance of the footnotes that crowded the bottom of the page. Footnotes are very convenient for those who love details, but it tends to make the text appear intimidating. To improve readability, all the footnotes have been moved to the back of the book. Another change is the overall layout. The backbone of the first edition was its chronological layout, tracing the history of the deuterocanon from Sirach (c. 200–150 B.C.) to Vatican I (1870). The chronological layout is still retained, but this edition focuses more on addressing specific issues or questions than on laying out a detailed history. The chapter arrangement is also slightly different, so that those who do not wish to know whether the writers of the tenth century accepted these books can safely skip to the next chapter without missing too much. New treatments are offered on important issues and less important data is compressed to a short summary or placed in the endnotes. All these measures will hopefully make the book a faster and more pleasant read.

The issue of the deuterocanon is perhaps *the* most important subject for anyone who takes the word of God seriously. The question of whether books were added or removed needs to be answered, and the only way to give you the full and complex answer is to present the data for your consideration. My hope is that this new edition will serve to make this fascinating issue more easily understandable and to finally give a definitive answer to whether Catholicism or Protestantism changed the Old Testament.

ACKNOWLEDGEMENTS

"Amico fideli nulla est conparatio et non est digna ponderatio auri et argenti contra bonitatem fidei illius."
Sirach 6:15

There are a number of people I would like to acknowledge and thank for bringing this book to completion. First and foremost, I would like to give thanks to the Holy Spirit who has spoken through the prophets and has given us the Sacred Scripture as a treasure of his love and wisdom. I would also like to thank Rod Bennett who patiently worked through this book and made it warm, accessible, and readable for all. I would also like to thank the team of editors, proofreaders, and designers who helped to turn this book from research to reality, especially Dennis Walters, Adele Brinkley, Gigi Mills, Brenda Polk, and Launa and Alan Wakenhut. Thank you also Paul, Cassandra, and the Husak family for the gift of your time, wisdom, and support for this project. My gratitude is also extended to Diane Everett and John McAlpine for all their hard work. To my good friend Robert Corzine, whose advice and encouragement helped guide me through the entire development of this book. Many thanks to Douglas Eiben for spending hours in front of a hot photocopier. I also owe Steve Ray and Patrick Madrid a very large debt of gratitude for the constant support and guidance. I would especially like to thank Todd Aglialoro and the team at Catholic Answers Press for making this second edition possible. They have been faithful friends indeed. Finally, I would like to thank my wife Chris, and my children, Paulina, Daniel, and Jennifer, for their patience and understanding while I was running off to libraries.

INTRODUCTION

One evening I had the sad duty of attending my neighbor's funeral. My neighbors were not religious, but apparently a local "mega-church" offered to conduct the eulogy for them. The assistant pastor from the church stood up and after a few short remarks about the deceased began to give a lengthy sermon. The first ten minutes were dedicated to how he knew that my neighbor believed in Jesus and was in heaven, so there was no need to pray for her or offer Masses or anything like that. The next thirty minutes or so (it's difficult to tell since it seemed like eternity) were dedicated to explaining why it doesn't matter which church one attends—Catholic, Presbyterian, Methodist, Episcopalian, Lutheran—they are all the same! None of them are more correct than any other. "We all believe in the same fundamental biblical truths about Jesus," he said, "such as the need to put our faith in Jesus," and so on. The sermon (eulogy) ended with an invitation to come join his church.

Speaking at a funeral must not be an easy thing to do, so I walked up to the assistant pastor to thank him. After dispensing with niceties and explaining that I am a Catholic, I said to him, "Pastor, I just want to share with you a biblical verse that has always given me comfort in times like these. The book of Wisdom, chapter 3 says, 'But the souls of the righteous are in the hand of God, and no torment will ever touch them. In the eyes of the foolish they seemed to have died, and their departure was thought to be an affliction and their going from us to be their destruction; but they are at peace.'" The pastor gave me an odd look. "Book of Wisdom?" he said. "That's not in the Bible!" To which I responded, "Well, I guess there *are* important differences between us."

Out of respect for the family, I left it at that. It wasn't the place to engage in a debate. My hope was to highlight a few things that the pastor seemed oblivious to. The assistant pastor, for example, seemed to be oblivious to the fact that Catholic and Orthodox bibles contain seven books in their Old Testament that Protestant bibles omit. These are the books of Sirach (sometimes called *Ecclesiasticus*), Wisdom, Sirach (or *ben Sira*), Tobit, Judith, and 1st and 2nd Maccabees along with a longer version of Daniel and Esther. Catholics call these books the deuterocanon. Protestants, however, have rejected these books as inspired texts and call them the *Apocrypha*.

Despite the assistant pastor's best efforts to be non-denominational and dispel the importance of religious dogmas, he and his church actually held a very dogmatic view on which books belonged to the Bible. Going by the generic name of "Christian" didn't release him from dogmatically committing himself to a particular doctrine on which books the Bible comprises. This position is undeniably important. Which collection or canon one adopts, whether Catholic or Protestant, will determine whether the first ten minutes of his sermon was "biblical" or a flight of fancy.

The question of which books belong to the Bible (especially the Old Testament, since Catholics and Protestant share the same New Testament books) is more fundamental of a question than anything in anyone's theology, because theology is to be based upon divine revelation. What makes up God's revelation, therefore, has a direct impact on one's theology. This is especially true for Protestants who believe in *sola scriptura*, which says that the Bible is the only source of Christian doctrine. It is, for nearly all Protestants, the norm that sets all norms and the standard that sets all standards: the highest court of appeal for judging all doctrine. But as we have painfully learned over the last few decades, those who are allowed to sit on the Supreme Court will affect how the court rules. This assistant pastor's "Supreme Court" (i.e., the Bible) informed him that we should not pray for the dead, but Catholic and Orthodox bibles affirm that we should. Each position is "biblical" given its respective Bible, but which Bible has the correct books? Which books are inspired by the Holy Spirit, and which ones are mere human apocrypha? This question needs to be settled first.

How did Protestants and Catholics end up with two different Old Testaments? Protestants claim that the Catholic Church added the seven books of the "Apocrypha" to the canon of Scripture in order to refute Protestantism. This is generally said to have occurred at the Fourth Session of the Council of Trent (April 8, 1546). Catholics make the opposite claim; they claim that these same books were always considered inspired Scripture, but they were rejected by Protestantism because their teaching contradicts certain areas of Protestant theology. Which is correct? Did the Catholic Church *add* books to the Old Testament, or did Protestantism *remove* these books from the canon of Scripture?

Both answers assume something about the status of these books prior to the Protestant Reformation. If the Council of Trent added these books to the Bible then they couldn't have been accepted as inspired Scripture before Trent, and if Protestant removed these books then they must have been accepted as inspired Scripture before. Therefore, in order to answer whether the deuterocanon was added or removed, we need to step back and look at its history, zeroing in every now and then on some pivot issues in order to answer this question.[1] The purpose of this book is not to prove or disprove the inspiration of the deuterocanon *per se*, but to determine how and why Protestants and Catholics have two different Old Testament canons.

ABBREVIATIONS

ABD	Anchor Bible Dictionary
ANF	Anti-Nicene Fathers (Robertson)
CBQ	Catholic Biblical Quarterly
CE	Catholic Encyclopedia (1908 ed.)
DS-H	Denzinger-Schonmetzer (Hünermann ed.)
EJ	Encyclopedia Judaica
FEF	Faith of the Early Fathers (Jurgens)
HTR	Harvard Theological Review
IDB	Interpreter's Dictionary of the Bible
IJA	International Journal of the Apocrypha
JE	Jewish Encyclopedia
JCB	Jerome Biblical Commentary
JTS	Journal of Theological Studies
JBR	Journal of Biblical Religion
NCC	New Catholic Commentary of the New Testament
NTS	New Testament Studies
PG	*Patrologia Graecae* (Migne)
PL	*Patrologia Latina* (Migne)
ZAW	*Zeitschrift für die Alttestamentliche Wissenschaft*

All emphasis in ancient sources is added.

1

Was the Old Testament Canon Closed Before Christ?

The first step on our journey to find out why Catholic bibles have seven more Old Testament books than Protestant bibles is to go back to the beginning, before the time of Christ. Opponents of the deuterocanon sometimes claim that the Old Testament was already a closed fixed collection of books long before the time of Christ, perhaps centuries before the first deuterocanonical book was written. If this is true, obviously, the deuterocanon could not be part of the Bible, or so it is argued.

It is easy to make such a claim, but it is very difficult (if not impossible) to substantiate it since there is nothing mentioned in the *protocanonical* books of the Old Testament (the books that Catholics and Protestants hold in common), nor are there any pre-Christian contemporary accounts of the closing of the Old Testament. But if there are no contemporary sources of this closure, how can the claim be made? Essentially, those who argue the point are forced to rely on Christian and post-Christian rabbinic sources, supposedly written centuries after the fact, as evidence.

In addition to late sources, the claim of a closed pre-Christian canon is riddled with ambiguity. If the Old Testament canon was definitively closed, who closed it, and when, and by what authority? The best answer to these questions is usually the vague and unhelpful response that "the Jewish community closed it."

If we cannot answer those questions about the closing of the canon, how do we know that a pre-Christian closure occurred? Three arguments are commonly given.

First, since all Scripture comes from God, all Scripture is revelatory or prophetic. But the deuterocanonical book of 1 Maccabees denies the existence of prophets in its day (late second century B.C.). Therefore, since 1 Maccabees denies that it can be "prophetic"—since it states that there were no prophets around when it was written—the canon must have been closed at that time.

The second argument is based on evidence from the New Testament. This argument claims that there are four passages in the New Testament (Matthew 23:35; Luke 11:50–51, 24:44; Romans 3:2) that indicate that the contents of Jesus' Bible is identical to what later became the rabbinic Bible. Since the rabbinic Bible excluded the deuterocanon, Jesus' Bible must have excluded it as well.

The third argument can be called the "cessation of prophecy" theory. It claims that all prophecy ceased in Israel after the time of King Artaxerxes (around the fifth century B.C.). Therefore, as in the first argument, since prophets and prophecy ceased centuries before Christ, Scripture could no longer be written beginning at that time. The deuterocanon cannot be Scripture.

Taken together, these three lines of argument seem persuasive. But since the word of God is our subject, we need to see whether each argument can stand up to scrutiny. Let's begin by taking a closer look at the claim that 1 Maccabees denies the existence of prophets in its time.

Did Maccabees Deny Its Own Inspiration?

Does 1 Maccabees deny its own inspiration by denying the

existence of a prophet? Three passages are usually adduced to substantiate this claim. The texts are:

> And they thought it best to tear it down, lest it bring reproach upon them, for the Gentiles had defiled it. So they tore down the altar, and stored the stones in a convenient place on the temple hill until there should come a prophet to tell what to do with them (4:45–46).
>
> And the Jews and their priests decided that Simon should be their leader and high priest forever, until a trustworthy prophet should arise (14:41).
>
> Thus there was great distress in Israel, such as had not been since the time that prophets ceased to appear among them (9:27).

If 1 Maccabees says that prophets no longer existed in Israel at this date, it is argued, then it cannot be "prophetic" Scripture. We will later encounter these same passages in the third argument as well.

Before we examine these texts more closely, let's give more thought to the premise that all prophetic writings (Scripture) must be written by prophets. Is this true? What does Scripture show us in this regard?

Prophets and Scripture

When we look at the protocanonical books of the Old Testament, we find that not all of its books were written by people who were known to be prophets. Ezra and Nehemiah are two good examples. They wrote inspired texts, yet neither of them was known to be a prophet. Ezra was a priest and a scribe (Ezra 7:6, 11–12; Neh. 8:1, 4, 9, 13; 12:26; 12:36) and Nehemiah was a cupbearer for the king (Neh. 1:11). The book of

Proverbs likewise mentions several people who contributed to this inspired work, but a few are not identified as prophets either. For example, the thirtieth chapter was written by a man named Agur. Was Agur a prophet? We know that his words are prophetic because they are recorded in Scripture, but that's about it. Likewise, Proverbs 31:1–9 is Scripture even though it is the words of the mother of King Lemuel of Massa, an Ishmaelite. Was this Ishmaelite mother a prophetess? Most probably she wasn't. However, she did write prophetic Scripture. If these people were known as things other than prophets (e.g., priest, scribe, cupbearer, king's mother, etc.), how can they compose prophetic Scripture?

The problem is a matter of equivocation. The word *prophet* is being used in two different senses. The title generally refers to someone who is publically recognized as holding the office of a prophet, such as Samuel, Isaiah, or Jeremiah. Their life's call is to give divine oracles. Since these people were publically known as prophets, we will call them—for lack of a better term—*public* prophets. But there is another meaning to the term that is much broader: any person (a wise man, a priest, a scribe, or even a king's mother) through whom God reveals himself. Although these people were never publically recognized as prophets during their lifetime, they were recognized as such later when their writings were acknowledged as being revelatory (i.e., inspired). We will call these people *post facto* prophets (after-the-fact prophets) because they were recognized as prophets *only after* their writings had been accepted as Scripture. Therefore, when it is asserted that "prophets ceased to appear in Israel," we must ask whether the statement is referring to *public* prophets or *post facto* prophets.

If *public* prophets ceased to appear in Israel, then it does not follow that inspired (prophetic) Scripture could not be written, since we know that Scripture can be written by people who were not known to be prophets or prophetesses (Ezra, Nehemiah, Lemuel's mother, etc.). If, on the other hand, the statement "prophets ceased to appear in Israel" refers to *post facto* prophets, then we have a circular argument, since it argues that no *post facto* prophets existed because there is no Scripture, and there is no Scripture because there were no *post facto* prophets to write it.

Looking at the three passages from 1 Maccabees, the author is clearly speaking about people who were *public* prophets. Therefore, 1 Maccabees still can be "prophetic" Scripture like the other texts that were written by *post-facto* prophets such as Ezra the priest or Nehemiah the cupbearer.

But didn't 1 Maccabees say that prophets were a thing of the past? Oddly enough, the first two passages quoted above (4:45–46; 14:41) actually imply the opposite. Re-read the passages. Both anticipate that a prophet would soon arrive and set things in order. If prophets permanently ceased, there would be no reason to expect their future arrival.

With this in mind, let's look at the third passage, 1 Maccabees 9:27. It speaks of a period of "great distress" when "all prophecy had ceased in Israel." Unfortunately, no further detail is given about this period. Was it a temporary or a permanent condition? We've already seen that the Maccabees expected the immediate arrival of a prophet, so we know that this period of distress was only temporary, not permanent. And indeed, we know of examples in Scripture where it is said that God temporarily withheld prophets or prophecy during periods of great distress. For example, Psalm 74:9 says, "We do not see our signs; there is no longer any prophet, and there is none among us who knows how long." We know that this period was not permanent, since prophets returned and prophesied and more inspired Scripture was written. The same can be said for Lamentations 2:9:

> Her gates have sunk into the ground; he has ruined and broken her bars; her king and princes are among the nations; the law is no more, and her prophets obtain no vision from the Lord.

Again, the condition was temporary, since prophets appeared and Scripture was written afterward. Given that the Maccabees expected the arrival of a prophet, the period of "great distress" mentioned in 1 Maccabees 9:27 is analogous to periods described in Psalm 74:9 and Lamentations 2:9 when no prophets prophesied. There is no need to read into this passage 400 years of prophetic silence.

Did Jesus Inherit a Closed Canon of Scripture?

What about the New Testament? Is there evidence in the New Testament that the Old Testament canon was closed and fixed long before the time of Christ, and so Jesus' Bible didn't include the deuterocanon? Three passages are often adduced to prove that such was the case. Let's look at each in turn.

Our first passage is from Luke 24:44, which reads,

> Then he said to them, "These are my words which I spoke to you, while I was still with you, that everything written about me in the Law of Moses and the prophets and the psalms must be fulfilled."

The argument runs like this: although it's true that the ancient Jews did not use the terms *Bible* or *canon*, they developed a stock idiom that they regularly employed when referring to the entire body of inspired Scripture; that idiom is "the Law, the Prophets, and the Writings," or *Tanakh* for short.[2] Jesus uses this stock phrase in Luke 24:44, which shows that his Bible followed the divisions of what was later known as the *Tanakh*. Since the *Tanakh* never included the deuterocanon, it is argued, Jesus' Bible likewise excluded the deuterocanon as well.

This argument reaches a bit when it assumes that "the Law, the Prophets, and the Writings" was a stock idiom during the time of Christ. The earliest known use of this idiom in Christian or rabbinic literature dates around the middle of the second Christian century.[3] It's never used in the deuterocanon or the New Testament.

The earliest known attempt to speak of Scripture as a whole by a three-fold division is found in the preface to the deuterocanonical book of Sirach (c. 200 B.C.). Curiously, Sirach's grandson, who wrote the preface, fails to provide a name for the third division later known as the Writings. Instead, he speaks of "the law, the prophets, *and the later authors*" or "the law, the prophets, *and the rest of the books of our ancestors*" or "the law itself, the prophets and *the rest of the books*."[4] In three attempts, the author fails to provide a consistent name for the third division, assigning it instead the rather open-ended descriptions of "the later authors," "the rest of the books of our ancestors," and "the rest of the books." Why this ambiguity? If the one normative collection of Old Testament books was settled centuries earlier, why hasn't the last division become formalized like the first two? The preface's ambiguity may suggest that the Old Testament canon was still open when Sirach's grandson wrote his preface.

When we move closer to the time of Jesus, we find 2 Maccabees (written around 150 B.C.) speaking of the whole of Scripture as "the law and the prophets" (15:9), and the same bi-partite division is found at Qumran as well.[5] The Jewish philosopher and contemporary of Jesus, Philo of

Alexandria, also didn't use the stock idiom that was adopted later in the rabbinic Bible.[6] The New Testament, like 1 Maccabees, usually refers to the whole of Scripture simply as "the law and the prophets."[7] If Jesus ever used a stock idiom of a three-fold divided Scripture, Luke 24:44 appears to be the only instance, which is strange given that it was supposedly well known.

The real problem is this: Jesus didn't use the standard phrase "the Law, the Prophets, and the Writings" in Luke 24:44! Instead, he says, "the Law of Moses and the prophets *and the psalms*." When Jesus says, "and the psalms" is he referring to a whole division of Scripture known as the "Writings" or is he referring to the book of Psalms?

The first rule of exegesis is not to go beyond the plain meaning of a text unless there is something in the context that demands such a change. The plain meaning of Luke 24:44 is "the law, the prophets and the [Book of] Psalms," not "the Law, the Prophets and [the writings that are being called] the Psalms." There is nothing in the context that demands that we understand the psalms to be a synecdoche for a whole division of books. Indeed, the context actually argues against it.[8]

Another problem is that Jesus isn't speaking about Scripture *as a whole*. If this verse is read in isolation, it would seem that Jesus is referring to the whole Bible since he seems to be speaking about "everything that is written about me" in Scripture. However, two verses later (Luke 24:46–47) Jesus recaps what he had just expounded from the scriptures: "Thus it is written, that the Christ should suffer and on the third day rise from the dead, and that repentance and forgiveness of sins should be preached in his name to all nations, beginning from Jerusalem." Since Jesus is not expounding on every prophecy about himself but only those that establish these points, there is no need to go beyond the plain understanding of Jesus' words since the law, the prophets, and especially the psalms contain more than enough information to establish these points. As Edward Reuss (1804–1891) wrote, "Commonly the attempt is made to prove the integrity of the Hebrew canon for the Apostolic Age, by the terms which Luke uses; but it is easy to see that in that passage he is simply enumerating the books in which messianic prophecies were found."[9]

The second premise of this argument is also fatally flawed. It assumes, as a matter of fact, that the later three-fold division always excluded the books of the deuterocanon; in reality, this common assertion is far from proved. For example, the Jewish work *Baba Kamma* 92b (written well into the Christian era) explicitly includes the book of Sirach among the Writings! Rabban ben Mari (320–350) told Raba (320–350),

> This matter is written in the Torah, repeated in the prophets, and repeated a third time in the *Hagiographa*, and was taught in the *Mishnah*, and was taught in a *Baraitha* . . . and repeated a third time in the *Hagiographa*, as it is written, "He will stay with you for a time, but if you falter, he will not stand by you" (Sir. 12:15).

Notice that Rabban ben Mari didn't see, as do those who argue this point, that that the three-fold division of the Law, the Prophets, and the Writings would necessarily exclude deuterocanonical books. On the contrary, he quotes Sirach as an authority as coming from the *Hagiographa* (the Writings). There is also evidence from the early Christian writers that the deuterocanon was retained within the collection of sacred writings long after the rabbis had rejected their authority.[10] Therefore, even if Luke 24:44 does affirm the tripartite division of Scripture, it does not, by that very fact, rule out the possibility that the deuterocanon was also included in that collection of Scripture.

Luke 11:49–51/Matthew 23:35—The Bookends Arguement

Although Luke 24:44 has received much scholarly attention, a more substantial argument is found in the "bookends" argument based on Luke 11:49–51 and its parallel in Matthew 23:35. The passages read,

> Therefore also the wisdom of God said, "I will send them prophets and apostles, some of whom they will kill and persecute," that the blood of all the prophets, shed from the foundation of the world, may be required of this generation, from the blood of Abel to the blood of Zechariah, who perished between the altar and the sanctuary. Yes, I tell you, it shall be required of this generation (Luke 11:49–51).
>
> [T]hat upon you may come all the righteous blood shed on earth, from the blood of innocent Abel to the blood of Zechariah the son of Barachiah, whom you murdered between the sanctuary and the altar (Matt. 23:35).

The "bookends" argument proposes that Jesus deliberately chose Abel and Zechariah as examples of the "blood of all the prophets shed upon earth" because Abel's martyrdom is found in the first book of the Bible (Gen. 4:8–11) and Zechariah's martyrdom is found in 2 Chronicles (24:20–22). Since Chronicles is traditionally placed at the end of the rabbinic Bible, it is argued, Abel and Zechariah show us that the first and last books of Jesus' Bible were identical to the first and last books of the rabbinic Bible. Therefore, Jesus' Bible, like the rabbinic Bible, did not include the deuterocanon.

This may sound pretty solid at first, but a closer look at each of its premises reveals that it's not a very good argument at all. What are its premises? There are three: first, the argument asserts that the Zechariah whom Jesus mentions in Luke 11:51 (Matt. 23:35) is the same Zechariah mentioned in 2 Chronicles 24:20–22. Second, that 2 Chronicles was the last book in the Bible of Jesus' day because it was traditionally placed at the end. Finally, that Jesus' reference to these two martyrs could only be for the purpose of delineating the limits of the Old Testament canon. Let us examine each of these individually.

Premise #1—*The Zechariah whom Jesus mentions is the same person mentioned in 2 Chronicles 24:20–22.*

Although the first premise is often stated with certainty, as if the Zechariah of 2 Chronicles is the only possible person Jesus could have been speaking about, there are actually five other candidates for the position. Although all of them are problematic, Zechariah of 2 Chronicles is one of the most problematic choices of the six.[11] One of the main reasons it is problematic is that Jesus identifies Zechariah as "the son of Barachiah" in Matthew 23:35, whereas 2 Chronicles twice identifies Zechariah as "the son of Jehoiada" (24:20, 25). Scripture does record a Zechariah, the son of Barachiah. He is the prophet Zechariah, the eleventh of the twelve minor prophets (Zech. 1:1, 7).

Two solutions are sometimes offered to save the Zechariah/2 Chronicles connection. One solution proposes that Jehoiada wasn't really Zechariah's father, but his grandfather; Zechariah's father was actually Barachiah. Therefore, when 2 Chronicles 24:20 speaks of "Zechariah, son of Jehoiada," it is using a rare but legitimate patronym formula that refers to Zechariah's grandfather. Jesus, however, used the customary patronym of "Zechariah, son of Barachiah" to reference Zechariah's actual father, Barachiah.

But although there may be rare cases in the Old Testament where the patronym formula refers to a grandparent, such is *not* the case in 2 Chronicles. We know this because 24:22 says, "Thus Joash the king did not remember the kindness which Jehoiada, *Zechariah's father*, had shown him, but killed his son."[12] There is no doubt, therefore, that Jehoiada was Zechariah's father and not his grandfather.

A second solution that is sometimes given is that "the son of Barachiah" is an error committed by a later copyist or Matthew or even Jesus![13] The problem here is that every major critical edition of the New Testament gives "the son of Barachiah" as its preferred reading. All the evidence points against it being a copyist error. As for the chance that an error occurred at its source, I think it would be wise to assume that Jesus and Matthew knew better who they were referring to than anyone living 2,000 years afterward. If Jesus said Zechariah was the "son of Barachiah," then he was the son of Barachiah.

The first premise, therefore, is not at all certain, and the identification of Zechariah as the Zechariah of 2 Chronicles is most likely incorrect. What about the claim that 2 Chronicles is traditionally the last book of the Hebrew Bible? Let's take a closer look.

Premise #2—*Second Chronicles is traditionally the last book of the Hebrew Bible.*

Apart from a single second-century rabbinic text (*b. Baba Bathra* 14b), all of the evidence argues *against* the proposition. Yes, you've read that correctly. *None* of the early Church Fathers, even those who attempted to reproduce the contents of the rabbinic Bible, lists Chronicles as the last book. Most of them put Esther or Ezra-Nehemiah at the end of the writings. Moreover, the two earliest complete Hebrew bibles (Aleppo and Leningrad [St. Petersburg] codices) place

Chronicles as the *first book* of the Writings, not the last.[14]

Since practically no one in the ancient world lists Chronicles at the end of the Writings, how can it be said that Chronicles was "traditionally" placed at the end? The answer is the printing press. Beginning in the 1400s, the first printed Hebrew bibles placed Chronicles but at the end, presumably following the order in *b. Baba Bathra.* Since every major printed copy since that time ended with Chronicles, it became the "traditional" order.

Since the uniform "traditional" placement of Chronicles at the end of the rabbinic Bible was the product of the printing press, those who lived before the era of the printing press (including the Church Fathers, medieval teachers and writers, even the Protestant Reformers) never made the "bookends" connection between Zechariah and the last book of the Bible. In fact, the connection wasn't made until 1780 (long after the printers established the "traditional" order) that a Protestant theologian, Johann Eichhorn (1752–1827), first proposed the "bookends" interpretation.[15]

Therefore, the second premise is based on the modern-era practices of the printing industry, and outside of a single rabbinic text from the second century, it has no foundation in antiquity. If anything, the evidence from antiquity runs against the claim.

Premise #3—*Abel and Zechariah were meant to function as bookends to define the canon.*

Once the "bookends" argument became a common feature in commentaries and apologetics works, scholars began to use it to *establish* that Chronicles was the last book in Jesus' Bible. [16] In other words, Jesus chose Zechariah because 2 Chronicles is the last book in Jesus' Bible, and 2 Chronicles must have been the last book in Jesus' Bible because Jesus chose Zechariah from 2 Chronicles! This is circular reasoning.

If, however, the "bookends" argument isn't true, why would Jesus chose Abel and Zechariah in the first place? Even if we grant the premise that Jesus did refer to Zechariah of 2 Chronicles, there is another plausible explanation that has nothing to do with the order of Old Testament books. H.G. Peels suggests that Jesus could have chosen Abel and Zechariah because they are two instances in Scripture where the shedding of blood calls out for divine retribution.[17] As examples of the kind of bloodshed that would be required of Jesus' hearers, the location of martyrdoms in the Bible really doesn't matter. Chronicles could be the first book of the Writings, and the point would remain unchanged. There are other possibilities as well. For example, if Jesus' Zechariah is Zechariah the father of John the Baptist or some otherwise unknown contemporary of Jesus, then the pairing of Abel and Zechariah could be referring to the first martyrdom and the last (i.e., the most recent). There are ancient stories about John the Baptist's father being martyred in the temple area, and Jesus sometimes references otherwise unknown contemporary events.[18] Both options are possible, and neither of them depends on the book order of the Old Testament.

Since the "bookends" argument is built on faulty and speculative premises, it simply isn't tenable.

The last New Testament text to be examined is Romans 3:1–2. This text doesn't pertain to the question of whether the deuterocanon is Scripture, but it is used to open the possibility that post-Christian Judaism had divine authority to reject the deuterocanon.

Romans 3:1–2—Jewish Province Argument

This argument is based on Romans 3:1–2, where St. Paul says that the Jews "were entrusted with the oracles of God."

There are several different versions of this argument, but the version most commonly given is that this passage establishes that God gave the Jews a divine mandate, a responsibility, to be the custodians of the Old Testament text. It is argued that since these texts were written by the Jews and for the Jews, the Jews alone are the ones who can recognize which of these books are sacred. Therefore, it wasn't up to the Christian Church to decide the contents of the canon; that authority was exclusively in the hands of the Jews, and they rejected the deuterocanon.[19]

Besides the fact that the New Testament clearly understands the Old Testament to be written for our sake (1 Cor. 10:6, 11) and that the New Testament books are part of "the other Scriptures" (2 Pet. 3:16), the argument goes beyond (and even contradicts) what Paul actually wrote:

> Then what advantage has the Jew? Or what is the value of circumcision? Much in every way. To begin with, the Jews are entrusted with the oracles of God (Rom. 3:1–2).

Let's look at the last line: "the Jews are entrusted with the oracles of God." *Which* Jews were entrusted with the oracles of God? The "Jewish province" argument assumes that first-century Judaism was more or less a monolithic religious body. It wasn't. First-century Judaism comprised several groups, sects, and schools, each claiming to be the true expression of Judaism. Although there was substantial agreement on many issues, all of these groups and sects held differing opinions, even on which books were to be considered Sacred Scripture. For example, the Samaritans (if they can be included in this list) believed that only the Pentateuch was Scripture, and it's quite possible that the Sadducees did as well.[20] The Essenes may not have accepted Esther, but possibly accepted Tobit,

Sirach, Enoch, and perhaps other books.[21] Even the Pharisees were not unified on this point. The Pharisaic schools of Shammai and Hillel were divided on Ecclesiastes, Song of Solomon, Esther, and possibly other books as well.[22]

Therefore, it is not enough to say "the Jews" were entrusted with the oracles of God. You need to first identify which sect (and which school within a sect) was "entrusted with these oracles" as well as to provide some sort of justification for why *they* were *the* authentic expression of Judaism and not some other sect. Furthermore, the diversity of opinions on the canon itself calls into question whether a centuries-old pre-Christian closed canon really existed. If it was closed for such a long time, it is strange that only one of these sects got the memo. Eventually, a single normative Judaism did emerge and proposed a normative Jewish canon, but this happened long after Paul wrote Romans.

Furthermore, the wording of Romans 3:2 shows that St. Paul is not speaking about an exclusive Jewish jurisdiction over the Old Testament that lasts into perpetuity, but rather about something that existed in the past. Here the *Revised Standard Version* does us a disservice. It translates that the Jews "are entrusted" with God's oracles. A more accurate translation is that the Jews "*were* entrusted with the oracles of God.[23] The Greek word translated "were entrusted" is a third-person, aorist, passive, indicative verb meaning that the "entrustment" was something that happened in the past; the Jews were *at one time entrusted* with the oracles of God. Paul surely believed that Christians are now entrusted with God's oracles.

When we examine the context of Romans 3:2, we find that Paul is not talking about the canon or the scriptures as a collection of books. Paul is naming the advantages that the Jews had over the Gentiles (Rom. 3:1). The Gentiles knew God's will through the dictates written in their hearts (Rom. 2:14–15); the

Jews, however, enjoyed the great advantage over the Gentiles in that they received "oracles" from God. The word translated "oracles" or "utterances" (Greek, *logia*) most certainly includes Sacred Scripture, but it is not restricted to Scripture. It can also include God's unwritten directions as well (Num. 24:3, 16; Ps. 105:19; Isa. 30:10–11; 1 Pet. 4:11). These unwritten instructions, like the written ones, were also a great advantage that the Jews enjoyed and the Gentiles lacked.

Although this broader interpretation may not fit the "Jewish province" argument, it does fit the context better and doesn't suffer from the strange pitfall of trying to pick and choose which one of the first-century Jewish sects got it right on the canon. All the sects of first-century Judaism enjoyed a great advantage over non-Jewish people in that God spoke to them and entrusted them with his utterances as recorded in Scripture and through divine direction through prophetic phenomena, such as the Urim and Thummim.[24]

Romans 3:2 is not giving *carte blanche* authority to the Jews in perpetuity to determine what is and is not canonical for the Old Testament. Whatever advantages the Jews possessed, Christians possess it as well, and the Old Testament Scripture is not exclusively *their* Scripture but *our* Scripture as well. Jesus said, "All authority in heaven and on earth has been given to me" (Matt. 28:18); that authority includes province over the Old Testament canon.

The Cessation of Prophecy Theory

The last argument for a pre-Christian closed canon is the "cessation of prophecy" theory. It is similar to the first argument in that both arguments assume that the absence of a "public" prophet means Scripture cannot be produced. It differs, however, by positing that there is a Jewish tradition that establishes that both prophets and prophecy ceased in Israel from the time of Artaxerxes or Esther (fifth century B.C.), where the first argument only spoke about the absence of prophets during the Maccabean period (first or second century B.C.).

This theory shares the same fatal flaw of the first argument—namely it equivocates on the word "prophet." As mentioned earlier, there are plenty of canonical texts that were written by people who were *not* known to be prophets (the *post facto* prophets), such as Ezra and Nehemiah. Therefore, even if all prophets and prophecy *did* cease to appear in Israel at some date, it doesn't follow that Scripture couldn't not be written during this no-prophet period.

But what about the ancient Jewish tradition that prophets and prophecy ceased? How solid is this assertion? Let's first look at the texts usually cited to establish this tradition.

The earliest and perhaps most important piece of evidence comes from the first-century Jewish writer Josephus in his apologetic work, *Against Apion*, written around A.D. 92. If he did teach the cessation theory, Josephus would be the earliest post-Christian source on the topic. Here is what Josephus wrote:

> For we have not an innumerable multitude of books among us, disagreeing from and contradicting one another [as the Greeks have], but only twenty-two books, which contain the records of all the past times; which are justly believed to be divine; and of them five belong to Moses, which contain his laws and the traditions of the origin of mankind till his death. This interval of time was little short of three thousand years; but as to the time from the death of Moses till the reign of Artaxerxes, king of Persia, who reigned after Xerxes, the prophets, who were after Moses, wrote

> down what was done in their times in thirteen books. The remaining four books contain hymns to God, and precepts for the conduct of human life. It is true, our history hath been written since Artaxerxes very particularly, but hath not been esteemed of the like authority with the former by our forefathers, because there hath not been an exact succession of prophets since that time.[25]

Josephus numerates twenty-two books of sacred history, hymns, and precepts recorded from the time of creation to the time of Artaxerxes. He concludes by stating that there are histories (in this context, *sacred* histories) that have been written since the time of Artaxerxes, but these later histories were not esteemed to be of like authority with the earlier histories "because there hath not been an exact succession of prophets since that time."

In addition to Josephus, there are several passages from rabbinic literature that are said to give support to the "cessation of prophecy" theory. They are:

> *b. Baba Bathra* 12b
> Said R. Abdimi of Haifa, "From the day on which the house of the sanctuary was destroyed, prophecy was taken away from prophets and given over to sages."[26]

> *Tosefta Sotah* 13:2
> "For our rabbis have taught: when Haggai, Zechariah, and Malachi died, the Holy Spirit departed from Israel; nevertheless they made use of the *Bath Kol*."[27]

> *Seder Olam Rabbah* 30
> That is Alexander the Macedonian who ruled for twelve years. Until that time there were prophets prophesying by

> the Holy Spirit; from there on (Prov. 22:10) "bend your ear and listen to the words of the wise," as it is said (Prov. 22:18–19): "How pleasant if you will preserve them in your body . . . that your trust shall be in the eternal."[28]
>
> *J. Ta'anith* 2, 1
> Rab Samuel bar Inia said, in the name of Rab Aha, "The second temple lacked five things which the first temple possessed, namely, the fire, the ark, the Urim and Thummim, the oil of anointing, and the Holy Spirit [of prophecy]."[29]

Therefore, the argument concludes, there is a well-established Jewish tradition that all prophet and prophecy ceased centuries before Christ, making the production of inspired writings impossible. The books of the deuterocanon, then, were never considered candidates for Scripture because they were written too late.

As with the previous two arguments, this argument suffers from overlooking, or perhaps ignoring, important details. A closer look will show you what I mean.

Josephus and the Succession of Prophets

Did Josephus teach that prophets and prophecy ceased in Israel after Artaxerxes so that no prophetic Scripture could be written? The odd thing is that Josephus never claims this. In fact, he seems to suggest the opposite.

It's true that the Jewish historian does state that twenty-two books chronicle the history of the Jews from creation down to Artaxerxes, and that the histories written after that time weren't as esteemed as the earlier ones, but why weren't they as esteemed? Was it because prophets and prophecy ceased and so these books lacked a prophetic author? That is what he should have said if he held on to the "cessation of prophecy" theory. But he didn't. Instead, Josephus says that they were not as esteemed as the former because they lacked "an exact succession of prophets." In other words, prophets and prophecy continued after Artaxerxes, but not in an exact succession. Josephus concedes the very point the "cessation" theorist claim he supports. As Lester Grabbe points out,

> "This [clause] implies breaks or gaps in the prophetic office, though *strictly speaking he does not say that prophecy ceased* in the time of Artaxerxes; *indeed, he implies the opposite*: there had been prophets in the period up to his own time but not the strict succession as formerly."[30]

Grabbe's comments are borne out in Josephus's historical work, the *Antiquity of the Jews*, where he speaks of prophets and prophecy continuing into the first Christian century.[31]

Why make this distinction? What was so important for Josephus to establish that an exact succession of prophets existed in the sacred histories prior to Artaxerxes I? Josephus wrote his comments on Scripture in the work *Against Apion,* which is his defense of his earlier work *The Antiquity of Jews.* Several pagan authors attacked Josephus *Antiquity* because, as Josephus says,

> [T]hey take it for a plain sign that our nation is of a late date, because they are not so much as vouchsafed a bare mention by the most famous historiographers among the Grecians; I therefore have thought myself under an obligation to write somewhat briefly about these subjects.[32]

The purpose of *Against Apion* was to vindicate the trustworthiness of the claims Josephus makes in his *Antiquities of the Jews*, specifically the claims prior to the time when the first Greek historians recognized the Jewish nation. Josephus mentions four of them: Herodotus and Thucydides (c. 460–400 B.C.) and Cadmus of Miletus and Acusilaus of Argos (c. 550–500 B.C.). All of these historians wrote around the time of Artaxerxes I (464–424 B.C.) or later.[33] Therefore, Josephus needs to vindicate the sacred histories of the Jews from the time of Artaxerxes I and earlier. Fortunately, the sacred histories within this period are impeccable from an ancient standpoint. Unlike the Greek sacred histories, which exist in a myriad of works that often contradicted each other, the Jewish histories were copied with great care and limited to only twenty-two books.[34] Furthermore, these books present history in a continuous, and sometimes overlapping, narrative. Hence, Josephus concludes, they enjoyed an "exact succession of prophets."[35] The pagans disputed the veracity of these earliest histories. Josephus brilliantly vindicates them by noting how the earliest histories are more highly esteemed, even more so than more recent histories because of their completeness and thoroughness in covering the historical period.

Therefore, Josephus's comments in *Against Apion* actually support the continuation of prophets and prophecy rather than establish their cessation.

Rabbinic Tradition?

Rabbinic literature now takes the center stage in our discussion. Let's look at each of the four texts quoted above.

b. Baba Bathra 12b reads,

Said R. Abdimi of Haifa, "From the day on which the

house of the sanctuary was destroyed, prophecy was taken away from prophets and given over to sages."

Aside from the fact that this Jewish tradition is quite late (third or fourth century A.D.), it doesn't teach that prophets or prophecy ceased. It says the opposite: after the destruction of the temple, "prophecy was taken away from prophets and *given over to sages*." Prophecy didn't cease; it just wasn't the exclusive property of prophets anymore. Sages now prophesy. In case there is any doubt about sages prophesying, the next line, which is almost always omitted by cessation theorists, places this interpretation beyond doubt:

> *So are sages not also prophets? This is the sense of the statement:* even though it was taken from the prophets, it was not taken from sages. Said Amemar, "And a sage is superior to a prophet: 'And a prophet has a heart of wisdom'" (Ps. 90:12).

What we see here is a transference of prophecy, not its extinction.

> *Seder Olam Rabbah*, 30
> That is Alexander the Macedonian who ruled for twelve years. Until that time there were prophets prophesying by the Holy Spirit; from there on (Prov. 22:10), "bend your ear and listen to the words of the wise."

Cessation of prophecy theorists focus on the words, "Until that time there were prophets prophesying by the Holy Spirit." What's often missed is that *Seder Olam Rabbah* then says to "listen to the wise." *Seder Olam Rabbah*, like the text above, is not talking about a cessation of prophecy, but a transference of the prophecy to others.

> *Y. Taanith* 2, 1
> Rab Samuel bar Inia said, in the name of Rab Aha, "The second temple lacked five things which the first temple possessed, namely, the fire, the ark, the Urim and Thummim, the oil of anointing, and the Holy Spirit [of prophecy]."

This text is one of a string of rabbinic texts that speak about five things that the second temple lacked. Notice that this text places the words "of prophecy" in brackets. This is because it is not present in the original. Jacob Neusner's translation of the passage simply reads "and Holy Spirit."[36] The same is given in another text.[37] A third text counts the Urim and Thummim as two distinct things and omits any reference to the Holy Spirit.[38] Why this disagreement?

The whole idea of five things missing in the second temple comes from the omission of the letter *he* in the Hebrew text in Haggai 1:8. Since this letter has a numerical value of five, it is thought that five things must be missing from the second temple. It's an interesting idea, but not exactly the type of thing you'd like to use to establish the biblical canon. The *Babylonian Talmud* gives a slightly different version of the five things missing and adds an important comment at the end:

> *But was it* [the sacred fire] *present in the second sanctuary?* Didn't R. Samuel bar Inia say, "What is the meaning of the verse of Scripture, 'And I will take pleasure in it and I will be glorified' (Hag. 1:8)? Why is the word for 'take pleasure in it' written without the expected H? It is to indicate that in five aspects, the first sanctuary differed from the second: the ark, the ark cover, the Cherubim, the fire, the presence of God, the Holy Spirit [prophecy], and the

> Oracle Plate"? Say: they were present, but they did not do so much good as they had."[39]

Notice the last line: the Holy Spirit ("prophecy" in brackets again) and other things *were present* in the second temple, "but they did not do so much good as they had." Prophecy (if the bracketed addition is correct) didn't cease; it continued, but it didn't do as much good as it did earlier.

Our last text is probably the most important.

> *Tosefta Sotah* 13:2
> For our rabbis have taught: when Haggai, Zechariah, and Malachi died, the Holy Spirit departed from Israel; nevertheless they made use of the *Bath Kol*.

What is the *Bath Kol* or "daughter's voice"? The prophets heard God's voice in two different fashions. Some heard God speak through a supersensible voice, such as when Moses heard God's voice in Deuteronomy 4:12. Others heard God speak in a more gentle voice, such as when Elijah heard God's voice as a whisper (1 Kings 19:12–13). According to *t. Sotah* 13:2, after the death of these prophets God continued to communicate with his people through the latter means (the "daughter's voice"). Prophecy, therefore, continues, but in a less distinct way.

That's one interpretation. John R. Levison offers another plausible explanation.[40]He argues that the best way to understand this passage is to interpret it in light of what is said earlier in chapter 10:

> When a righteous person comes into the world, good comes into the world . . . and retribution departs from the world; and when the righteous person leaves the world,

retribution comes into the world and goodness departs from the world.

The consequences of the death of the righteous may sound permanent, Levison argues, but they are actually only temporary. He gives three examples where the same text states that the deaths of three righteous teachers (Rabbis Eliezer, Joshua, and Akiva) are said to cause the glory of the Torah to cease.[41] Obviously, the glory of the Torah couldn't permanently cease three times. If this is true with these three teachers in regard to the Torah's glory, the same can be said of the Holy Spirit departing after the death of Haggai, Zechariah, and Malachi. In fact, immediately after it says that the Holy Spirit departed, it speaks of Hillel the Elder and Samuel the Little as "deserving that the *Shechinah* [Holy Spirit] should alight upon them though their respective generations were unworthy."[42] This adds further weight to Levison's contention that the consequences of the death of the righteous were only temporary.

When Did It Happen?

Not only do these texts *not* establish the cessation of prophets and prophecy—some of them actually affirm that prophecy continued—but they disagree with each other in regard to when this cessation supposedly took place. Josephus, for example, speaks of the time of Artaxerxes (between 465–424 B.C.). Others, such as *b. Baba Bathra* 12b and the "five things missing" texts, speak about the destruction of the first temple in 587 B.C. *Tosefta Sotah* 13, 2 says that it ended with the deaths of Haggai (520–522 B.C.), Zechariah (520 B.C.), and Malachi (445 B.C.). *Seder Olam Rabbah*, 30 mentions the time of Alexander the Great (c. 334–301 B.C.)! Why is there such disagreement? It is because each of them is talking about something other than a cessation of prophecy.

There is also a question about how reliable these sources are about relating a tradition that is said to pre-date Christianity. All of these sources are post-Christian. Most of them were written long after the establishment of the rabbinic bibles (c. A.D. 100–135).[43] It is difficult, if not impossible, to determine whether they really are passing on an ancient tradition or reading their current situation back into history, which occasionally occurs in rabbinic literature.

Given that the "cessation of prophesy" theory equivocates on the word "prophet," it is unable to pinpoint when the cessation occurred, and because the sources that it relies upon teach that prophecy continues, the theory is simply not tenable.

More to Consider

Now that we have seen that the three major arguments for a closed pre-Christian canon are untenable, it's time to switch gears and look at evidence that inspired Scripture continued to be written up until the time of Christ. Our investigation begins with the deuterocanonical book of Sirach.

Sirach (also called *Ecclesiasticus*) is the oldest book in the deuterocanon. It was written in Hebrew (most likely in Palestine) sometime around the beginning of the second century before Christ. Like the book of Proverbs, Sirach falls under the category of wisdom literature and was very popular in the Jewish world—so much so that Sirach's grandson translated the book into Greek (probably in Egypt) about fifty years after its composition.[44] This grandson also added a Greek preface to his translation, which we already examined earlier in regard to his ambiguous reference to the category later known as the "writings."

The preface also speaks of his grandfather's work in a way that suggests that his grandfather wrote the work as an inspired author, just like the authors of the Old Testament. The preface reads,

> [M]y grandfather Jesus, after devoting himself especially to the reading of the Law and the prophets and the other books of our fathers, and after acquiring considerable proficiency in them, *was himself also led to write something pertaining to instruction and wisdom*, in order that, by becoming conversant with this also, those who love learning should make even greater progress in living according to the Law.[45]

The phrase "was himself also let to write" sounds suspiciously like 2 Peter 1:21, which says, "no prophecy ever came by the impulse of man, *but men moved by the Holy Spirit* spoke from God?"[46] Could Sirach have been likewise led to write by the Holy Spirit?

Sirach himself also seems to believe that he was writing an inspired work. Speaking in the voice of divine wisdom, Sirach wrote,

> I went forth like a canal from a river and like a water channel into a garden. I said, 'I will water my orchard and drench my garden plot'; and behold, my canal became a river, and my river became a sea. I will again make instruction shine forth like the dawn, and I will make it shine afar; I will again pour out teaching like prophecy, and leave it to all future generations. Observe that I have not labored for myself alone, but for all who seek instruction (24:30–34).

The book of Sirach teaches, "All wisdom comes from the Lord and is with him forever" (1:1), and later we find divine wisdom saying, in Sirach 24:28–31, "I will again pour out teaching like prophecy" for "all future generations." Doesn't this suggest that Sirach's teachings came "from the Lord," and the book is claiming to be a prophetic writing that is written for all future generations? That certainly sounds like a claim to inspiration.[47] But how could Sirach (or anyone else for that matter) claim inspiration when the Old Testament canon was supposedly closed centuries earlier and prophecy was no longer possible?

The Judean Desert Manuscripts

Another indication that Scripture could be written after Malachi comes by way of two ancient texts found in the Judean desert. Both of the fragments are from the book of Sirach. One was discovered in a casement within the East fortress wall of Masada (*MasSir, Mas1h*), which dates to sometime between 10 B.C. and A.D. 50. The other fragment comes from Qumran (*2QSir*). It was found in Cave 2, and it dates to sometime between 50 B.C. and 1 B.C.

What's significant about these two fragments is that the texts are laid out in a special stichographic format that is used almost exclusively for poetic biblical passages.[48]

The fact that two copyists from two separate Jewish communities (likely pre-Christian communities) copied Sirach using this special format indicates an acceptance of Sirach as Sacred Scripture. We also should note that fragments of the deuterocanonical books of Tobit (*4Q197–200*) and the Epistle of Jeremiah (Bar. 6) (*7Q2*) were also discovered at Qumran.[49]

Prophets and Prophecy in the New Testament

The New Testament also has something to say about the idea of a pre-Christian cessation of prophets and prophecy. If all prophets and prophecy ceased hundreds of years before Christ, one would expect that the arrival of a prophet or prophetic utterances would be greeted with surprise or even incredulity. However, the New Testament speaks as if this were an ordinary occurrence. For example, when the people identified John the Baptist was a prophet[50] or Jesus as a prophet,[51] there wasn't the slightest hint that prophets and prophesy were no longer a possibility.

The Gospel of Luke also introduces us to a man named Simeon, who was "righteous and devout . . . and the Holy Spirit was upon him. And it had been revealed to him by the Holy Spirit that he should not see death before he had seen the Lord's Christ. And inspired by the Spirit he came into the temple" (2:25–27). If prophesy had ceased, how could Simeon receive the revelation from the Holy Spirit? Moreover, Luke doesn't feel need to explain or defend Simeon's prophetic gifts, which is the opposite of what one would expect if prophets and prophecy were no longer possible. Likewise, Anna, the daughter of Phanuel, is even more revealing. Luke identifies Anna as a prophetess (Luke 2:36). Apparently, Anna enjoyed the reputation for being a prophetess before she met Jesus in the temple. But how could Anna have a reputation as a prophetess when all prophets and prophecy were a thing of the past?

Had the idea of the "cessation of prophecy" really been a well-known fact, it is odd that no one in the New Testament bothers to point it out, even when it was in their best interest. For example, the Pharisees said about Jesus, "If this man were a prophet, he would know who and what sort of woman this is who is touching him" (Luke 7:39). But wouldn't it have been easier to say, "He can't be a prophet. Prophets and prophesy ceased centuries ago!" Likewise, when Nicodemus was speaking about Jesus to the Sanhedrin, a member of the Sanhedrin said that "no prophet arises from Galilee" (Luke 7:52). Why not say, "Prophets are no longer possible, much less one from Galilee"? The New Testament indirectly shows that prophets and prophesy were a common feature of the time and not a relic of the past.

What About the Deuterocanon?

Does the New Testament have anything to show us about its view of the deuterocanon? Does it ever quote, reference, or use the deuterocanonical books? Is there any evidence that Jesus, the apostles, and the inspired authors may have believed the deuterocanon to be Scripture? Or does the New Testament bear out the Protestant canon? Does it ever reject these books as "apocrypha" or deny their ability to confirm doctrine? We will look for the answers to these questions in the next chapter.

2

The Deuterocanon and the New Testament

Since the claim of a pre-Christian closure of the canon is not tenable, we now turn our attention to the New Testament to see what it can tell us about the earliest Christians' views on the deuterocanon.

People sometimes think that the New Testament is devoid of any reference to the deuterocanon. Not only is this false, but it wasn't even the view of early Protestantism. Many of the earliest Protestant English translations of the Bible included cross-references in the New Testament to the deuterocanon as well as cross-references from these books to the New Testament. These cross-references show us that the Protestant editors knew that the New Testament used, referenced, and alluded to the deuterocanon. For example, the original 1611 edition of the King James Bible boasts ten New Testament cross-references to the deuterocanon (and 102 from the deuterocanon to the New Testament). These cross-references remained in Protestant bibles until the "Apocrypha" were eventually removed.

Although some still claim that the New Testament is utterly devoid of any contact with the deuterocanon, most people would not go that far. They'll admit that the New Testament does use these books, but they will usually focus all the attention on direct quotations, pointing out that the New Testament never directly quotes the deuterocanon or that it never formally introduces a reference to it with the words "It is written," "Thus saith the Lord," or "the Scripture says."

Although the New Testament does make numerous such formal quotations, these are taken from only a few books. Informal quotations are far more frequent. However, even if all the quotations, both formal and informal, were combined, there still would remain a substantial number of Old Testament books that are never quoted (Ruth, 1 and 2 Chronicles, Ezra, Esther, Song of Solomon, Ecclesiastes, Lamentations, Ezekiel, and perhaps Daniel) and three of these books (Ecclesiastes, Song of Solomon, and Esther) do not appear to receive so much as an allusion! What this shows is that the absence of a quotation, or even an allusion, proves nothing in regard to a book's inspired status. Otherwise, none of these other books should be considered Scripture, either.

But even if the New Testament did directly and formally quote from the deuterocanon, these quotations would still be indecisive because the New Testament freely quotes (even formally) non-canonical writings. If quotation equaled inspiration (and canonicity) then no one would have a correct Bible, since the New Testament passes over several protocanonical books and quotes a few non-canonical works.[52]

Where does this leave us? Is there anything in the New Testament that can help us understand whether the earliest Christians understood the deuterocanon to be Sacred Scripture? The presence or absence of a quotation in itself tells us very little. What matters, however, is *how* the New Testament quotes or uses a book. That tells us a great deal.

So that there can be no argument from Protestants about whether a particular passage of Scripture is referencing a deuterocanonical text, we will use the venerable King James Bible (KJB) as our guide.[53] Let's look at each of the ten New Testament cross-references to deuterocanonical books in the KJB and see what each can tell us.

1) Matthew 6:7 and Sirach 7:14

> And in praying do not heap up empty phrases as the Gentiles do; for they think that they will be heard for their many words (Matt. 6:7).
>
> Do not prattle in the assembly of the elders, nor repeat yourself in your prayer (Sir. 7:14)

Matthew makes a distant allusion to Sirach's advice to be as brief as possible when talking to superiors. As you can see, this allusion is quite weak, representing little more than a mere correspondence in thought.

2) Matthew 27:43 and Wisdom 2:15,16

Matthew 27:39–43

> And those who passed by derided him, wagging their heads and saying, 'You who would destroy the temple and build it in three days, save yourself! If you are the Son of God, come down from the cross." So also the chief priests, with the scribes and elders, mocked him, saying, "He saved others; he cannot save himself. He is the king of Israel; let him come down now from the cross, and we will believe in him. He trusts in God; let God deliver him now, if he desires him; for he said, 'I am the Son of God (Matt. 27:39–43)."

Wisdom 2:17–22

> "Let us see if his words are true, and let us test what will happen at the end of his life; for if the righteous man is God's son, he will help him, and will deliver him from the hand of his adversaries (Wis. 2:17–22).

In the Matthew passage, many modern bibles will direct the reader to the Suffering Servant passage in Psalm 22:7–8, which reads,

> All who see me mock at me, they make mouths at me, they wag their heads; "he committed his cause to the Lord; let him deliver him, let him rescue him, for he delights in him."

Bibles that include the deuterocanon will likely provide a second cross-reference to Wisdom 2:17–18. No one would deny that the two texts have a certain affinity with one another. For example, both Psalms 22:8–9 and Wisdom 2:17–18 speak about God rescuing the just man who places his trust in him.[54] However, the taunts of the chief priests, scribes, and elders in Matthew 27:43 suggest something more specific; Christ is being mocked not merely for being "loved by God" (as a comparison to Psalm 22:7–8 would suggest), but specifically because he "said 'I am the Son of God.'" Notice how Wisdom 2:17 takes the truthful claim to be the "Son of God" as a condition for God's deliverance:

> For if the just one be the Son of God, he will defend him and deliver him from the hand of his foes.

This is the only passage in the Old Testament that expresses a direct expectation that the true Son of God would be rescued and delivered from persecution by mockers and detractors; and it is precisely Christ's claim of divine sonship that led the Jewish leaders in Matthew 27:43 to express their feigned expectation of such a rescue. Given this close interconnection, it is not surprising to find Protestant sources recognizing this dependency on Wisdom in Matthew 27:41–43. What, if anything, however, does this usage tell us about the inspired status of Wisdom?

First, the elders must have understood the book of Wisdom to be an authoritative, perhaps even predictive, sacred text; otherwise, their taunt would have been meaningless, perhaps even blasphemous, since it would then have amounted to a demand for a miraculous rescue that God never promised. Only a recognized inspired text would have given these words power and avoided blasphemous presumption.

Second, the chief priests, scribes, and elders must have had a reasonable expectation that those present would recognize their citation of Wisdom 2:17–18; otherwise, their words would have been lost on their hearers. Third, Matthew's inclusion of these words in his Gospel narrative indicates that he saw them as having some significance for Jewish Christian readers, seeing perhaps, as the apostle Paul did, Christ's ultimate rescue in the Resurrection as a vindication or demonstration of his divine sonship.[55] Finally, Matthew apparently expected his readers to know this text as well and accept it as a genuine prophecy. From earliest times, Christians used Wisdom 2:17–18 as a genuine prophecy of Christ's passion.

There is something stronger than an allusion or even a quote here; Matthew is *employing* Wisdom in this text (or rather the Jewish elders are employing Wisdom, and Matthew records it). It suggests that Matthew, the chief priests, scribes, and elders, as well as their hearers and readers, understood this text to be prophetic. Yet despite the significance of this employment, by Matthew and others, this reference to the inspired book of Wisdom has been systematically omitted from most Protestant bibles.[56]

3) Luke 6:31 and Tobit 4:15

And as you wish that men would do to you, do so to them (Luke 6:31).[57]

And what you hate, do not do to anyone (Tob. 4:15).

The KJB draws the obvious comparison between our Lord's "Golden Rule" and the negative form of it that appears in Tobit 4:15.

4) Luke 14:13 and Tobit 4:7

But when you give a feast, invite the poor, the maimed, the lame, the blind, and you will be blessed, because they cannot repay you. You will be repaid at the resurrection of the just (Luke 14:13).

Give alms from your possessions to all who live uprightly, and do not let your eye begrudge the gift when you make it. Do not turn your face away from any poor man, and the face of God will not be turned away from you (Tob. 4:7).

5) John 10:22 and 1 Maccabees 4:59

It was the feast of the Dedication at Jerusalem (John 10:22).

Then Judas and his brothers and all the assembly of Israel determined that every year at that season the days of the dedication of the altar should be observed with gladness and joy for eight days, beginning with the twenty-fifth day of the month of Chislev (1 Macc. 4:59).

The Feast of the Dedication, mentioned in John 10:22,

known today as Hanukkah, was established during the time of the Maccabees and prescribed as an annual feast in 1 Maccabees 4:59. Antiochus IV, king of Syria, had defeated Egypt and turned his wrath toward Israel. He took for himself the golden altar, lamp stands, and sacred vessels of the temple and sacrificed a pig to the god Zeus in the Holy of Holies. The Syrian king forbade circumcision, Sabbath observance, and the keeping of the kosher laws. Judas Maccabees refused to submit to the king's oppressive rules and led a successful rebellion on behalf of God's people against their oppressors. On the twenty-fifth of Kislev, the Jews rededicated the temple. A special lamp called the *ner tamid* or "eternal light" was relit, but there was barely enough consecrated oil to keep it burning for a day, and a week would be needed to prepare more. Jewish tradition records that God miraculously sustained the burning lamp for eight days until a new supply had been prepared, and commissioned the celebration of a feast on this date.

The origin of the feast is found nowhere in the Protestant Bible, yet our Lord not only attended this Feast of Lights but also used it as a backdrop for his "Light of the World" discourse.[58] In a sense, this feast is fulfilled in Jesus, who is the true light that enlightens every man.[59]

6) Romans 9:20–22 and Wisdom 15:7

> But who are you, a man, to answer back to God? Will what is molded say to its molder, "Why have you made me thus?" Has the potter no right over the clay, to make out of the same lump one vessel for beauty and another for menial use (Rom. 9:20–22).

> For when a potter kneads the soft earth and laboriously

> molds each vessel for our service, he fashions out of the same clay both the vessels that serve clean uses and those for contrary uses, making all in like manner; but which shall be the use of each of these the worker in clay decides (Wis. 15:7).

This cross reference may not at first seem very impressive. The same imagery of the potter and the clay is used in several other passages in the protocanon (Isa. 29:16; 45:9; Jer. 18:6, etc.). Protestant theologian Bruce M. Metzger notes, however, that although the image of the potter and clay can be found elsewhere, only Romans and Wisdom agree in the "twist": that both good and bad are made from the *same lump of clay*. Indeed, this is more than just a twist, it is one of the major points Paul is trying to establish in Romans 9, namely that "not all who are descended from Israel belong to Israel, and not all are children of Abraham because they are his descendants" (Rom. 9:6–7).[60] Metzger further bolsters this observation by noting between these two texts several linguistic parallels that are sustained through three consecutive verses from Romans 9:20–22.[61]

7) Romans 11:34 and Wisdom 9:13

> For who has known the mind of the Lord, or who has been his counselor? (Rom. 11:34).

> For what man can learn the counsel of God? Or who can discern what the Lord wills? (Wis. 9:13).

Here Paul is apparently quoting Isaiah 40:13 (Septuagint). However, there is a more distant echo of the same thought in Wisdom 9:13.

8) 2 Corinthians 9:7 and Sirach 35:9

Each one must do as he has made up his mind, not reluctantly or under compulsion, for God loves a cheerful giver (2 Cor. 9:7).

With every gift show a cheerful face, and dedicate your tithe with gladness (Sir. 35:9).

The Septuagint version of Proverbs 22:8 and Sirach 35:9 echoes Paul's thoughts in 2 Corinthians 9:7. It is interesting that both of these texts are absent in the Hebrew *Masoretic Text* (MT) of the Old Testament.

9) Hebrews 1:3 and Wisdom 7:26

He reflects the glory of God and bears the very stamp of his nature upholding the universe by his word of power (Heb. 1:3).

For she is a reflection of eternal light, a spotless mirror of the working of God, and an image of his goodness (Wis. 7:26).

Like Proverbs, Wisdom 7:26 personifies the wisdom of God.[62] The writer of Hebrews appears to have adopted Wisdom 7:26's description of divine wisdom and applies it to Jesus. He is the *refulgence* of God's glory. The word translated "refulgence" [Greek, *apaugasma*] is extremely rare in the Septuagint, appearing only in Wisdom 7:26, thus linking the two passages.[63]

10) Hebrews 11:35 and 2 Maccabees 7:7

Women received their dead by resurrection. Some were

tortured, refusing to accept release, that they might rise again to a better life (Heb. 11:35).

It happened also that seven brothers and their mother were arrested and were being compelled by the king, under torture with whips and cords, to partake of unlawful swine's flesh . . . When he too had died, they maltreated and tortured the fourth in the same way. And when he was near death, he said, "One cannot but choose to die at the hands of men and to cherish the hope that God gives of being raised again by him. But for you there will be no resurrection to life" (2 Macc. 7:1, 13–14).

The writer of Hebrews provides a long list of figures from sacred history whose faithfulness gained approval. In near chronological order, the author arranges a series of illustrations from the following biblical figures: Abel (Gen. 4:4), Enoch (Gen. 5:21–24), Noah (Gen. 6:13–22), Abraham (Gen. 12:1–4, 8; 13:3, 18; 18:1–9 et al.), Sarah (Gen. 17:19; 18:11–14; 21:1), Isaac (Gen. 22:1–10; 21:12; 27:27–29), Jacob and Esau (Gen. 27:27–29; 48:1, 5, 16, 20), Joseph (Gen. 50), Moses (Exod. 2:2, 10–11, 15), Joshua (Josh. 6:20), Gideon (Judg. 6–7), Barak (Judg. 4–5), Samson (Judg. 13–16), Jephthah (Judg. 13–16), David (1 Sam. 16:1–13), Samuel (1 Sam. 1:20), and the prophets. Hebrews continues his list of these great biblical figures by recounting their exploits rather than listing their names. In Hebrews 11:35, the writer refers to Maccabean martyrs depicted in 2 Maccabees 7:1–42.

This identification of the Maccabean martyrs with those described in Hebrews 11:35 is of a high degree of certainty because there are no other examples presented in the Greek Old Testament of persons undergoing torture and not accepting deliverance for the hope of a better resurrection. Twice in the episode of the Maccabean martyrs this hope for a better resurrection is explicitly stated.[64]

Hebrews 11:35 and 2 Maccabees are also linked linguistically as well:

> The word in Heb. xi. 35, rendered "tormented," is a peculiar one (*tumpanizw*) . . . is used here in reference to the *tumpanon*, in the account of Eleazar's martyrdom in Maccabees, which the Dean does not hesitate to assert is the case especially intended. Also the word for "cruel mockings" in verse 36 is peculiar to this verse and 2 Macc. 7:7. Other of the deeds and suffering enumerated are also based upon the Maccabean history.[65]

Apart from dogmatic prejudice, this reference to 2 Maccabees is unquestionable, and both Catholic and Protestant scholars rightly acknowledge it.

Protestant apologists often argue that the citation of these Maccabean martyrs is really nothing more than a simple historical reference, and that it has no bearing on the discussion of whether 2 Maccabees ought to be considered divinely inspired Scripture. The context of the eleventh chapter of Hebrews would indicate the contrary. We are not dealing here with a mere historical factoid; Hebrews 11 provides a panoramic view of *sacred* history beginning with Abel in Genesis and continuing through (more or less chronologically) to 2 Maccabees. None of the previous verses refers to any mere historical personage; each and every prior reference is to some biblical figure renowned for supernatural acts of faith. So we must ask: If the writer of Hebrews had wished us to accept only the shorter Protestant canon and had accepted such a canon himself, would he have placed, as he does, the heroes of an apocryphal book on the same list with Noah, Abraham, Moses, and David—the greatest figures of salvation history? Or would he not, rather, have avoided any reference to such a book, as most Protestants do, fearing to give it a false impression of authority, and concluded his list instead with biblical figures from before the time of Ezra?[66]

Because the book of Hebrews does extend its panorama of "the men of old who gained approval" from Abel to the Maccabees, we must honestly conclude that the writer of Hebrews appears to have accepted the larger Catholic canon.

Other Points of Contact

The editors of the KJB might well have included many other similar connections, all of which have been known and commented upon since the days of the Church Fathers. Several of these additional points deserve mention in this section.

The first is a rather lengthy parallel between the thought of the apostle Paul in Romans 1:20–32 and that contained in the thirteenth and fourteenth chapters of the book of Wisdom. There are several points of contact between these two sections, the breadth of which led the famed Protestant exegete J.B. Lightfoot, to comment, "All which follow in this chapter shows a remarkable correspondence with Wisdom 13–15, a passage which St. Paul *must* have had in his mind."[67]

Paul, who learned his Hebrew theology at the feet of Gamaliel, would certainly have known the book of Wisdom well, as did all learned Jews, whatever they may have thought of its status as inspired Scripture. That the great apostle was willing to echo the thoughts of such a book so directly, borrowing them almost wholesale for use in his own arguments, speaks volumes about his opinion of the supposedly apocryphal writings in question. At the very least, however, this remarkable correspondence is an example of something that (according to the argument we are examining) is not supposed to have happened: a direct allusion to, if not a quotation from, the deuterocanonical books within the pages of the New Testament.

2 Corinthians 5:1–9 and Wisdom 9:10–18

For we know that if the earthly tent [Greek, *epigeios . . . skenos*] we live in is destroyed, we have a building from God, a house not made with hands, eternal in the heavens. Here indeed we groan, and long to put on our heavenly dwelling, so that by putting it on we may not be found naked. For while we are still in this tent, we sigh with anxiety [Greek, *baroumenoi*, "weighed down"]; not that we would be unclothed, but that we would be further clothed, so that what is mortal may be swallowed up by life. He who has prepared us for this very thing is God, who has given us the Spirit as a guarantee (2 Cor. 5:1–9).

Send her forth from the holy heavens, and from the throne of your glory send her, that she may be with me and toil, and that I may learn what is pleasing to you. For she knows and understands all things, and she will guide me wisely in my actions and guard me with her glory. Then my works will be acceptable, and I shall judge your people justly, and shall be worthy of the throne of my father. For what man can learn the counsel of God? Or who can discern what the Lord wills? For the reasoning of mortals is worthless, and our designs are likely to fail, for a perishable body weighs down [Greek, *barynei*] the soul, and this earthy tent [Greek, *geōdes skénos*] burdens the thoughtful mind. We can hardly guess at what is on earth, and what is at hand we find with labor; but who has traced out what is in the heavens? Who has learned your counsel, unless you have given wisdom and sent your Holy Spirit from on high? (Wis. 9:10–18).

Metzger sees here both a parallel in thought and linguistic contacts:

> But the presence of certain verbal coincidences in the Greek of both passages points to a literary connection. For example, it is significant that the word *skénos*, translated "tent" or "tabernacle," appears only in these two passages in all of biblical Greek—the entire Septuagint and the New Testament.[68]

Although Metzger does not go as far as to say that Paul was dependent upon the book of Wisdom for his teachings, he does admit that the apostle borrowed thoughts and phrases from the deuterocanonical books.[69] The renowned Protestant exegete E.H. Plumptre echoed Metzger's thoughts when he wrote, "The whole passage [2 Cor. 5:4] is strikingly parallel to Wisdom 9:15."[70]

James 1:13 and Sirach 15:11–13

> Let no one say when he is tempted, I am tempted by God; for God cannot be tempted with evil and he himself tempts no one (James 1:13).

> Say not: "It was God's doing that I fell away"; for what he hates he does not do. Say not: "It was he who set me astray"; for he has no need of wicked man. Abominable wickedness the Lord hates, he does not let it befall those who fear him (Sir. 15:11–13).

James and Sirach both record a similar accusation against God.[71] The relationship between these two passages seems to be tenuous at best until the reader takes into account that

James 1:13 is only one of a series of such contacts between the letter of James and the book of Sirach, as we will see illustrated below.

James 1:19 and Sirach 5:11 [13]

> Know this, my beloved brethren. Let every man be quick to hear, slow to speak, slow to anger (James 1:19).

Sirach 5:11

> Be quick to hear, and be deliberate in answering (Sir. 5:11).

Both James 1:19 and Sirach 5:11 recommend that the godly be quick to hear and slow to speak or give answer.

James 3:5 and Sirach 28:12

> So the tongue is a little member and boasts of great things. How great a forest is set ablaze by a small fire! (James 3:5).

> If you blow on a spark, it will glow; if you spit on it, it will be put out; and both come out of your mouth (Sir. 28:12).

Commenting on the power of speech for good or ill, both the James and Sirach use the same distinctive imagery: the kindling of a potentially destructive fire. Other parallels continue throughout this chapter (e.g., James 3:6, 10). The Protestant scholar Alfred Edersheim notes, "The result is to prove beyond doubt the familiarity of St. James with Ecclus [Sirach]."[72]

James 3:6, 3:10, and Sirach 5:13 [15]

> And the tongue is a fire. The tongue is an unrighteous world among our members, staining the whole body, setting on fire the cycle of nature, and set on fire by hell (James 3:6).
>
> From the same mouth come blessing and cursing. My brethren, this ought not to be so (James. 3:10).
>
> Glory and dishonor come from speaking, and a man's tongue is his downfall (Sir. 5:13).

James 5:3 and Sirach 12:11; 29:9–10

> Your gold and silver have rusted, and their rust will be evidence against you and will eat your flesh like fire. You have laid up treasure for the last days (James 5:3).
>
> Even if he humbles himself and goes about cringing, watch yourself, and be on your guard against him; and you will be to him like one who has polished a mirror, and you will know that it was not hopelessly tarnished (Sir. 12:11).
>
> Help a poor man for the commandment's sake, and because of his need do not send him away empty. Lose your silver for the sake of a brother or a friend, and do not let it rust under a stone and be lost (Sir. 29:9–10).

Metzger notes three areas in which James 5:3 has an affinity with no other book in the Greek Bible but Sirach. For example, the verb translated in the NASB as "have rusted" is used in the Greek Old Testament only in Sirach 12:11.[73] Likewise, the illustration of rust corroding unused gold and silver appears nowhere else in the Greek Old Testament or in the New Testament outside of these two books. Although Metzger does not consider the views presented in Sirach and James to be compatible, he does conclude that James drew his material from Sirach.[74]

Consider the past few allusions, all of which trace from James to Sirach:

James 1:13–Sirach 15:11–13
James 1:19–Sirach 15:11 [13]
James 3:5–Sirach 28:12
James 3:6–Sirach 5:13
James 3:10–Sirach 5:13
James 5:3–Sirach 12:11

Within the relatively short five chapters of James there are a half-dozen allusions or references to the deuterocanonical book. Taken individually, one or two of these may be dismissed. Taken collectively, it is difficult not to get the impression that James is deliberately drawing from and making use of material found in Sirach.

A similar string of contacts exists between Matthew and Sirach.

Matthew 11:28–30 and Sirach 6:24–25; 51:23–27

> Come to me, all who labor and are heavy laden, and I will give you rest. Take my yoke upon you, and learn from me; for I am gentle and lowly in heart, and you will find rest for your souls. For my yoke is easy, and my burden is light (Matt. 11:28–30).

> Put your feet into her [Wisdom's] chains, and your neck

> into her collar. Put your shoulder under her and carry her, and do not fret under her bonds. Come to her with all your soul, and keep her ways with all your might (Sir. 6:24–26).

> Come aside to me, you untutored, and take up lodging in the house of instruction; how long will you be deprived of wisdom's food, how long will you endure such bitter thirst? I open my mouth and speak of her [i.e. Wisdom]: again, at no cost, wisdom for yourselves. Submit your neck to her yoke, that your mind may accept her teaching. For she is close to those who seek her, and the one who is in earnest finds her. See for yourselves! I have labored only a little, but have found much (Sir. 51:23–27).

Our Lord's words in Matthew 11:28–30 has a strong affinity to Sirach 6 and 51. Both Jesus and Sirach invite their disciples to "come" and receive the yoke of wisdom that they have to offer. For both, the yoke of instruction is light and fruitful, but where Sirach is merely sharing the divine wisdom he has received, our Lord directs his disciples to himself: "learn from me, for I am gentle and lowly heart."

John 6:35 and Sirach 24:18–22

> Jesus said to them, "I am the bread of life; he who comes to me shall not hunger, and he who believes in me shall never thirst. But I said to you that you have seen me and yet do not believe" (John 6:35).

> Come to me, you who desire me, and eat your fill of my produce. For my teaching is sweeter than honey, and my inheritance sweeter than the honeycomb, and my remembrance lasts throughout all generations. Those who

> eat me will hunger for more, and those who drink me will thirst for more (Sir. 24:19–21).

Our Lord both adopts the same language as Sirach in regard to eating and drinking, however, he changes it in a very important way. Sirach tells his disciples that those who partake of wisdom will find it so desirable that they will hunger and thirst for more. However, Jesus, who is the Wisdom of God (1 Cor. 1:24), says that whoever comes to him and believes will be forever satisfied, never hungering or thirsting for more.

John 3:12 and Wisdom 9:16

> If I have told you earthly things and you do not believe, how can you believe if I tell you heavenly things? (John 3:12).

> We can hardly guess at what is on earth, and what is at hand we find with labor; but who has traced out what is in the heavens? (Wis. 9:16).

John 3:12 appears by itself to be a mere statement of fact; yet if we consider Wisdom 9 to be its background we may find in Jesus' words a profound statement about who he is—and where he came from.

Revelation 8:2 and Tobit 12:15

> Then I saw the seven angels who stand before God, and seven trumpets were given to them (Rev. 8:2).

> I am Raphael, one of the seven holy angels who present the prayers of the saints and enter into the presence of the glory of the Lord (Tob. 12:15).

There are, of course, other ways in which the author of Revelation could have learned of the seven who stand before the Lord; it might have been revealed to him in the vision itself, or he could have learned it through Jewish tradition. Even so, the fact remains that the reference to seven angels standing before God is found nowhere else in the Greek Bible except this passage in Tobit.

Ephesians 6:13–17 and Wisdom 5:17–20

> Therefore take the whole armor of God, that you may be able to withstand in the evil day, and having done all, to stand. Stand therefore, having fastened the belt of truth around your waist, and having put on the breastplate of righteousness, and having shod your feet with the equipment of the gospel of peace; besides all these, taking the shield of faith, with which you can quench all the flaming darts of the evil one. And take the helmet of salvation, and the sword of the Spirit, which is the word of God (Eph. 6:13–17).

> The Lord will take his zeal as his whole armor, and will arm all Creation to repel his enemies; he will put on righteousness as a breastplate, and wear impartial justice as a helmet; he will take holiness as an invincible shield, and sharpen stern wrath for a sword, and Creation will join with him to fight against the madmen (Wis. 5:17–20).

The "armor of God" motif used in Ephesians 6:13–17 is found also in Isaiah 59:17 and Wisdom 5:17–20—both of which have points of dissimilarity with Paul along with their affinities. Interestingly enough, however, Ephesians uses the Greek word *panoplian* (translated "armor") in verse 13, a word found only in Wisdom's description, not the Septuagint version of Isaiah.

The New Testament and the Deuterocanon

What do all these cross-references and other passages show us? They show that the New Testament did not ignore the deuterocanon. Quite the opposite. The inspired authors of the New Testament referenced, used, and integrated the deuterocanon into their work just as they did the other Old Testament texts. Perhaps this is why those who reject the deuterocanon so often carefully qualify their objections when it comes to the New Testament. To evade this very salient point, they will redirect their readers' attention to matters of little consequence by saying that "the New Testament never directly quotes the deuterocanon" or "it's never quoted formally with phrases like 'thus saith the Lord' or 'it is written.'" But as we've noted, since several books in the Protestant Old Testament are never directly quoted and some non-canonical books *are*, such things prove nothing.[75]

These references show us that the New Testament authors used the deuterocanon in a way indistinguishable from Sacred Scripture. True, not all cross-references from the KJB are of equal value in this regard. A few are nothing more than a mere correspondence in thought. However, others are quite revealing. For example, only an inspired text could legitimately propose the promise that God would rescue the true Son of God (see Wis. 2:17–22; Matt. 27:43) or lead the author of Hebrews to include the Maccabean martyrs, as described in 2 Maccabees, among his list of Old Testament saints (Heb. 11:35). More can be said in this regard, but the material presented in this chapter shows that the New Testament's inspired authors didn't regard the deuterocanon as human apocrypha, but as an integral part of Sacred Scripture.[76]

3

The Closing of the Rabbinic Bible

If Jesus and the earliest Christians didn't inherit a closed, fixed collection of Sacred Scripture that excluded the deuterocanon, and if the New Testament uses the deuterocanon like Scripture, how is it that the Jews don't accept these books? Why do Christians and Jews have two different Old Testaments?

Earlier, we noted that a single normative canon could not have existed within first-century Judaism because there wasn't a single normative version of Judaism to propose a single normative canon. Judaism during this period was anything but a monolithic religious body. It was composed of several different religious sects, each claiming to be the true expression of Judaism. Some of these sects held different opinions about which books were part of the Old Testament. The Sadducees, like the Samaritans, only accepted the five books of Moses as sacred. The Essenes appear not to have accepted Esther, but accepted Tobit, Sirach, Enoch, and other works as well.[77] Moreover, some of these sects weren't even in agreement among themselves. The Pharisees, for example, had two schools (Shammai and Hillel) that disagreed on the sacredness of Ecclesiastes, Song of Solomon, Esther, and possibly others.[78] Since different sects had different collections, there wasn't a single normative canon until one sect emerged and dominated all the others. This didn't happen until well into the Christian era.

The Birth of Rabbinic Judaism

Judaism during the time of the New Testament was a cultic religion. It operated according to the dictates of the Old Covenant, which made previsions for a functioning priesthood, a temple and altar, various sacrifices, and sacrificial feasts that were to be celebrated throughout the year. The temple was at the center of Jewish life in and around the area of Judea. This form of Judaism came to an abrupt end around forty years after the Crucifixion.

In A.D. 66, Jewish Zealots rose up in rebellion against the pagan Roman Empire. Not everybody was behind this revolt. The Sadducees, who had ties with the priesthood, were friendly toward the Romans. They may not have cared for being under the heel of these pagan occupiers, but they nevertheless were willing to make the best of the situation. The Pharisee party didn't care for the Romans either, but they also did not back the revolt. Despite the lack of unity, the Zealots went ahead and attacked the Romans, and so began the First Jewish Revolt.

The revolt took the Romans by surprise, and the Zealots won a few initial victories. Seeing this as a sign from God, they believed that victory was assured even though the Romans were a military superpower. The Romans struck back and slowly began to take back Judea, eventually laying siege to the city of Jerusalem. However, all was not lost. Jerusalem was well fortified and well supplied. Under normal circumstances, it may have been able to bring the Roman counter-offensive to a stalemate. The Zealot leadership was not unified, however, and the Zealots broke into factions, fighting against each other and destroying each other's food stores. Jerusalem quickly fell into a state of starvation.

It was during this turmoil that Rabban Yahanan ben Zakkai—ruler of the Sanhedrin and leading member of the

Pharisees—escaped the city by being taken out in a coffin. Since Yahanan was against the revolt from the beginning, he was able to win favor with Vespasian, predicting that the Roman would eventually become emperor. He asked Vespasian for permission to allow him to set up a rabbinic school in the city of Jamnia (Yavne). Vespasian agreed. The Romans eventually breached the walls of Jerusalem and destroyed the Jerusalem temple. A few years later the revolt was finally crushed after the taking of the fortress at Masada.

The destruction of the temple was nothing short of cataclysmic. Without the temple, it would be impossible for Judaism to practice the faith as prescribed by the Mosaic Law. Moreover, the aftermath of the first revolt had serious ramifications for several sects within Judaism. The Zealots were wiped out by the Romans. The Qumran community was decimated by the Romans as well. Without the priesthood and the temple, the Sadducees became disenfranchised and disappeared from history. Only two Jewish sects survived the first revolt intact, and even a bit emboldened: the Christians and the Pharisees.

The Christians survived because Jesus had warned his followers about the coming destruction and commanded them to flee for safety at its outset (Matt. 24:2ff.; Mark 13:2ff.; Luke 19:43–44; 21:5–6). The early Christians who heeded Christ's words were largely untouched by the hostilities. Moreover, the fulfillment of Christ's predication surely emboldened Christians and gave them a powerful apologetic for the truth of the gospel.

The Pharisees survived through the brokered deal with the Romans, allowing them to set up a school at Jamnia. After the dust settled from the First Jewish Revolt, the school at Jamnia became the new center for Jewish religion and politics. The Sanhedrin, which had previously operated in Jerusalem, was effectively moved to Jamnia, and the leadership of this body became dominated by the Pharisees.

The Second Jewish Revolt (A.D. 132–135)

The failure of the First Jewish Revolt left the Jewish nation in an intolerable situation. Either another revolt needed to be waged so that the Jerusalem temple could be rebuilt and its cultic practices restored or Judaism needed to re-define itself along non-sacrificial, non-cultic lines; that is, it needed to become a religion of the book.

History tells us that *both* paths were chosen. And curiously enough, both endeavors happened under the direction and auspices of one of the most famous rabbis in rabbinic history: Akiva (or Akiba) ben Joseph (c. A.D. 50–137).

Perpetration for the Second Revolt began almost as soon as the first one had failed. The failure had taught the Jews a very valuable lesson. If the Second Revolt were to have any chance at success, it needed to be led by a single strong leader. That leader was Simon bar Kokhba (d. A.D. 135). Rabbi Akiva, the head of the school at Jamnia, proclaimed that bar Kokhba was the long-awaited messiah who would defeat the Romans and rebuild the temple. Simon became known as *bar Kokhba* (Aramaic, "son of the star") because Numbers 24:17 prophesied, "There shall come a star out of Jacob."[79]

Akiva's identification of Simon bar Kokhba as the messiah had a direct impact on the nature of the Second Jewish Revolt. The first revolt was a national uprising; this second revolt would be a messianic movement.[80] A large number of Jews joined in the rebellion; after all, the head rabbi had identified the messiah! Enthusiasm for the Second Revolt was so great, in fact, that even Samaritans and pagans joined in the fighting. However, there was one Jewish sect that refused to join: an obstinate sect known as the Christians.

The Christians, a majority of whom were ethnically Jewish, were pressed to join the revolt, but they refused. To accept bar Kokhba as messiah, as Akiva insisted, would have been nothing short of apostasy; and because of their refusal to do so, Christians were treated by the Jews not only as heretics but traitors as well.[81]

The False Prophet and the Beast

The drama surrounding the Second Revolt sounds from a Christian perspective much like something out of the book of Revelation. Akiva is a false prophet who declares Simon bar Kokhba to be the messiah, and all the people in the land are pressed to serve him in the revolt. Bar Kokhba, like the beast in Revelation 13:7, had authority to wage war against the holy ones and did so by persecuting Christians and pressing them to join his ranks. Even the length of the revolt echoes Revelation; the Second Jewish Revolt (A.D. 132–136) lasted roughly forty-two months (or three and a half years).[82]

The point here is not to identify Akiva or bar Kokbah with any particular character in Revelation, but to show that—from a Christian perspective—Akiva was not what one may call a "gospel-friendly" character. In fact, both he and bar Kokhba had committed serious acts of blasphemy, and their revolt caused a great deal of suffering and persecution of the Jewish people for decades afterward.

Redefining Judaism

The second course headed by Rabbi Akiva was to re-define Judaism in order to meet new challenges. It was under the auspices of Akiva that Jewish oral tradition was, for the first time in history, consigned to writing. Akiva not only advocated that this be done, but it seems that he even played a role in selecting which oral traditions were to be preserved and which ones were not. The *Avot of Rabbi Natan* says of Akiva,

> What was Rabbi Akiva like? A worker who goes out with his basket. He finds wheat—he puts it in, barley—he puts it in, spelt—he puts it in, beans—he puts it in, lentils—he puts it in. When he arrives home he sorts out the wheat by itself, barley by itself, spelt by itself, beans by themselves, lentils by themselves. So did Rabbi Akiva; he arranged the Torah rings by rings.[83]

The earliest layers of oral tradition were selected by Akiva, and whatever was not selected or preserved was soon forgotten and lost forever.[84]

Another part of the transition from cultic Judaism to rabbinic Judaism concerned the interpretation of Scripture. Rabbinic Judaism faced new and unique challenges, and it needed flexibility to deal with them. The solution came through an interpretive method, adopted by Akiva, called *inclusion and exclusion*.[85] This method gave the interpreter an enormous power to read vast amounts of legislation *into* the minutest features of the Hebrew text. As John Bowman notes,

> It was a mighty key that R. Akiba provided to unlock the Torah, so that a never-ending stream of *halakoth* could be derived from it. . . . The written Torah, thanks to R. Akiba, kept its central place in Judaism without its hampering the development of the oral law. . . . He supplied the principles for justifying this abandoning of absolute reliance on tradition without breaking with the alleged fount of all tradition.[86]

The inclusion and exclusion method, however, requires a single, stable, authoritative sacred Hebrew text—something that first-century Judaism didn't have. The Old Testament circulated in a number of different versions and translations, the most popular being an ancient Jewish Greek translation known as the Septuagint (or LXX). A single authorized or normative text was needed.

Closing the Rabbinic Bible

It is here that we find a convergence of several lines of evidence that point to the Rabbi Akiva being the one who closed the canon of the rabbinic Bible. It was during Akiva's tenure that a single normative text was first adopted, which corresponds roughly to the Hebrew Masoretic Text (or the MT) that we have today.[87] Akiva was also instrumental in the rejection and replacement of the Greek Septuagint. His disciple, a Jewish proselyte named Aquila, produced a new hyper-literal Greek translation from the MT that was meant to replace the Greek Septuagint for Greek-speaking Jews. Aquila's hyper-literal translation reflects Rabbi Akiva's peculiar interpretative methods.[88]

The adoption of a normative text also entailed the adoption of a single normative canon. With the selection of one text as rabbinic Judaism's norm, all the books found within this text were to be considered sacred—even if some disputed their sacredness—and all the books not found in this text—even if some held them to be sacred—were to be rejected.[89] Here again, we find Akiva at the center of this process. Consider this passage from the Mishnah, *Yadayim* 3:5 concerning the sacred status of the books of Ecclesiastes and Song of Songs [Solomon]:

> All Holy Scriptures defile the hands. Song of Songs and Ecclesiastes defile the hands. Rabbi Judah (A.D. 135–170) says, "Song of Songs defiles the hands but there is a dispute regarding Ecclesiastes." Rabbi Jose [A.D. 135–170]

> says, "Ecclesiastes does not defile the hands, and there is a dispute about Song of Songs." Rabbi Simeon [A.D. 135–170] says, "[The status of] Ecclesiastes is one of the lenient rulings of the School of Shammai, and one of the strict rulings of the School of Hillel." Rabbi Simeon ben Azzai [110–135] said, "I have a tradition from the seventy-two elders (of the Sanhedrin) that on the day when Rabbi Eleazar ben Azariah [A.D. 110–135] was appointed head of the Academy, it was decided that Song of Songs and Ecclesiastes defile the hands." Rabbi Akiba [A.D. 110–135] said, "God forbid! No one in Israel disputed about Song of Songs, saying that it does not defile the hands. For all of eternity in its entirety is not as worthy as the day on which Song of Songs was given to Israel, for all the Writings are holy, but Song of Songs is the Holy of Holies. And if they disputed at all, they disputed only regarding Ecclesiastes." Rabbi Yohanan ben Joshua (A.D. 135–170) the son of Rabbi Akiba's father-in-law said, "As according to Ben Azzai, so did they dispute and so did they determine."

These debates took place between the First and Second Jewish Revolts. Some disputed the sacredness of Ecclesiastes and Song of Solomon, even though they were part of what became the normative Hebrew text. Akiva's predecessor at Jamnia, Rabbi Eleazar ben Azriah, had already ruled that both books were sacred ("defiled the hands"), but apparently his ruling didn't end the disputes, so Rabbi Akiva, in a rather hyperbolic statement, places the Song of Solomon beyond disputed and Akiva appears to have made his predecessor's decision final.[90]

Even more important for our discussion, Akiva also is instrumental in rejecting the New Testament and the deuterocanon. Akiva states,

> The Gospels and heretical books do not defile the hands. The books of ben Sira and all other books written from then on, do not defile the hands.[91]

Here Akiva rejects as not sacred (i.e., not defiling the hands)[92] the Gospels (and also the books of the New Testament), the book of Sirach (the oldest book of the deuterocanon), and all books written afterward.

Why did Rabbi Akiva pair the rejection of the Gospels with the rejection of the deuterocanon? Akiva's decree suggests that there must have been a sizable percentage of Jewish Christians in Judea during this time (c. A.D. 132) who held the deuterocanon to be sacred along with the Gospels and the New Testament. It also shows that either some Jews may have already accepted some of these books or that there was a danger that they might be accepted in the future. Therefore, a decision was needed.

Here we have a "hostile witness" confirming through his actions that the earliest Christians accepted both the Gospels and the deuterocanon as inspired Sacred Scripture. It was this watershed event—the naming of the false messiah Simon bar Kokhba and the anathematizing of those who rejected him—which occasioned the closing of the rabbinic Bible and the rejection of the deuterocanon.

Jewish scholar Louis Ginzberg poses that the reason Akiva repudiated the use of the Greek Septuagint and the deuterocanon was

> the desire to disarm Christians—especially Jewish Christians—who drew their "proofs" from the Apocrypha, must also be attributed his wish to emancipate the Jews of the Dispersion from the domination of the Septuagint, the errors and inaccuracies in which frequently distorted

> the true meaning of Scripture, and were even used as arguments against the Jews by the Christians.[93]

The circumstantial evidence seems to back up Ginzberg's claim. After all, Christians refused to follow Akiva's messiah in the Second Jewish Revolt; they also continued to use the Septuagint, which was incompatible with Akiva's interpretive method of Scripture; and Christians drew proofs for Christ not only from the protocanonical books but from the deuterocanon as well.[94]

Whatever Akiva's motives were, we can agree with Ginzberg's assertion that he "was the one who definitely fixed the canon of the Old Testament books."[95]

Akiva's repudiation of the New Testament and the deuterocanon shows that the advent of the rabbinic Bible produced not one normative canon but two. One "canon"—if we can use that word so early in Christian history—was the books included in the new normative text for rabbinic Judaism, which excluded the deuterocanon. The second "canon" was an older collection of books that predated the first two Jewish revolts. This was the Christian "canon," which as Akiva's decree suggests, included the Gospels and the rest of the books of the New Testament and the Old Testament with the deuterocanon. Christians and rabbinic Judaism now have two different Old Testaments.

The Aftermath of the Second Jewish Revolt

The bar Kokhba revolt failed. Simon bar Kokbah was killed in battle at Betar. Rabbi Akiva was martyred a few years later by the pagan Romans. Emperor Hadrian (A.D. 76–138), wishing never to deal with this problem again, launched a campaign to annihilate Jewish communities in Judea.[96] Jerusalem was renamed the *Aelia Capitolina*, and temples to the emperor and Venus were erected. The Jews were expelled from Jerusalem and weren't allowed even within eyesight of it so that they could not mourn at what was lost. Before Hadrian's decree, the names of the Christian bishops of Jerusalem were Hebrew. Afterward, the names became uniformly Gentile. Judea was renamed *Philistinian Syria* (or "Palestine" for short). Thousands of Jews were either slaughtered or sold into slavery. As Finkelstein describes it,

> The savagery of the repressions grew from month to month. It was probably in the year 134, just before the capitulation of Betar, that the Romans issued their drastic decree, forbidding not only the practice, but also the study of the Torah.[97]

Judaism was in a fight for its life. Rabbis were martyred, and the authorities at Jamnia ran into almost constant interruptions, being forced to relocate back and forth between Jamnia and Usha.[98] As Louis Ginzberg observes,

> The religious persecutions of Hadrian had devastated the country, depopulated the cities, and made the intellectual development of the Jews impossible. Had these conditions lasted much longer there would have been an end to the Jewish people in the Roman Empire.[99]

The "intellectual development" that Ginzberg mentions certainly entails the codification and dissemination of all the reforms enacted under Akiva. The confusion was finally lifted sometime around A.D. 145 when Simeon ben Gamaliel II became the president of the Sanhedrin in Usha. He was followed by Judah the Prince, who, around 200, completed the work that Akiva started in organizing a written record of early oral rabbinic tradition known as the *Mishnah*.

Almost immediately, Christians became aware that the Jews now had a different Old Testament from their own. However, the horrible aftermath of the Second Jewish Revolt appears to have caused some confusion as to exactly which books belonged to the new rabbinic Bible. If Akiva indeed wished to "disarm Christians," it seems to have worked, at least for a few decades. Christians could no longer indiscriminately appeal to the sacred texts as they had done in the past.

The emergence of the new normative rabbinic Bible impacted Christian apologetics and evangelism. In order to evangelize the Jews and defend the Christian faith effectively, Christians needed to know which Old Testament books were still accepted by the Jews. After all, it wouldn't do very much good to appeal to books that the rabbis no longer accepted. The aftermath of the Second Jewish Revolt made this investigation all the more difficult since it also hampered the implementation of the new normative text throughout the synagogues of the Diaspora. Some synagogues continued to use their older texts while others quickly adopted the new ones (e.g., the *Aquila* or another Jewish translation called the *Symmachus*).

In the next chapter, we will see how the advent of the rabbinic Bible and the aftermath of the Second Jewish Revolt affected the early Christian writers. It will help explain some of the strange twists and turns concerning the deuterocanon in Church history.

4

The Bible of the Earliest Christians

Having outlined the birth of rabbinic Judaism and the closing of the rabbinic Bible, we now turn our attention back to Christian sources, beginning with the earliest extra-biblical Christian writers known as the *Apostolic Fathers.* There is no official list of those who are to be considered Apostolic Fathers, although it is generally agreed that they include Clement of Rome, Ignatius of Antioch, Polycarp of Smyrna, Barnabas, the *Didache*, the *Shepherd of Hermas*, and the *Letter to Diognetus.* The Apostolic Fathers are not just ancient: they are important witnesses because some of them personally knew the apostles or were taught by a disciple of an apostle. Therefore, their use of the deuterocanon is very important since it likely reflects the how the apostles used these books.

First Epistle of Clement (c. A.D. 80)

St. Clement of Rome was the third bishop of that city after the apostle Peter.[100] Several ancient accounts state that Clement was baptized by St. Peter himself. Sometime around the year A.D. 80, Clement wrote a letter from Rome, correcting and admonishing those in the church in Corinth who wrongfully dismissed certain elders from their Church offices. The letter, called 1 Clement, was obeyed by the Corinthian church and subsequently was held in high esteem.

This letter makes use of the deuterocanon as an inspired text, twice quoting the deuterocanonical book of Wisdom.[101] There is a disputed third possible quotation of Wisdom 11:21 or 12:12 in 1 Clement 27:5–7, followed immediately by a quote from Psalms 19:1–3.[102] If Wisdom is being quoted, then the introductory words and the unqualified quotation from the Psalms would show that Clement accepted Wisdom as Scripture.[103]

Clement also references the book of Judith and the deuterocanonical version of Esther as sacred texts in 1 Clement 55:2–6, which reads,

> Many women also, *being strengthened by the grace of God*, have performed numerous manly exploits. *The blessed Judith*, when her city was besieged, asked of the elders permission to go forth into the camp of the strangers; and, exposing herself to danger, she went out for the love which she bare to her country and people then besieged; and the Lord delivered Holofernes into the hands of a woman. *Esther also*, being perfect in faith, exposed herself to no less danger, in order to deliver the twelve tribes of Israel from impending destruction. *For with fasting and humiliation she entreated the everlasting God, who sees all things; and he, perceiving the humility of her spirit, delivered the people for whose sake she had encountered peril.*[104]

Some may be tempted to dismiss St. Clement's use of Judith as an example drawn from secular history, not Scripture. On the contrary: just as we saw with the Maccabees in Hebrews 11, Judith is linked directly with Esther, who is found in the *protocanonical* books. Moreover, secular history is not concerned with the acts of God, but Clement holds up Judith and Esther as examples of women who were "strengthened by the grace of God."[105] Likewise, God delivered Holofernes into the hands of Judith to save his chosen people, just as he spared the Jews through the humility of Esther. There is not the slightest hint in this passage that Clement considers the ancient account of Judith's heroics to be one whit less reliable, one whit less religious in nature, than the similar story found in Esther. Furthermore, Clement calls Judith "blessed"—quite a significant appellation, since the only other persons given this title in his letter are the towering figures of the "Blessed" Paul and the "Blessed" Moses.[106] In short, Clement assumes that his Corinthian readership will understand and accept his use of Judith as a biblical figure worthy of mention alongside some of the greatest names in Scripture. As a side note: this passage also suggests that Clement accepted the longer Septuagint version of Esther as well (which includes sections omitted from Protestant bibles) since that version better suits his rhetorical purposes.[107]

The Epistle of Barnabas (c. A.D. 70)

The title of this work is something of a misnomer; modern scholars do not consider the *Epistle of Barnabas* to have been written by the great companion of St. Paul (largely because of marked differences in viewpoint). Nevertheless, the letter is very ancient, and it was highly regarded in the early Church—so highly, in fact, that some ancient writers considered it a canonical New Testament book. Its author and place of composition are unknown; it may have originated in Alexandria, Palestine, or even Syria.

Barnabas, like Clement, seems to hold a favorable view of the deuterocanon. Barnabas 6:7 appears to quote Wisdom 2:12, as if Wisdom were part of Isaiah 3:9–10 LXX. If this identification is correct, then the intermixing of the two prophecies from Wisdom and Isaiah would strongly suggest that the author understood them both to be divine and prophetic in origin.[108] We saw a similar intertwining of Wisdom and the Psalms in Matthew 27:42–43 where the psalmist's Suffering Servant appears to be linked to Wisdom's binding of the Just One (Wis. 2:15–16).

Epistle of St. Polycarp to the Philippians (c. A.D. 69–155)

St. Polycarp, who was the bishop of the church in Smyrna, was martyred by the Romans around the year A.D. 157. The second-century Father Irenaeus of Lyons says that Polycarp was "instructed by the apostles and conversed with many who had seen Christ" and that he died a martyr, "having always taught the things which he had learned from the apostles, and which the Church has handed down, and which alone are true."[109] This being the case, Polycarp's use of the deuterocanonical book of Tobit is particularly important since it reflects the practices of the apostles and the earliest Christians. Polycarp wrote,

> When you can do good, defer it not, because "alms delivers from death" [Tob. 4:10; 12:9]. "Be all of you subject one to another? [1 Peter 5:5] having your conduct blameless among the Gentiles," [1 Pet. 2:12] that you may both receive praise for your good works, and the Lord may not be blasphemed through you. But woe to him by whom the name of the Lord is blasphemed! [Isa. 52:5] Teach, therefore, sobriety to all, and manifest it also in your own conduct.[110]

Polycarp shows no scruples about using Tobit 4:10 or 12:9 to confirm the spiritual efficacy of almsgiving; as we will see later, it is one teaching rejected by the Protestant Reformers. He makes no distinction or qualification between Tobit and the other quotations from the New Testament and Isaiah, indicating that Polycarp understood Tobit to be part of the same body of authoritative texts.

Although the dating is not very precise, 1 Clement and the epistles of Barnabas and of Polycarp were written sometime shortly before or during the time when the rabbinic Judaism adopted a single normative Hebrew text. As you can see, Christians during this period use the deuterocanon as Scripture, much like the authors of the New Testament.

The Shepherd of Hermas (c. A.D. 140)

The Shepherd of Hermas is a Christian apocalyptic writing composed in the first half of the second century A.D. In this book, Hermas receives several visions from our Lord in which he explains various mysteries and doctrines, especially that of penance. Scholars note several points of contact between the *Shepherd of Hermas* and the deuterocanonical books.[111] However, most of these allusions are too indistinct to insist upon. There is one worthy of note, however; it comes at the beginning of a section titled *First Commandment,* in which Hermas writes,

> First of all, believe that there is one God who created and finished all things, and made all things out of nothing.[112]

The doctrine that God made all things out of nothing (creation *ex nihilo*) is never explicitly stated in the protocanonical books of Scripture, although it is implied in several passages.[113] However, 2 Maccabees 7:28 does explicitly teach this great and foundational Christian doctrine:

> I beseech you, my son, look upon heaven and earth, and all that is in them: and consider that *God made them out of nothing*, and mankind also.[114]

The phraseology in *Hermas* would seem to echo that of 2 Maccabees, but it is impossible to determine with certainty whether he used the deuterocanonical book as his source.

The *Didache* (c. A.D. 140)

The *Didache* (or the *Teaching of the Twelve Apostles*) is the earliest surviving document outlining rules for Church government. However, it is difficult to date. Scholars generally place the date of composition sometime during the first half of the second century (though much earlier dates are widely accepted). This book contains two possible points of contact with the book of Sirach.

The first instance is debatable. *Didache* 1:6 appears to be quoting Sirach, but the wording is imprecise (Protestant exegete J.B. Lightfoot, in his work *The Apostolic Fathers,* believes this to be an inexact quote from memory).[115] The second citation is more discernible than the first. It reads,

> "Be just in your judgment" [Deut. 1:16, 17; Prov. 31:9]: make no distinction between man and man when correcting transgressions. Do not waver in your decision. "Do not be one that opens his hands to receive, but shuts them when it comes to giving" [Sir. 4:31].[116]

Also significant is the fact that the Didachist makes no distinction between this quotation and the quotations from Deuteronomy and Proverbs that preceded it. The transition between the quotes is seamless.

Second Clement (c. A.D. 150)

This early document has come down to us as the Second

Epistle of Clement to the Corinthians. Its traditional title, nowhere included within the text of the work itself, is now almost universally held to be incorrect; the book does not seem to be an epistle at all, but rather the earliest preserved Christian homily outside the pages of the New Testament; and the identification with Clement is almost certainly an error. It may have been composed in Corinth and included in a collection of writings along with the authentic letter of Clement. There is no doubt at all, however, that it dates from the second century A.D. at latest.

Scholars do note a few points of contact between the disputed books and 2 Clement. These allusions are a bit vague and may, again, have been quoted from memory. For example, Lightfoot believes the writer of 2 Clement 16:4 to have had Tobit 12:8 in mind.[117] Likewise, 2 Clement 16:4 appears to be more of an echo of Tobit 12:8 than a direct quote or allusion.

What Do the Apostolic Fathers Show Us?

Although the Apostolic Fathers wrote shortly before or during the time that the rabbinic Bible was formalized, none of them appear to have knowledge of its closing. They freely use the deuterocanon much in the same way as they do the other books of Scripture, which mirrors what we found in the New Testament. Clement of Rome holds up Judith (a person in the deuterocanonical book of the same name) and Esther as examples of courage just as the letter to the Hebrews held up the Maccabean martyrs among the other Old Testament saints. Polycarp of Smyrna quotes the deuterocanonical book of Tobit to explain the spiritual efficacy of almsgiving just as Hebrews uses Wisdom 7:26 to explain its Christological point in verse 1:3.

As Ralph Brabban concludes after a thorough examination of the Apostolic Fathers, their "canon" was not restricted to the contents of the rabbinic Bible (or later the Protestant canon), but it appears to be much larger, including the book of Wisdom, Sirach, Judith, Esther (expanded version), Tobit, 4 Esdras, (1) Enoch, an expanded Jeremiah, and perhaps others as well.[118] There are no signs of hesitancy among these early apostolically informed writers about using the deuterocanon. They never disparaged, distinguished, or in any way qualified these books when they used them. The deuterocanon is used as Scripture and not rejected as apocrypha.

Newfound Awareness of the Rabbis' Canon

Up until now, the early Christians didn't record anything that would tip us off that they were aware of the new rabbinic Bible. All this will change with our next Father, Justin Martyr. Justin became a Christian shortly before the Second Jewish Revolt. One of his works, known as the *First Apology*, is a defense of Christianity addressed to Emperor Antoninus Pius, who was the emperor who retracted Hadrian's anti-Jewish laws. Justin, therefore, is uniquely situated to observe the adoption of rabbinic Judaism's new biblical norm and interact with it.

Justin Martyr (c. A.D. 100–163)

Born to pagan parents, Justin grew up with a love for philosophy. While walking on a beach one day, Justin met an old man who explained Christianity to him. Justin became a Christian and an ardent defender of the Faith. He became a Christian around A.D. 130. Sometime shortly after the Second Jewish

Revolt, Justin encountered a Jew named Trypho and his companions from the city of Ephesus. Justin's *Dialogue with the Jew Trypho* was written a few years later (around 155–160).[119]

Justin's *Dialogue* is particularly important. In it, he notes that Trypho's teachers "refuse to admit that the interpretation made by the seventy elders" (i.e., the Greek Septuagint) and have "taken away many Scriptures" from that translation.[120]

Justin, nevertheless, made ample use of the Greek Septuagint in his *Dialogue with Trypho,* although he never appeals to the deuterocanon. At first blush, this omission might appear to speak against the early Christian acceptance of these books, but Justin states that he intended to dialogue with Trypho and his companions "by means of those passages which are *still admitted by you.*"[121] In other words, the apologetic purpose of the dialogue prevented Justin from appealing to texts that the rabbis rejected.

Later in the *Dialogue*, Justin is challenged to produce some of the passages that were removed. He responds by quoting a few otherwise unknown texts from Ezra and Jeremiah, stating,

> And since this passage from the sayings of Jeremiah is still written in some copies [of the Scriptures] in the synagogues of the Jews (for it is only a short time since they were cut out).[122]

Justin's words appear to be directed at the ongoing transition of older texts to newer texts in the synagogues of the Diaspora. The new texts had "cut out" portions of the Septuagint that Justin believed were authentic. Later in the same work, Justin makes another curious remark:

> I do not proceed to have a mere verbal controversy with you, as I have not attempted to establish proof about

> Christ from the passages of Scripture which are not admitted by you which I quoted from the words of Jeremiah the prophet, and Esdras, and David; but from those which are even now admitted by you, which had your teachers comprehended, be well assured they would have deleted them, *as they did those about the death of Isaiah, whom you sawed asunder with a wooden saw.*[123]

The story of Isaiah being sawed in two isn't recorded anywhere in the Septuagint, but it is recorded in a pseudepigraphic work called the *Ascension of Isaiah*. The letter to the Hebrews (11:32) mentions this episode. It's unclear why Justin believed that this book was "deleted" by Trypho's teachers, but he is surely mistaken on this point.[124] Be that as it may, Justin believed that Trypho's teachers "deleted" whole books. Justin's mistake about the *Ascension of Isaiah* shows that although he knew that whole books were removed by Trypho's teachers, he wasn't sure exactly which ones were removed. The chaos that followed the failed Second Jewish Revolt may have prevented him from having a clearer picture of the situation.

The next early Church Father appears to have encountered the same uncertainty about the new rabbinic canon a few decades later.

Melito of Sardis (d. c. A.D. 170)

Little is known about Melito other than that he was a well-respected bishop of the church at Sardis (one of the seven churches mentioned in Revelation 3:1–6). Only fragments of his works have come down to us. One such fragment, relevant to our current discussion, is preserved in Eusebius's *Church History*:

But in the Extracts made by him the same writer [Melito] gives at the beginning of the introduction a catalogue of the acknowledged books of the Old Testament, which it is necessary to quote at this point. He writes as follows:

"Melito to his brother Onesimus, greeting: since you have often, in your zeal for the word, expressed a wish to have extracts made from the law and the prophets concerning the Savior and concerning our entire Faith, and have also desired to have an accurate statement of the ancient books, as regards their number and their order, I have endeavored to perform the task, knowing your zeal for the Faith, and your desire to gain information in regard to the word, and knowing that you, in your yearning after God, esteem these things above all else, struggling to attain eternal salvation. Accordingly when I went east and came to the place where these things were preached and done, I learned accurately the books of the Old Testament, and send them to you as written below. Their names are as follows: of Moses, five books: Genesis, Exodus, Numbers, Leviticus, Deuteronomy; Jesus Nave, Judges, Ruth; of Kings, four books; of Chronicles, two; the Psalms of David, the Proverbs of Solomon, Wisdom also, Ecclesiastes, Song of Solomon, Job; of Prophets, Isaiah, Jeremiah; of the twelve prophets, one book; Daniel, Ezekiel, Esdras. From which also I have made the extracts, dividing them into six books."

Such are the words of Melito.[125]

Melito's list frequently appears as a witness for the shorter Protestant canon, even though the contents of Melito's list are different.[126] Such an appeal, however, is misplaced since Melito was not giving us a list of the Christian Old Testament canon, but what Melito believed rabbinic Judaism accepted at that time. How do we know this?

The fact that Melito needed to investigate which books belong on the list is our first clue. If Melito was simply reproducing the books accepted by all Christians, there would be no need for an investigation; the venerable bishop certainly would have known which books were read as Scripture in his own church! Moreover, if Melito was ignorant of the canon, why did it take Onesimus's inquiry to motivate him to find out which books were to be read as Scripture? It's difficult to imagine, much less believe, that this venerable bishop didn't know (or showed little interest in) which books were and were not considered the word of God until he was asked!

But even if Melito didn't know which books were read in his own church, why did he feel that it was necessary to travel all the way to Palestine to learn which books are Scripture? Surely, he could have consulted the Jews in Sardis, especially if, as some assume, both Jews and Christians accepted the same canon that was supposedly closed centuries before Christ. Sardis had a very large Jewish population in the second century; it even had one of the largest synagogues from the Greco-Roman period. What prevented Melito from simply knocking on the door of this synagogue and asking one of its members for an answer? Moreover, why didn't Melito consult with any of the Christian churches and Jewish synagogues on his way to Palestine?[127] If Melito was trying to find out which books were part of the Christian Old Testament, these questions suggest an ignorance on Melito's part so profound that it strains credulity. Surely, something else is going on.

Melito's list wasn't meant to describe which books *Christians* accepted as Scripture, but what *rabbinic Judaism* accepted as Scripture. Melito's list is found in a book he composed for Onesimus called *Extracts*, and it appears to be part of a well-known genre of Christian anti-Jewish apologetic literature. As Arthur C. McGriffith's notes in his *Dialogue Between a Christian and a Jew*,

> The nature of the work is clear from the words of Melito himself. It was a collection of testimonies to Christ and to Christianity, drawn from the Old Testament law and prophets. It must, therefore, have resembled closely such works as Cyprian's *Testimonia,* and the *Testimonia of Pseudo-Gregory,* and other anti-Jewish works, in which the appeal was made to the Old Testament—*the common ground accepted by both parties*—for proof of the truth of Christianity. Although the *Eclogae* [Extracts] of Melito were not anti-Jewish in their design, their character leads us to classify them with the general class of anti-Jewish works whose distinguishing mark is the use of Old Testament prophecy in defense of Christianity.[128]

Melito's *Extracts* was a Christian apologetic work, and since it is necessary for there to be "common ground accepted by both parties," Onesimus, in his zeal for the Faith, needed to know which books could be used in Christianity's defense against Jewish contentions. Origen of Alexandria, who wrote only a few decades later, spoke of how the Jews "scornfully laugh at Gentile believers" when they quoted texts that differ from their own. Melito's list was to help Onesimus avoid such scornful laughter.

Why is this important? Because it means that Melito's list isn't telling us about what *Christians* believed about the Old Testament canon or the Christian canon, but what *the rabbis* currently accepted. The omission of the deuterocanon from Melito's list, therefore, only shows that rabbinic Judaism had rejected it.

Athenagoras (c. A.D. 133–190)

Very little is known about Athenagoras. He was an Athenian philosopher who had converted to Christianity around the first half of the second century. His main surviving works—*The Plea for Christians* and a *Treatise on the Resurrection*—are addressed to pagan audiences. In the former, he speaks about Moses, Isaiah, Jeremiah, and the other prophets "who, lifted in ecstasy above the natural operations of their minds by the impulses of the divine Spirit, uttered the things with which they were inspired, the Spirit making use of them as a flute player breathes into a flute; what, then, do these men say? 'The Lord is our God; no other can be compared with him. [Bar. 3:35]." [129] Athenagoras follows his quote from Baruch with a series of quotations from Isaiah. There is no indication that Athenagoras recognized any differentiation between the authority of Baruch and that of the other texts.

Irenaeus of Lyons (c. A.D. 115–190)

Irenaeus was born in Proconsular Asia and converted to Christianity during the first half of the second century. When he was a young man, he was a hearer of Polycarp, the bishop of Smyrna, who was a disciple of the apostle John.[130] Irenaeus is somewhat unique in that he provides eyewitness testimony regarding the condition of the second-century Church in both the eastern and western parts of the empire. His life straddles the watershed period from the end of the Apostolic Fathers (via his acquaintance with Polycarp) right up to the turn of the third century.

Irenaeus's writings indicate clearly that he accepted the deuterocanon as Scripture. The books of Wisdom, Baruch, and the deuterocanonical portions of Daniel are freely cited as Scripture.[131] And as the early Church's great expert on

Gnosticism, Irenaeus also provides evidence for acceptance of the deuterocanon even among the early splinter groups; he records that Gnostic Ophites and Sethians included the book of Tobit among the writings of the prophets.[132]

The *Muratorian Fragment* (c. A.D. 155)

L.A. Muratori discovered this famous fragment in 1740; a somewhat mysterious fragment of second-century writing that could very well be the oldest surviving list of New Testament books.[133] And even though the *Muratorian Fragment* never addresses the subject of the Old Testament at all, we must include a discussion of it here—if only because it includes, among the books of its recommended New Testament, the Old Testament book of Wisdom![134]

The Catacombs (Early Second Century–Third Century)

Christian art dates back to the beginning. Tombs of the earliest Christians were adorned with biblical images drawn from the Old and New Testaments, including the deuterocanon. Although fewer in number, the images from the deuterocanon are also present among the works, some dating as far back as the early second century. The earliest themes are drawn from Susannah, Bel and the Dragon, and Tobit.[135] This does not prove that the deuterocanon was accepted as inspired Scripture, but it does give us a glimpse into the biblical worldview of the earliest Christians, and we see that it was deuterocanon-friendly.

Tertullian of Carthage (A.D. 155–250)

Quintus Septimius Florens Tertullianus, better known as Tertullian, was born around A.D. 160 to the family of a Roman centurion. He grew up in Rome and later became involved in the Roman legal system, either as a lawyer or as someone schooled in the ways of the court. Tertullian converted to Christianity near the end of the second century and became an ardent apologist, writing numerous defenses of the Faith. Sadly, this career was short-lived; brilliant as he was, he was also a hot-headed perfectionist, impatient with human frailty. Around 210, Tertullian abandoned the Church for a heretical group called the Montanists. This early, "quasi-charismatic" sect believed that the work of the apostles had largely come to nothing and looked for a fuller, more complete revelation through their latter-day "prophet" Montanus and two of his female adepts. Among their more spectacular departures from orthodoxy: a belief that the New Jerusalem would soon descend out of the heavens and come to rest somewhere in the vicinity of Phrygia. Needless to say, they were wrong. Because of Tertullian's departure from orthodoxy, his writings are generally divided into three distinct periods: Catholic, semi-Montanist, and Montanist.[136]

Catholics and Protestants both agree that Tertullian accepted the deuterocanon as inspired Scripture; there is really no doubt about the matter.[137] For example, he extols the zeal of Joshua and the Maccabees without distinction or qualification, suggesting that he saw them both as figures in the same inspired history. What's interesting here is that this is found in his apologetic work against the Jews.[138]

Hippolytus of Rome (A.D. 170–235)

Hippolytus was a presbyter in Rome at the beginning of the third century. His unorthodox Christology sparked a conflict between himself and Pope Zephyrinus (A.D. 198–217) along with a majority of the priests in Rome. After the pope's death,

Callistus I (r. 218–223), who played a role in Hippolytus/Zephyrinus conflict, succeeded to the Chair of Peter. After Hippolytus separated from the Church, his followers elected him pope (more accurately, elected him as anti-pope since this was an illicit election). Hippolytus's reign as anti-pope lasted through the pontificates of Callistus and Urban (222–230). It was not until the reign of Pope Pontian (230–235) that Hippolytus was reconciled with the Church, while he was in exile in Sardinia.

Hippolytus unquestionably accepted the deuterocanon as Scripture.[139] He also used the deuterocanonical books to establish doctrine. For example, he appealed to passages from Susanna and Tobit as proofs that God immediately hears our prayers.[140]

His use of Wisdom in a polemic against Jews may demonstrate that Hippolytus was either unaware that the Jews no longer accepted this book, or that he felt that the substance of the quote was so strong that he was compelled to include it, even though the appeal was likely to fall on deaf ears. In conclusion, Hippolytus uses the deuterocanonical works as authentic portions of Scripture, just as profitable for the confirming of doctrine as any other Old Testament book.

Clement of Alexandria (A.D. 150–216)

Titus Flavius Clemens was a native of Athens who traveled widely as a philosopher. He converted to Christianity, believing it superior to pagan philosophy. While in Alexandria, he met a man named Pantaenus, who so impressed him that Clement became his pupil. He studied and taught at the famed catechetical school of Alexandria until the persecution of 202 and died in Cappadocia around the year 216. Like Irenaeus, Clement was only one generation removed from the apostles, receiving, as he wrote, "the shadow and outline of what he had heard from men . . . who persevered the true tradition of the blessed John and Paul . . . the holy apostles, from father to son, even to [his] time."[141]

Clement, in his writings, affirms in the strongest possible language the inspiration and scriptural status of the deuterocanon.[142] There is simply no dispute; this tremendous apologist, so close in time to the apostles themselves, honored the deuterocanon as the inspired word of God. He quotes nearly every deuterocanonical book at one time or another and calls them "Scripture" in so many words.[143]

Cyprian of Carthage (c. 200–258)

Born to pagan parents around the year 200, Cyprian became a skilled rhetorician and lawyer in Carthage, North Africa. He converted to Christianity in his middle forties and was later elected bishop of Carthage. Enamored with Tertullian's writings, Cyprian exhibited the same tenacity in his own works. Cyprian, however, is more eloquent and refined than his master. His reign as bishop was fraught with dangers; the intense persecution under Decius forced Cyprian to flee for his life. He eventually returned to his see, where he remained a stalwart defender of the Faith until his martyrdom in 258.

Like Irenaeus, Tertullian, and Hippolytus, Cyprian is firmly in the pro-deuterocanonical camp, often explicitly quoting the deuterocanon as "divine Scripture" and using it to confirm doctrine.[144]

Julius Africanus (c. A.D. 160–231)

Julius is the father of Christian chronography. Little is known about his life, other than that he was North African and perhaps a priest.

It is here, during the first decades of the third Christian century, that we find for the first time a Christian disputing the deuterocanon; specifically the section of Daniel known as Susanna. In a letter to Origen, Africanus upbraids the Alexandrian teacher for appealing to Susanna in a discussion with a mutual friend. The reason for his objection is linguistic; namely he believed Susanna to be written in Greek, not Hebrew. Africanus based this belief on the presence of a wordplay that is present in Greek but not in Hebrew.

What is most interesting in the tale of this ancient debate is the way in which Origen responds to the charge: Africanus attacked Susanna on linguistic grounds, Origen defends Susanna on linguistics and especially *Christian usage.* After addressing Africanus's concerns about the wordplay, Origen reminds him that Susanna (and, by extension, the rest of the deuterocanon) is found and read as Scripture "*in every* Church of Christ."[145] Origen acknowledges that Jews did not currently accept Susanna or the other books of the deuterocanon; because the Church, however, receives them as Scripture, we can have confidence in their authenticity.[146] Indeed, Origen actually mocks that idea that Christians ought to reject any portion of Scripture because it is not accepted by the Jews:[147]

> And, forsooth, when we notice such things [portions of Scripture not found in Hebrew manuscripts], we are forthwith to reject as spurious the copies in use in our churches, and enjoin the brotherhood to put away the sacred books[148] current among them, and to coax the Jews, and persuade them to give us copies which shall be untampered with, and free from forgery! Are we to suppose that that providence which in the Sacred Scriptures has ministered to the edification of all the churches of Christ,

> had no thought for those bought with a price, for whom Christ died; whom, although his Son, God who is love spared not, but gave him up for us all, that with him he might freely give us all things? In all these cases consider whether it would not be well to remember the words, "You shall not remove the ancient landmarks which your fathers have set."[149]

It is God's providential concern for the Church, according to Origen, that prevents the original deposit of Scripture from being corrupted. Therefore, it is an offense against God to consider that the Jews, who rejected Christ, could somehow have preserved the true collection in pristine purity over and against the Spirit-filled Church.[150] The scriptures are a set collection, given by the apostles, that no one is permitted to change.[151] And like Justin Martyr and Tertullian, Origen contends that the Jews tampered with the Scripture.[152]

Origen of Alexandria (A.D. 185–232)

Origen was raised in a Christian home and was the student of Clement of Alexandria. He became a pioneer in biblical textual criticism and created the famed *Hexapla,* a manuscript with various translations of the Bible running in parallel columns for the purposes of comparison. For this reason, he is known as the father of Textual Criticism. Origen's motivation for this work was to aid Christians in Jewish apologetics.[153]

Given Origen's stringent defense of the deuterocanon in his *History of Susanna,* it may be surprising to find that Protestants often appeal to Origen as one example of a Church Father who rejected the deuterocanon. But this appeal is made for two reasons. First of all (and in marked contrast to everything we have seen so far) Origen does, on occasion, qualify his use of the book of Wisdom. For example, in his *First Principles*, Origen states that Wisdom is "a work which is certainly not esteemed authoritative by all."[154] By qualifying his use of Wisdom, it is argued, Origen demonstrates that the early Church had its doubts about this book and that it should not, therefore, be received as Scripture. The second reason is that in a portion of his *Commentary on the Psalms* (preserved in Eusebius), Origen produces a list of twenty-two Old Testament books that omits the deuterocanon.[155] This passage, according to proponents of the shorter Protestant list, represents Origen's dispassionate judgment on the subject; his defense of Susanna, and the abundant use he makes of the deuterocanonical elsewhere, is simply loose talk generated by careless enthusiasm. Both of these reasons lack cogency.

Why does Origen qualify his use of Wisdom? Clearly, he does it because the statement as it stands is literally true: not everyone did accept the authority of Wisdom at that time. But what sorts of people rejected it—and why? Jews rejected it, to be sure, for reasons we have already addressed; and at least a few Christians, too, since we have already seen Origen himself disputing over it with Africanus. The question, really, is just how many third-century Christians Africanus may reasonably be supposed to represent. After all, we could probably find some isolated group today, or some modernist scholar, willing to reject one portion or another of the Protestant canon (as Luther himself did for a while!). Would it be safe to conclude from such a discovery that twenty-first-century Protestants are seriously divided over the canon, or that opinions on it vary widely? Of course not.

As we have seen, Africanus never even claimed to base his rejection of Susanna on anything other than his own private study; whereas Origen's defense of it is based on an appeal to near-universal acceptance in all the churches of

God. It is wise, therefore, not to read into this phrase from *First Principles* any notion that a large number of Christians rejected the book of Wisdom in Origen's day; actually, his argument against Africanus shows he believed just the opposite to be true—that any rejection of the deuterocanon represented a privately held opinion at variance with traditional Christian ideas. This is underscored by one additional fact about Origen's *First Principles*: both before and after the passage in which he supposedly casts doubt of the book of Wisdom, the author quotes from it and describes the quotes as "Scripture."[156]

Origen's list in Eusebius is likewise misunderstood. His actual *Commentary on the Psalms* is lost, so we are forced to rely on the two brief quotes included in Eusebius to understand why Origen made up this list. Here is how Eusebius framed the quotes:

> When expounding the first psalm, he [Origen] gives a catalogue of the Sacred Scriptures of the Old Testament as follows: "It should be stated that the canonical books, as the Hebrews have handed them down, are twenty-two; corresponding with the number of their letters." Farther on he says: "The twenty-two books of the Hebrews are the following: that which is called by us Genesis, but by the Hebrews, from the beginning of the book, Bresith, which means, 'in the beginning'; Exodus, Welesmoth, that is, 'these are the names'; Leviticus, Wikra, 'and he called'; Numbers, Ammesphekodeim; Deuteronomy, Eleaddebareim, 'these are the words'; Jesus, the son of Nave, Josoue ben Noun; Judges and Ruth, among them in one book, Saphateim; the First and Second of Kings, among them one, Samouel, that is, 'the called of God'; the Third and Fourth of Kings in one, Wammelch David, that is,

'the kingdom of David'; of the Chronicles, the First and Second in one, Dabreiamein, that is, 'records of days'; Esdras, First and Second in one, Ezra, that is, 'an assistant'; the book of Psalms, Spharthelleim; the Proverbs of Solomon, Me-loth; Ecclesiastes, Koelth; the Song of Solomon, Sir Hassirim; Isaiah, Jessia; Jeremiah, with Lamentations and the epistle in one, Jeremia; Daniel, Daniel; Ezekiel, Jezekiel; Job, Job; Esther, Esther. And besides these there are the Maccabees, which are entitled Sarbeth Sabanaiel." He gives these in the above-mentioned work.[157]

Is this list a catalogue of the books accepted by Jews alone, or is it also intended to represent the list received by Christians as well? Look closely at the wording of the passage above; notice that Origen twice describes this as a list of canonical books "*as the Hebrews have handed them down. . . .* The twenty-two books *of the Hebrews* are . . ." Origen's list in Eusebius, then, reflects rabbinic usage, not Christian; and we have already seen what Origen believed about allowing unbelieving Jews to fix the limits of Scripture for Christians. Notice, too, that the list as Eusebius quotes it does not even succeed as an accurate representation of the *rabbinic* canon accepted in the third century! Origen omits the twelve minor prophets (which would have been reckoned as one book in the practice of that time) and then inexplicably *includes* (under its Hebrew title) the book of 1 Maccabees (though he does separate it from the other books). Shall we conclude then, that Origen denied the authority of the minor prophets as well as the deuterocanon? Or has a mistake been made somewhere?

It would be nice if we could examine the rest of Origen's *Commentary on the Psalms*, for clearly the passage as it stands in rather mysterious. Sadly, the original work no longer exists. There is, however, at least one way to gain insight into its contents: both contemporaries and modern critics agree that the *Prologue to the Book of Psalms* by Hilary of Poitiers (which has survived) follows Origen's *Commentary of the Psalms* "in all things."[158] What do we find in Hilary's book corresponding to the passage of Origen in question?

> And this is the cause that the law of the Old Testament is divided into twenty-two books, that they might agree with the number of letters. These books are arranged according to the tradition of the ancients, so that five are of Moses . . . complete the number of twenty-two books. To some it has seemed good to add Tobias and Judith, and thus constitute twenty-four books according to the Greek alphabet.[159]

One does not find here a dispassionate, literal-historical investigation of the Old Testament collection, but rather a typical Alexandrian contemplation of the mystical correspondences between numbers, letters, and sacred books. Hilary's primary concern was this correspondence of numbers and alphabets and not so much an accurate computation of an Old Testament catalogue. Tobit and Judith are added to the list so as to produce the number of letters in the Greek alphabet. As Breen observes,

> We see here [in Hilary] an excessive mysticism impelling a man to reject or admit a book for the sole purpose of completing a mystic number. This tendency had been brought into patristic thought by Origen and the Alexandrian school.[160]

Hilary's dependence on Origen's *Commentary* suggests that Origen had the same priorities in mind when he composed his list. While writing down the books and their Hebrew names, Origen seems to have accidentally skipped over the twelve minor prophets, so when he ended the compilation, he only had twenty-one names. Unable to find the omission, Origen included the Hebrew name for Maccabees in order to have twenty-two names for twenty-two letters.[161] It is difficult to believe that Origen would be so careless in providing a catalogue, until we recall that Hilary added Sirach and Wisdom to fit the Greek alphabet into the same catalogue of books. It is the mystical correspondences of alphabets, and not the strict enumeration of the Christian canon, that the great Alexandrian wished to leave his Christian readers.

The strongest proof of Origen's full acceptance of the deuterocanon is to be found in the manner in which he employed them. So far in our survey, we have placed the specifics of how an early Father used the deuterocanon in the endnotes. For Origen, however, we will keep this section in the main text to underscore how emphatically positive Origen's use of the deuterocanon truly is.

Origen's Use of the Deuterocanon

Looking at how Origen used the deuterocanon, there cannot be any doubt that he accepted them as nothing less than inspired Scripture, capable of confirming doctrine.[162] He believed the deuterocanonical sections of Esther to be an authentic part of the book of Esther.[163] Origen quotes Wisdom as the word of God[164] and uses it to confirm and summarize Christian doctrine.[165] On numerous instances, Origen quotes Wisdom and the protocanonical books without qualification or distinction.[166] Origen calls Sirach "holy Scripture" and "the divine word." In regard to the latter term, Protestant scholar Edward Reuss noted that elsewhere the same Greek description *ho theios logos* not only indicates "the intrinsic value of the passage quoted, but ought certainly to remind us of its supernatural origin."[167] A similar phrase is applied elsewhere to both Sirach 21:18 and 1 Peter 3:15.[168]

Sirach is called "divine Scripture" in *Contra Celsum*, 8.50 and "Scripture" in *Homily 1 in the Book of Kings, 4*. The formal appellation "It is written" is applied to Sirach on numerous occasions. Again, no distinction or qualification is ever given to Sirach when other books are quoted in the same context. When Origen applies that formula to quotes from Tobit, again he makes no distinction or qualification. He presents Judith as a noble figure worthy of Christian imitation, and cites Baruch with the formula "It is written" without qualification.[169] For Origen, sacred history does not terminate at the time of Esther, as would be the case with the Protestant canon, but continues down through to the time of Maccabees. In *Contra Celsum*, 8.46, Origen writes that there is no need to quote "all the princes and private persons of Scripture history who fared well or ill according to their obedience to the prophets." He then presents Abraham and Sarah, King Hezekiah and Isaiah, Elisha and the childless women who received him and bore a son, a general statement about the maimed man whom Jesus cured, and the Maccabees. Origen elsewhere cites Maccabees as scriptural warrant for the doctrine of creation *ex nihilo*.[170]

Finally, in a very important passage from Origen's *Homily on the Book of Numbers*, the Alexandrian teacher gives guidance to those who had recently entered the Church on how to read the "divine volumes." He suggests that they start with the books of Esther, Judith, Tobit, Wisdom, the Gospels, the writings of the apostles, and the Psalms, but he warns against reading Numbers and Leviticus until later.[171] Clearly, Origen saw the deuterocanon on par with the other inspired books of Scripture.

Dionysius the Great of Alexandria (A.D. 190–c. 260)

Dionysius was a convert to Christianity and disciple of Origen in Alexandria. He became the head of its catechetical school, and in 247, became bishop of Alexandria. Although he was a prolific writer, only a few of his works have survived the ages. Even from these works, however, we readily demonstrate his acceptance of the deuterocanon.[172]

The Council of Antioch (269)

The Council of Antioch was convened to condemn the anti-trinitarian heresy of Artemon as introduced by Paul of Samasota. An official letter sent to Dionysius of Rome and Maximus of Alexandria contains a quote introduced with the formal appellation "It is written" followed by what appears to quote the ninth chapter of Sirach. The Council of Antioch, if this contention is true, is the earliest known local council to officially use a deuterocanonical book in an authoritative manner.

Archelaus (*ante* c. 277)

Little is known about this early Father other than that he was bishop of Mesopotamia. In his debate with the heretic Manes, recorded by an unknown writer, Archelaus uses Wisdom 1:13 against Manes's contention that death did not begin in time, but was "unbegotten" or part of God's nature.[173] By his use of this quote, Archelaus demonstrates an expectation that both Manes and his wider readership would accept the book of Wisdom as an authoritative source, capable of confirming doctrine.

Methodius of Tyre (*ante* c. 311)

A native of Olympius in Lycia, Methodius was the bishop of Philippi. He suffered martyrdom in Greece about the year 311. Methodius, like those who preceded him, fully embraced the deuterocanonical books as inspired Scripture capable of confirming doctrine.[174]

Lactantius (250–326)

Born to a pagan family in North Africa, Lactantius excelled in the discipline of rhetoric. Emperor Diocletian himself requested that he become an official professor of rhetoric at the imperial city of Nicomedia; he converted to Christianity either shortly before or after he left this chair. When the emperor began his great persecution of Christians in 303, Lactantius was financially ruined. Later, he was raised up by Emperor Constantine, who appointed him tutor of his son Crispus. Lactantius died around the year 326. Because most of his works are defenses against paganism, Lactantius uses relatively few Old Testament quotations. He did, however, leave one surviving reference from the deuterocanon: a quotation from Sirach which he uses, in his *Institutes*, to confirm doctrine in an authoritative manner.[175]

The Council of Nicaea (325)

The first and perhaps greatest of the ecumenical councils, that of Nicaea, was called primarily to refute the heresy of Arius, and it left no official record of having attempted to settle any questions of canonicity.[176] Cassiodorus seems to claim, however (along with the thirty-sixth canon of the later Council of Hippo), that the Nicene Fathers did take up the issue of the Christian canon; and Jerome (in a much more reliable text) believes that Nicaea ruled in favor of the book of Judith.[177] Be that as it may, it seems exceedingly unlikely (as Breen notes) that so great a council made any official decree on the subject without the action having become widely known; if it had done so, the result would have been a much more unified understanding of the canon in the East.[178] (It may be that Jerome only means the council fathers made use of Judith in their deliberations without incorporating their approval into any official statement.)

Eusebius Pamphilus (260–341)

Eusebius was likely of a noble birth and became a disciple of Pamphilus, who established the famed library of Caesarea. Eusebius later became the head of the school in Caesarea and its library. In 315, he was elected bishop and became deeply entangled in the Arian controversies of that era.

Eusebius's view of the deuterocanon is difficult to determine. Most of the evidence is taken from his *Church History*, where he reproduces the lists of Josephus, Melito, and Origen. Since these lists do not agree with one another (and he makes no indication of which he prefers), none can be taken to represent his own true opinion. At times, Eusebius seems to separate the books of the Maccabees from the "divine Scriptures," and reports some dispute over Sirach and Wisdom. In other places, he quotes Baruch and Wisdom as if they were Scripture.[179] Therefore, Eusebius's views cannot be determined with anything like certainty.[180]

Aphraates the Persian (280–345)

Aphraates is one of the oldest Syrian Fathers. There is no solid biographical information available, and only a single work of his has survived the ages.

In *Demonstrations*, 5.19, Aphraates refers to the martyrdoms of the Maccabees, and later in the same work quotes Sirach 29:17. He does not segregate these quotations from those taken from the protocanon and uses them without qualification or distinction. Aphraates assumes throughout that his readers will be familiar with deuterocanonical texts and makes no apology for using them.

Alexander of Alexandria (250–326)

Alexander of Alexandria was bishop of that city at the time (c. 312) when Arius first began his agitations concerning the nature of the Christ. Alexander acted slowly but firmly against his unruly presbyter, yet his countering statements on the great subject were careless and imprecise, leaving him open to Arian charges of Modalism.[181] Alexander thus left matters at Alexandria worse than when he found them. It was letters from this bishop to Constantine that convinced the emperor to convene the Council of Nicaea and settle the matter of Arianism (or so he thought) once and for all.

In one of his surviving works, Alexander makes an important use of the book of Sirach. He actually sandwiches a quote from 1 Corinthians between two different quotes from that deuterocanonical work:

> Therefore, I do not think men ought to be considered pious who presume to investigate this subject, *in disobedience to the injunction*, "Seek not what is too difficult for you, neither enquire into what is too high for you" [Sir. 3:21]. For if the knowledge of many other things incomparably inferior is beyond the capacity of the human mind, and cannot therefore be attained, as has been said by Paul, "Eye has not seen, nor ear heard, neither have entered into the

> heart of man, the things which God has prepared for them that love him" [1 Cor. 2:9], and as God also said to Abraham, that the stars could not be numbered by him; and it is likewise said, "Who shall number the grains of sand by the seashore, or the drops of rain?" [Gen. 15:5].[182]

As we can clearly deduce from this fragment, Alexander saw no distinction in status between Sirach and 1 Corinthians; and Sirach's "injunction" is plainly being used to confirm an important doctrine of the Church—that of God's incomprehensibility.

The Early Christians, The Deuterocanon, and the Rabbis

Did the earliest Christians believe that the deuterocanon was human apocrypha? Not at all. The earliest extra-biblical Christian writings show a marked acceptance of the deuterocanon. The books of Tobit, Judith, Wisdom, Sirach, and 2 Maccabees are used and quoted in a way indistinguishable from the rest of Scripture, including being used to confirm doctrine.

The first trace of any disagreement comes by way of a private dispute between Julius Africanus and Origen. Julius's problem with deutero-Daniel was that it appeared to be written in Greek and not Hebrew. Origen disagreed and appealed to the universal use of these books as Scripture in the Church, which he believed was sufficient proof to overcome whatever doubt Julius may have had about their place in Scripture.

Origen's point is illustrated by the rest of our survey. Athenagoras, Irenaeus, the Muratorian Fragment, Tertullian, Cyprian, Hippolytus, Clement of Alexandria, Dionysius the Great, Archelaus, Lactantius, Aphraates, and Alexander of Alexandria all accepted the deuterocanon as Scripture, capable of being used in debate to confirm doctrine.

Almost immediately after the Second Jewish Revolt, we saw a few early Christian writers recognizing that the rabbis held to a different collection of sacred texts than Christians. Justin Martyr was first. Onesimus requested that Melito of Sardis compose a book of extracts (prooftexts from the Old Testament that could be used in Christian/Jewish dialogues) also include a list of the books. Both Justin and Onesimus appear to be uncertain as to which books were part the rabbinic canon. This was during the reign of Antoninus Pius, who rescinded Hadrian's anti-Jew laws and stopped the persecution of the Jews.[183] Justin also notes that the sacred texts read in the synagogues of the Diaspora were in a state of transition, which fits well with what we've seen in the previous chapter. Even under ideal conditions, implementation of Akiva's work would take a couple of decades to filter out to the rest of the Jewish world. The disastrous aftermath of the Second Revolt could certainly account for a bit of confusion, which may explain why Melito was unable to obtain a definitive answer for Onesimus from the Jews at Sardis or on the way to Palestine.

The Christian inability to meet rabbis in dialogue using a common text that both groups accepted as authoritative motivated Origen, in his *Hexapla*, to compare and contrast the various Greek texts with the Hebrew text.[184] By this time—the beginning of the third Christian century—Akiva's reforms began to fit into place. Origen recognizes only one Hebrew text in his *Hexapla*; the other Hebrew texts that had once been in circulation apparently fell into disuse and were replaced by the normative text. Also, the hyper-literal Greek translation of Aquila, Akiva's disciple, finally usurped the Septuagint in prominence among the Greek-speaking Jews.[185]

Origen's detailed work revealed exactly where the Christian Old Testament stood in regard to the rabbinic Bible and the other Greek translations in circulation. Thanks to Origen, Christian bishops and teachers could now pass on this information to the faithful for more fruitful and effective evangelism and apologetics. Moreover, it served a pastoral need as well. In areas where there might be a large Jewish population, it would be unwise for new Christians, who are just beginning to study the Faith, to become entangled in disputes with Jews over which books are sacred. Therefore, it became important for these Christians to know that the deuterocanon could only be used effectively within the Church and even to instruct catechumens to focus their studies primarily on the books that the Jews did not dispute, leaving them to study the deuterocanon at their own leisure.

But as we will see in the next chapter, this distinction, as helpful as it was, also lead to confusion.

5

When Contents Became Canon

With the exception of Julius Africanus and a pair of qualified quotations from Origen, early Christian acceptance of the deuterocanon as Scripture was uniformly positive. Origen's systematic study of the different Old Testament texts allowed Christians not only to recognize that rabbinic Judaism had a different collection of sacred books—which Christians knew long before Origen—but also what was included within that collection. Armed with this knowledge, Christian writers needed to pass on this information by making a distinction within the Old Testament between the books that are accepted by Christians and Jews and those that are accepted only by Christians.

We begin this chapter with St. Athanasius for two reasons. Athanasius was the first early Church Father to construct a comprehensive list of Sacred Scripture to include a distinction within the inspired Old Testament corpus. He also appears to be the first (or one of the first) early Church Father to use the word *canon* to describe the contents of Scripture.[186]

What Is a Canon?

Canon comes from a Greek term originally referring to a reed or measuring stick. A canon is used to measure things, or, if you will, it is a rule by which people must abide. The word is used twice in the New Testament and by the early Fathers in a generic sense, as in the "canon of the Faith" or the "canon of doctrine" or the "canon of tradition," but it was not applied to the contents of Scripture until the period now under consideration.

It's important to know that the "canon of Scripture" is really a Christian way of speaking. Rabbinic Judaism never uses this word in that way. Rabbis preferred to speak of Scripture in terms of its holiness or sacredness. For them, a book was either holy ("defiles the hands") or profane ("not defiling the hands").[187] Christians adopted the same binary (holy or profane) from the Jews, only they didn't adopt the language of ritual uncleanness. For Christians, a writing is either sacred (inspired) Scripture or apocrypha (ordinary human writings). The sacredness of Scripture is tied to its use in worship. Both the Jews and Christians had a special place in their respective liturgies for the reading of Sacred Scripture, usually from an elevated platform or pulpit.[188] Profane books were excluded from public reading.

The same binary is used today. The canon of Scripture is an authoritative list of inspired books, co-extensive with inspired writings.[189] If a writing is inspired, it is canonical. If a writing is not inspired, it is not canonical. The modern use of *canon* took time to develop. As we will see, its earliest wasn't necessarily co-extensive with inspired works. Therefore, it was possible for a book to be not canonical but still inspired.

Athanasius (295–373)

Athanasius succeeded Alexander as bishop of Alexandria. His bishopric there lasted forty tumultuous years, during which he was four times deposed and exiled from his see by Arian opponents. Athanasius is best known in Church history for his staunch and heroic defense of the full divinity of

Christ against the overwhelming tide of heresy that threatened to engulf the world during those decades.

It was the custom in ancient Alexandria that a letter from the bishop be circulated throughout the churches of Egypt to help prepare the faithful for the Easter season. In one of these letters, the *Thirty-Ninth Festal Letter* (January 7, 367), Athanasius addresses what had become a nagging concern at that time. It seems that a spate of suspicious books had been circulating among the churches, a state of affairs in which (according to the letter) some "which are called apocrypha" had been mixed together with the sacred texts. Athanasius wished to separate undoubted Scripture from apocrypha:

> There are, then, of the Old Testament, twenty-two books in number; for, as I have heard, it is handed down that this is the number of the letters among the Hebrews; their respective order and names being as follows. In this order [lists all the protocanonical books, adding Baruch and the epistle of Jeremiah and omitting the book of Esther] thus far constitutes the Old Testament.[190]

Athanasius continues by enumerating the books of the New Testament. At the end of this list, he concludes,

> These are fountains of salvation, that they who thirst may be satisfied with the living words they contain. In these alone is proclaimed the doctrine of godliness. Let no man add to these, neither let him take ought from these. For concerning these the Lord put to shame the Sadducees, and said, "You err, not knowing the Scriptures" (Matt. 22:29). And he reproved the Jews, saying, "Search the Scriptures, for these are they that testify of me" (John 5:39).[191]

Athanasius's quotations from Matthew 22:29 and John 5:39 suggest that the books listed are the ones that are capable of being used to "put to shame" and "reprove the Jews." In other words, they comport with the rabbinic Bible.

Oddly enough, Athanasius's "canonical" list is a bit different from the rabbinic Bible as it is known today. He deliberately excluded Esther from the "canon" category (placing it instead in the second category), and he includes the deuterocanonical book of Baruch and the epistle of Jeremiah (Baruch 6) among those that are in the canon. Not only does this not match the rabbinic Bible, but Athanasius's list is unique in antiquity. No other early Church Father gives exactly the same list.[192] Could it be possible that the Jewish population in Alexandria still had yet to fully adopt the new normative rabbinic canon and still accepted Baruch while having doubts about Esther?[193]

Had Athanasius ended the *Festal Letter* at this point, it would seem that only the books that he called "canonical" were divine scriptures. However, Athanasius felt compelled to add, for greater accuracy, other books that were not listed among "those that are canonized" that the Fathers also handed on to be read:[194]

> But for greater exactness I add this also, writing of necessity; that there are other books besides these not indeed included in the canon, but appointed by the Fathers to be read by those who newly join us, and who wish for instruction in the word of godliness. The Wisdom of Solomon, and the Wisdom of Sirach, and Esther, and Judith, and Tobit, and that which is called the Teaching of the Apostles, and the Shepherd. But the former, my brethren, are included in the canon, the latter being [merely] read;

> nor is there in any place a mention of apocryphal writings. But they are an invention of heretics, who write them when they choose, bestowing upon them their approbation, and assigning to them a date, that so, using them as ancient writings, they may find occasion to lead astray the simple.[195]

The books of the second category were not among the books that could be used to "put to shame" and "reprove the Jews," but they were to be read only by Christians, especially catechumens, who needed catechesis in the "word of godliness." Among these books are the deuterocanonical books of Wisdom, Sirach, Judith, and Tobit (Baruch is listed among the canonical books).[196]

Notice that Athanasius's first two categories—"those canonized" and "those that are read"—share some things in common: they both were handed down or appointed by the Fathers to be read in Church, they both are said to pertain to the study of the "word" or "teaching" of godliness, and they both were distinguished from the third category of apocrypha. But did Athanasius accept the deuterocanon as inspired Scripture? There are several reasons to believe that he did.

With few rare exceptions, all of the Church Fathers up to this point accepted the deuterocanon as Scripture in its fullest sense. This doesn't prove that Athanasius also accepted them, but it does open the possibility. Also, Athanasius's comment about the Fathers recommending the second category to be read by catechumens likely came from Origen of Alexandria. In Origen's *Homilies on the Book of Numbers*, he suggests that catechumens should read the "divine volumes," starting with Esther, Judith, Tobit, Wisdom, as well as the Gospels, the writings of the apostles, and the Psalms, leaving difficult books like Numbers and Leviticus for last.[197]

Origen's advice sounds suspiciously like Athanasius's, especially since Esther is among the first listed by Origen, and Athanasius places Esther among the books that catechumens are to read. If this is so, Athanasius, like Origen, must have understood that these books belong to the "divine volumes" (i.e., inspired Scripture).

Athanasius's Use of the Deuterocanon

A stronger and more decisive indicator that Athanasius accepted of the deuterocanon as inspired Scripture is how he uses these books in his other writings. He not only explicitly calls the deuterocanonical books "Scripture,"[198] but he uses them to confirm doctrine both in defense of the Faith against pagans and against his most vociferous opponents, the Arians. For example, Athanasius quotes Wisdom 6:18 as a proof that knowledge of God leads to immortality.[199] In his work, *Concerning the Opinion of Dionysius*, 9, Athanasius defends the orthodoxy of Dionysius by using Wisdom 7:25.[200] In his work, *Defense of the Nicene Definition*, 5, 20, Athanasius explains that the fathers of the Council of Nicaea wished to define the relationship of the Son to the Father using images from Wisdom 7:26.[201] He even uses Baruch and Wisdom to explain the consubstantiality of the Father and Son![202] Yes, you read that correctly. Athanasius is explaining the consubstantiality of the Father and Son using two deuterocanonical books! Baruch is not surprising since Athanasius places it among "those that are canonized," but Wisdom is in the second category. Clearly, both categories are capable of confirming doctrine and thus are inspired Scripture.

Unless Athanasius was repudiating his former use of these books, which he used to establish certain core theological doctrines, the *Thirty-Ninth Festal Letter* should be understood as a tacit acceptance of the deuterocanon rather than a rejection.

Athanasius is also the first early Father to use the threefold division of Scripture. This is a feature that other early Church Fathers will use during this period. Instead of dividing religious literature into the two categories that we use today, he divides it into three: the "canonized," "those that are read," and apocrypha. For Athanasius, the canonical books were those that were read as Scripture *both* in the synagogue and in Christian churches. The "books that were read" referred to Scripture that was read only in church. Apocrypha were those writings that were not read in either.

The Council of Sardica (c. 342/343)

Pope Julius asked Emperor Constans to convene a local council, the Council of Sardica, to help clear up new difficulties caused by the ongoing Arian heresy. Ninety bishops from the West and about eighty from the East attended this local council, with bishops representing some forty-eight provinces of the empire. This council formally employs a quote from the book of Wisdom in its decrees:

> We cannot deny that he was begotten; but we say that he was begotten before all things, which are called visible and invisible; and that he is the Creator and artificer of archangels and angels, and of the world, and of the human species. It is written, "Wisdom which made all things has taught me" [Wis. 7:22] and again, "All things were made by him" [John 1:3].[203]

Clearly, these council fathers understood Wisdom to be authoritative Scripture, capable of confirming doctrine.[204]

It ought to be noted that a quotation does not constitute an official declaration of a book's inspiration or canonicity, but it does indicate that there must have been a very wide acceptance of Wisdom as Scripture.

Cyril of Jerusalem (315–386)

Cyril was ordained a priest and became bishop through the appointment of Acacius, who was metropolitan of Caesarea and an Arian. Like Athanasius's church, Cyril's diocese was wracked by the Arian controversy. Although Cyril always held to the orthodox Faith, his reign as bishop was a stormy one.

Like Athanasius, Cyril of Jerusalem had a problem with apocrypha in his district, and he composed a list much like that of Athanasius.[205] Cyril writes,

> Learn also diligently, and from the Church, what are the books of the Old Testament, and what are those of the New. And, pray, read none of the apocryphal writings: for why do you, who knows not those which are acknowledged among all, trouble yourself in vain about those which are disputed? Read the divine scriptures, the twenty-two books of the Old Testament, these that have been translated by the seventy-two interpreters . . . *Of these read the two and twenty books, but have nothing to do with the apocryphal writings. Study earnestly these only which we read openly in the Church.* Far wiser and more pious than yourself were the apostles, and the bishops of old time, the presidents of the Church who handed down these books . . .
>
> And of the Old Testament, as we have said, study the two and twenty books, which, if you are desirous of

> learning, strive to remember by name, as I recite them. For of the Law the books of Moses are the first five, Genesis, Exodus, Leviticus, Numbers, Deuteronomy. And next, Joshua the son of Nave, and the book of Judges, including Ruth, counted as seventh. And of the other historical books, the first and second books of the Kings are among the Hebrews one book; also the third and fourth one book. And in like manner, the first and second of Chronicles are with them one book; and the first and second of Esdras are counted one. Esther is the twelfth book; and these are the historical writings. But those which are written in verses are five, Job, and the book of Psalms, and Proverbs, and Ecclesiastes, and the Song of Solomon, which is the seventeenth book. And after these come the five prophetic books: of the twelve prophets one book, of Isaiah one, of Jeremiah one, including Baruch and Lamentations and the epistle; then Ezekiel, and the book of Daniel, the twenty-second of the Old Testament.
>
> Then of the New Testament [the books of the New Testament are listed]. *But let all the rest be put aside in a secondary rank. And whatever books are not read in churches, these read not even by you, as you have heard me say.* Thus much of these subjects.[206]

Cyril's list, like that of Athanasius, divides Scripture into three categories: 1) the twenty-two books, 2) those put in secondary rank, not among the twenty-two but still read openly in the churches, and 3) the apocryphal books, which are not to be read at all, not even privately.

Why did Cyril encourage the reading of the twenty-two books while putting most of the deuterocanon in "second rank"? One has to remember that Cyril's *Catechetical Lectures* were primarily meant to instruct new converts. Being a good pastor, he naturally wished to protect these new Christians by steering them away from the controversies caused by a recent flood of apocryphal literature as well as the books disputed by the Jews. This is good advice indeed for newly catechized Christians in fourth-century Jerusalem. But was Cyril's advice meant to be the standard for all Christians at all times?

If we look to see how Cyril treats the deuterocanon in the same book, we find that he quotes Baruch 3:27 as "the prophet."[207] He also uses Sirach, Wisdom, and Baruch to confirm doctrine.[208] And he even uses the deuterocanonical sections of Daniel that are occasionally cited with the solemn introduction, "It is written."[209] Everywhere else, he quotes the deuterocanon without distinction or qualification.[210]

The fact that Cyril did not restrict himself to the twenty-two protocanonical books, but rather uses the deuterocanon in the same work as inspired Scripture, shows that the distinctions made within his list are meant to help catechumens—*not* to be an objective statement on the canon.

The Council of Laodicea (343/381)

The Council of Laodicea took place in Pacatian of Phrygia sometime in the latter half of the fourth century. It is not known how many bishops attended this local council. Laodicea issued no doctrinal decrees; it only passed disciplinary canons. Laodicea was also plagued by apocrypha, which had crept into the usage of certain churches. The fifty-ninth canon of Laodicea dealt with this problem:

> That psalms of private origin are not to be read in the church, nor uncanonical books, but only the canonical books of the Old and New Testaments.

As mentioned earlier, Christians inherited the practice of having a special station in their liturgy for the reading of Sacred Scripture. Therefore, it was imperative that *only* Sacred Scripture be read in the liturgy and not apocryphal documents. The fifty-ninth canon reinforced the dividing line between sacred and profane books by forbidding the latter to be read.[211] Which books did this council consider canonical? The sixtieth canon reads,

> These are all the books of the Old Testament appointed to read: [it lists the protocanonical books Baruch and the Epistle] . . . and these are the books of the New Testament.

This sixtieth canon has some affinity with Athanasius's list, in that it includes Baruch and the Epistle of Jeremiah, but differs by including Esther.[212] It also differs from Cyril, Athanasius, and Origen in that it omits any mention of the deuterocanon.[213] These oddities only serve to highlight the fact that this canon may very well be spurious; scholars have long noted that this sixtieth canon is missing in an important Greek manuscript and in two early Syriac versions; also in one of two later Latin manuscripts. The consensus among Catholic and Protestant scholars alike is that this canon is *not* genuine, but likely represents a gloss that was incorporated into the text at later date.[214]

Furthermore, even if it could be proved to represent the authentic view of the council, this sixtieth canon may have been a *disciplinary* measure and not a *doctrinal* one.[215] The deliberations of this council have been lost, however, and it is impossible to know if the lists given in the sixtieth canon were to be temporary or permanent or if they were intended to be enforced locally or universally.

Hilary of Poitiers (315–c. 367)

Born into a wealthy pagan family in Gaul, Hilary was well educated, and later in life converted to Christianity along with his wife and children. Around 350, he was elected bishop of Poitiers, where he became famous as a valiant defender of orthodoxy against the Arian heresy. The Arian metropolitan sent Hilary into exile in Phrygia for his beliefs, but he proved too much to handle for the Arians in the East, so he was sent back to Gaul, where he was received as a hero.

We have already visited Hilary's *Prologue on the Psalms*, in which he enumerated the twenty-two books of the Old Testament, adding, "To some it has seemed good to add Tobias and Judith, and thus constitute twenty-four books according to the Greek alphabet."[216] Outside of this eccentric Alexandrian computation of the canon, Hilary's deuterocanonical usage reveals that he accepted all of the books in question as inspired Scripture.[217] He uses Baruch as an authentic part of Jeremiah.[218] Hilary refers to Wisdom as the words of a prophet.[219] He also quotes it side by side with the protocanonical books without distinction or qualification.[220] Sirach is likewise used without qualification or distinction.[221] Judith is quoted as Scripture.[222] Tobit is used without any qualification.[223] The deuterocanonical sections of Daniel are used in a manner indistinguishable from the protocanonical books and sections.[224] Hilary also quotes the books of Maccabees with protocanonical quotations without any qualification or distinction.[225] In one significant passage from *On the Trinity*, Hilary uses 2 Maccabees to refute erroneous opinions that God did not create all things from nothing:

> Since, therefore, the words of the apostle, one God the Father, from whom are all things, and one Jesus Christ, our Lord, through whom are all things, form an accurate

> and complete confession concerning God, let us see what Moses has to say of the beginning of the world. His words are, "And God said, let there be a firmament." If you deny it, you must tell us through whom it was that God's work in Creation was done, or else point for your explanation to an obedience in things yet uncreated, which, when God said, "Let there be a firmament," impelled the firmament to establish itself. Such suggestions are inconsistent *with the clear sense of Scripture.* "For all things," *as the prophet says*, "were made out of nothing"; it was no transformation of existing things, but the creation into a perfect form of the non-existent.[226]

Not only is 2 Maccabees 7:28 used to confirm doctrine, but Hilary introduces the quote by stating that it is the words of "the prophet" and part of the clear sense of divine Scripture.[227]

Basil the Great (329–379)

Basil was born into a distinguished Christian home. Along with Gregory of Nyssa and Gregory of Nazianzus, he is counted as one of the three Cappadocian Fathers. Excelling in his studies, Basil traveled to Caesarea, Constantinople, and Athens. In 370, he became bishop of Caesarea, where he become renowned for his teaching and administration.

Basil quotes the book of Judith in his treatise, *On the Holy Spirit.*[228] He follows this quote with quotations from the Gospel of John without any distinction or qualification. Basil holds up the mother of the seven Maccabean martyrs as an example for Christians.[229] Basil also employs the book of Wisdom to confirm doctrine: for example, he uses Wisdom 1:7 to prove that the Holy Spirit is infinite.[230] Wisdom

1:4 is adduced to show that faith and works are necessary to see the Lord.[231] Likewise, he uses Wisdom 7:26 to explain how the Son is the same "prototype" of the Father, yet different from him.[232] He also quotes Sirach 27:12 explicitly as "Scripture."[233] In other words, Basil uses the deuterocanon as inspired Scripture.[234]

Gregory of Nazianzus (330–374)

Another one of the Cappadocian Fathers is Gregory of Nazianzus, the quieter counterpart of Basil the Great. Gregory's father had been a member of a heretical sect but later converted to orthodox Christianity and was ordained a priest. While at the famed school of Caesarea, Gregory met Basil, who became his lifelong friend. He traveled to Palestine and completed his studies in Alexandria (where Athanasius was then bishop) and Athens. Gregory became bishop in Nazian and was later invited to be bishop of Constantinople, but internal bickering prevented him from accepting the position.

Gregory uses the deuterocanon the same as his friend Basil. He quotes Baruch 3:35–37 to counter his opponent's position concerning the doctrine of the Trinity.[235] Wisdom is used as a definition from Solomon.[236] Wisdom is frequently quoted among other texts without qualification or distinction and is often used to confirm doctrine.[237] The deuterocanonical sections of Daniel are used as an authentic part of Daniel.[238] Sirach is also cited in an authoritative manner. Gregory uses Sirach to expound on the commandment, "Honor your father and your mother." Elsewhere, Sirach and Proverbs are quoted without qualification in order to demonstrate that the Holy Spirit is not a created being.[239] He also introduces a passage from the book of Judith as Scripture.[240]

In *Orations* 43, 70, Gregory recounts numerous examples drawn from sacred history:

> Come then, there have been many men of old days illustrious for piety, as lawgivers, generals, prophets, teachers, and men brave to the shedding of blood. Let us compare our prelate with them, and thus recognize his merit.[241]

He continues by expounding with the examples of Adam, Enos, Enoch, Noah, Abraham, Isaac, Jacob, Joseph, Job, Moses, Aaron, Joshua, the Judges, Samuel, David, Solomon, Elijah, and the seven Maccabean martyrs. In chapter 75, with examples taken from the New Testament, Gregory's panorama covers the whole of biblical history, beginning with Genesis and continuing through the New Testament. The inclusion of the Maccabees in this context strongly suggests that Gregory's Old Testament included the deuterocanon. Outside of a single qualified quotation, Gregory speaks and uses the deuterocanon as inspired Scripture.[242]

This usage seems to be contradicted, though, by a poem written by Gregory where he lists twenty-two Old Testament books.[243]

Gregory's list appears to be pastoral and theoretical, however, since the poem begins with what appears to be a personal recommendation: "Receive, O friend, this my approved number." Notice he didn't say, "Receive, O friend, this *the* approved number." If he had said this, he would be testifying to an objective standard. Instead, he is giving pastoral counsel. The pastoral nature of Gregory's list is further evidenced by the fact that he himself did not follow it; he used the deuterocanon as nothing less than inspired Scripture.

Amphilochius of Iconium (c. 339–394)

Amphilochius is not counted as one of the three great Cappodocian Fathers, but he was an integral member of their company. In 374, Amphilochius became bishop of Iconium. He was known for his learning and for his close friendship with Basil. The majority of his works are lost, and the few that have survived are in fragments. One work (long considered the writing of Gregory of Nazianzus but now attributed to Amphilochius) is called the *Iambics to Seleucus*. The *Iambics* lists the protocanonical books of the Old Testament canon (including Esther) in verse and the New Testament canon, although it states that some considered the book of Revelation spurious.

Amphilochius's list is meant to describe what he believed were the most certain of the books of Scripture.[244] This is why he qualifies Esther and Revelation as being doubted by some. However, the *Iambics* does not exclude the deuterocanon entirely. As Breen notes, Amphilochius places the deuterocanon in an intermediate place between inspired and non-inspired writings.[245] This intermediate category, which Amphilochius describes as those that have acquired the name of Scripture and are neighbors of the "word of truth," is neither listed among the most certain books nor rejected as aocrypha.

Amphilochius, like Athanasius and Cyril of Jerusalem, divides religious writings into three categories. For him these categories are: books that are most certainly Scripture, those that are called Scripture and neighbors to the word of truth, and apocrypha (unsafe and spurious books).

He also, like Athanasius and Cyril of Jerusalem, seems to have accepted the books of the intermediate category as Scripture. Even though the book of Baruch is omitted from Amphilochius's "most certain" category, he nevertheless quotes Baruch 3:37 explicitly as the voice of a prophet and a prophecy about the Incarnation.[246] His intermediate category, therefore, appears to include inspired prophetic works capable of confirming doctrine.

Pope Damasus I (r. 366–384) and the Council of Rome (c. 382)

Around the year 382, a list of canonical Scriptures was compiled that contained the deuterocanon. This list is identical to the canon held by Catholics and is found in a work called the *Decree of [Pope] Damasus*.[247] Some believe this *Decree* to be a papal pronouncement, whereas others contend that it was part of a decree from the local Council of Rome that was held in the same year. It is impossible to prove or disprove either of these propositions. The *Decree* reads,

> Likewise, it has been said: now indeed we must treat of the divine scriptures, what the universal Catholic Church accepts and what she ought to shun. The order of the Old Testament begins here [lists all of the protocanon and deuterocanon].[248]

If the *Decree of [Pope] Damasus* is truly the product of the Council of Rome, then it would represent the first list of Scripture known to be officially promulgated by such a council.[249] The Anglican scholar H.H. Howorth notes, "This pronouncement, as we have seen, does not profess to enunciate any new views on the matter, but merely to declare what the Universal Church accepted as divine Scripture."[250]

Epiphanius (310–403)

During his youth, Epiphanius joined a monastery in Egypt and later returned to Palestine, where he founded his own monastery. In 367, he became bishop of Constantia or Salamis on the island of Cyprus, where he reigned as bishop until his death. He traveled frequently to other countries in order to combat heresy, especially that heresy of Origenism, which, no doubt, won him the admiration of Jerome.

In regard to the Old Testament canon, Epiphanius gives us three lists; two of these lists come from his work in Christian heresiology called *Panarion* and the third from his work *On Weights and Measures.*

In his *Panarion*, under the heading *Against Judaism*, Epiphanius reproduces the books that the Jews possessed *on return from the Babylonian exile*:

> By the time of the captives' return from Babylon these Jews had acquired the following books and prophets, and the following books of the prophets: [lists the protocanonical books and Baruch] . . . And they [the Jews] have two more books of disputed canonicity, the Wisdom of Sirach and the Wisdom of Solomon, apart from certain other apocrypha. All these holy books also taught Judaism the things kept by the law until the coming of our Lord Jesus Christ.[251]

Epiphanius's list of only the protocanonical books (plus Baruch) isn't surprising, since he is listing the books the Jews acquired when they returned from exile. The deuterocanon was written long afterward. Surprisingly, after recounting the "books and prophets" of the Jews, Epiphanius adds that the Jews "have" Sirach and Wisdom as two books of disputed canonicity. This may be another sign that the rabbinic norm had yet to achieve universal acceptance throughout the Diaspora.[252]

The second list is part of Epiphanius's argumentation *Against the Arian Anomoeans* where he challenges them:

> For if you were begotten of the Holy Ghost, and taught by the apostles and prophets, this should you do: examine all the sacred codices from Genesis to the times of Esther, which are twenty-seven books of the Old Testament, and are enumerated as twenty-two; then the four holy Gospels . . . and the books of Wisdom, that of Solomon, and of the son of Sirach, and in fine all the books of Scripture [Greek, "divine writings"], and realize that you have come to us with a name, "ingenerate," which Scripture never mentions.[253]

Epiphanius invalidates the Arian Anomoeans' use of the term "ingenerate" because it is never used in the "divine writings." What are the "divine writings" that are capable of validating it? The twenty-two books of the Old Testament (from Genesis to Esther), the New Testament, Wisdom, Sirach, and others. Unlike the list given in *Against Judaism* that reproduces the rabbinic canon, against the Arians Epiphanius appeals to the Christian canon, which includes the books of Wisdom, Sirach, and others. The assumption is that the Anomoeans would also see these books as "divine writings."

The third list comes from his work *On Weights and Measures.* It is a complex work and at times difficult to follow. After explaining how Origen used the obelisk to indicate where the Greek Septuagint had material that was not found in the Hebrew, he recounts the story of the miraculous translation of the Septuagint under Ptolemy II Philadelphus and how the Hebrews divided the sacred text (of the Septuagint) into twenty-seven or twenty-two books, which corresponds to the number of letters in the Hebrew alphabet. Sounds involved? It is very involved, because the rabbinic Bible was divided differently from the Septuagint. As a result, Epiphanius's description is repeatedly qualified with references to the Hebrew practice.

In regard to Wisdom and Sirach, he writes,

> For there are two [other] poetical books, that by Solomon called "most excellent," and that by Jesus the son of Sirach and grandson of Jesus—for his grandfather was named Jesus [and was] he who composed Wisdom in Hebrew, which his grandson, translating, wrote in Greek—which also are helpful and useful, but are not included in the number of the recognized; and therefore they were not kept in the chest, that is, in the Ark of the Covenant.[254]

The "number of the recognized" refers to those books recognized in rabbinic Judaism. The remark about being placed in the "Ark of the Covenant" likewise refers to Jewish practice.

Therefore, Epiphanius twice reproduces the books of the rabbinic Bible (in *Against Judaism* and *On Weight and Measures*), noting that they also "have" Sirach and Wisdom. He gives an incomplete list of the Christian canon in the section *Against the Arian Anomoeans* where he appeals to the "divine writings" accepted by Christians. Epiphanius's use of the deuterocanon throughout the same work confirms his acceptance of the deuterocanon as inspired Scripture. He frequently quotes from it explicitly as Scripture[255] and uses it to confirm Christian doctrine and refute heresies.[256]

Theodore of Mopsuestia (c. 350–428)

Theodore became a monk at the age of eighteen, then over his life drifted out of and back into the contemplative life more than once. This inconstancy and his impetuous character, along with a propensity for an overly literalistic reading of Scripture, eventually led him into theological error. He is perhaps best known for his espousal of the Nestorian heresy.[257] Theodore's writings eventually suffered condemnation at the Second Council of Constantinople in 533.

The canon of Scripture also suffered under his hand. Theodore rejected the letter of James in the New Testament; and in the Old, he appears to have discarded the books of Job, Song of Solomon, and Chronicles, along with the deuterocanon.[258]

Theodore's canon is just that—Theodore's canon. Like that of Julius Africanus, it represents the outworking of his own research and reflects his own private opinion, not that of his contemporaries. As such, it offers us little more than a historical curiosity.

John Chrysostom (347–407)

Born in Antioch, Chrysostom was one of two children of a high-ranking officer in the Syrian army. About the year 367, Chrysostom underwent a spiritual conversion, and through his bishop Meletius, he studied Scripture and was eventually baptized. He was ordained a priest and became renowned for his sermons, hence the surname *Chrysostom* ("golden-mouthed"). In 397, John Chrysostom was consecrated bishop of Constantinople.

Few contest Chrysostom's acceptance of the deuterocanon as Scripture. He uses Tobit in his work *Concerning Statues*.[259] Baruch is quoted as an authentic portion of Jeremiah.[260] The deuterocanonical sections of Daniel are included among a series of quotes from Scripture, without qualification.[261] Wisdom is quoted as "divine Scripture."[262] Although this prominent Father cannot be shown to have used the other disputed books, he likely accepted them as Scripture along with the rest.

Ambrose of Milan (c. 340–397)

Born of a Roman Christian family, Ambrose became bishop of Milan in 374. He mastered the Greek language and was an assiduous student of Scripture and the writings of the Fathers, particularly Origen and Basil. Ambrose combated and extinguished the Arian heresy in his diocese and defeated a short-lived pagan uprising in 391. Ambrose's godliness and humility made a tremendous impact on Augustine of Hippo.

Like John Chrysostom, Ambrose indisputably accepted the deuterocanon as inspired Scripture.[263]

Mommsen Catalogue (Cheltenham List) (c. 350–359)

In 1885, Theodor Mommsen discovered a manuscript containing a list of Scripture. The manuscript was then housed among the Phillips Collection at Cheltenham in England; therefore, it is sometimes referred to as the *Cheltenham List.* The author is unknown, and the manuscript was probably composed in North Africa during the middle of the fourth century.

The list contains the following Old Testament books: Genesis, Exodus, Numbers, Leviticus, Deuteronomy, Joshua, Judges, Ruth, 1–4 Kings,[264] 1–2 Chronicles, Solomon, Job, Tobit, Esther, Judith, Psalms, Isaiah, Jeremiah, Daniel, Ezekiel, twelve minor prophets, and 1–2 Maccabees.

The word *Solomon* denotes the books attributed in the ancient Church to Solomon (Proverbs, Ecclesiastes, Song of Solomon, Wisdom, and Sirach).[265] Baruch is likely included with the book of Jeremiah, as was commonly practiced. If this is so, the Cheltenham List reflects the same contents that would be given later at the North African Councils of Hippo Regius (393) and Carthage III (397), except for three books, which were undoubtedly accepted, but for some unknown reason were omitted in this list (Ezra, Nehemiah, and Lamentations).

Rufinus of Aquileia (345–410)

Born in Concordia in Italy, Rufinus studied in the town of Aquileia, known for its institutions of higher learning. It was at Aquileia that Rufinus met Jerome and where they formed a strong friendship. When Jerome left Aquileia, Rufinus traveled to Egypt, learning Greek there, and then to Palestine, where he built a monastery on Mount Olivet. For a time, both Jerome and Rufinus embraced the teaching of Origen of Alexandria. However, after some of Origen's less-than-orthodox ideas came under attack, Jerome abandoned and turned on his former master, but Rufinus remained faithful. Sadly, the two friends became bitter enemies.

Rufinus provides a list of the Old Testament books in his *Commentary on the Symbol of the Apostles*, which reads,

> This then is the Holy Ghost, who in the Old Testament inspired the law and the prophets, in the New the Gospels and the epistles. Whence also the apostle says, "All Scripture given by inspiration of God is profitable for instruction." And therefore it seems proper in this place to enumerate, as we have learnt from the tradition of the Fathers, the books of the New and of the Old Testament, which, according to the tradition of our forefathers, are believed to have been inspired by the Holy Ghost, and have been handed down to the churches of Christ. . . . Of the Old Testament, therefore, first of all there have been handed down five books of Moses, Genesis, Exodus, Leviticus, Numbers, Deuteronomy . . . and Esther . . . These are the books which the Fathers have comprised within the canon, and from which they would have us deduce the proofs of our faith.
>
> But it should be known that there are also other books which our Fathers call not "canonical" but "ecclesiastical":

> that is to say, Wisdom, called the Wisdom of Solomon, and another Wisdom, called the Wisdom of the Son of Sirach, which last-mentioned the Latins called by the general title Ecclesiasticus, designating not the author of the book, but the character of the writing. To the same class belong the book of Tobit, and the book of Judith, and the books of the Maccabees . . . all of which they would have read in the churches, but not appealed to for the confirmation of doctrine. The other writings they have named "apocrypha." These they would not have read in the churches. These are the traditions which the Fathers have handed down to us, which, as I said, I have thought it opportune to set forth in this place, for the instruction of those who are being taught the first elements of the Church and of the Faith, that they may know from what fountains of the word of God their draughts must be taken.[266]

Rufinus's list gives us much to unpack.

The most noticeable feature is that it doesn't use the modern binary of canonical/apocryphal, but rather adopts a three-fold division similar to that of Athanasius, Cyril, and others. As with all three-fold divisions of Scripture, a book being omitted from the "canon" category doesn't necessarily mean that it is not inspired Scripture. But did Rufinus believe the deuterocanonical books to be inspired Scripture? There are several reasons to believe that he did.

First, Rufinus calls the deuterocanon "ecclesiastical books," which he claims came from the Fathers of the Church. But the only known instance of "ecclesiastical books" is found in a writing from Rufinus's master, Origen of Alexandria. In his *First Principles* Origen discusses the use of the word "incorporeal" in an apocryphal book called *The Doctrine of Peter.* Origen states that this book "is not included among ecclesiastical books; for we can show that it was not composed either by Peter or by any other person *inspired by the Spirit of God.*"[267]

The "ecclesiastical books," for Origen, are those books known to be written by an apostle or a person "inspired by the Spirit of God." Given that Rufinus was a devotee and staunch defender of Origen, it's quite likely that he too understood the "ecclesiastical books" to be inspired by the Spirit of God.

Second, Rufinus quotes the "ecclesiastical books" explicitly as holy Scripture. He speaks of Baruch, for example, as the words of the prophet Jeremiah.[268] He quotes from Sirach explicitly as "Sacred Scripture."[269] Wisdom is said to contain a prediction made by a prophet.[270]

Third, Rufinus defends the deuterocanonical sections of Daniel against Jerome, who deliberately removed them from his Latin translation. In defending them, he affirms that they are authentic members of the inspired Scripture:

> In all this abundance of learned men, has there been one who has dared to make havoc of the divine record [Latin, *instrumentum divinum*] handed down to the churches by the apostles and the deposit of the Holy Spirit [Latin, *depositum Sancti Spiritus*]? For what can we call it but havoc, when some parts of it are transformed, and this is called the correction of an error? For instance, the whole of the history of Susanna, which gave a lesson of chastity to the churches of God, has by him been cut out, thrown aside, and dismissed. The hymn of the three children, which is regularly sung on festivals in the Church of God, he has wholly erased from the place where it stood. But why should I enumerate these cases one by one, when their number cannot be estimated?[271]

Had Rufinus restricted Scripture to only what is found in the rabbinic Bible, he should have praised Jerome for restoring the authentic Old Testament text, instead of castigating him and accusing him of wreaking "havoc on the divine record." As far as he was concerned, deuterocanonical texts like Susanna and the hymn of the three children were part of the "deposit of the Holy Spirit" and authentic members of the "divine record" handed on by the Fathers. If this is true for the deuterocanonical chapters of Daniel, it is even more true for the rest of the deuterocanon.

Finally, Rufinus claims to have received his understanding of these books from the early Church Fathers, yet we've seen that the early Church Fathers, with rare exceptions, accepted the deuterocanon as inspired Scripture. If Rufinus's comments rejected their inspiration, his view would be in conflict with the very Fathers he claims to have followed.

But if Rufinus believed that the deuterocanon was inspired, why would he deny that they could confirm doctrine? St. Paul teaches that all Scripture is inspired and profitable for teaching, reproof, correction, etc. (2 Tim. 3:16). If they are inspired, they should be able to confirm doctrine. Why the denial?

What's even more curious is that Rufinus uses the deuterocanon to confirm doctrine in the very same work! For example, Rufinus uses Wisdom 7:22, 26 to explain the consubstantial relationship of the first and second Persons of the Trinity:

> [W]hy should it be inconceivable for the substance of that eternal light, which has always existed because it contains nothing insubstantial in itself, to produce from itself a brightness which is substantial? Hence the correctness of the Son's being described as *only*; because he was born in this way, he is unique and alone.[272]

In the same work Rufinus quotes Baruch 3:36–38 to refute the Patripassianists, showing that although the Son is "invisible and impassible," he took on flesh and became visible and suffered.[273]

How can Rufinus claim that the deuterocanon cannot be used to confirm doctrine, when in the same book he uses it to teach, reproof, and correct? Either Rufinus is being hypocritical or there is a distinction that we are missing. Rufinus wasn't being hypocritical. The distinction we are missing is this: a book can be said to be capable of confirming doctrine in two ways. It can be intrinsically (objectively) qualified to confirm doctrine, and it can be extrinsically (subjectively) qualified to do the same. A book is *intrinsically* capable of confirming doctrine in virtue of its inspiration; the very nature of the book (having God as its primary author) makes it authoritative.

Although a book may be inspired and objectively qualified to confirm doctrine, this doesn't mean that everyone will subjectively recognize its inspiration and authority. It may truly have God as its author, but it cannot be fruitfully used to confirm doctrine with someone who doesn't recognize it as such. If Rufinus had this distinction in mind, the perceived tension within his writings is resolved, since he is using the deuterocanon to explain and defend doctrine to Christians and Christian heretics, not to Jews. In this sense, they truly are ecclesiastical books ("Church books") because they can only be used fruitfully for those *within the Church.*

Distinctions and Doubts

We've reached the brink of a watershed moment in the history of the deuterocanon, but before we cross that threshold, it's best to take a moment and review what has been presented so far.

Origen's work of textual comparison enabled Christians to distinguish which parts of the historic Christian Bible were and were not accepted in rabbinic Judaism. Today, Catholics make this same distinction without thinking about it. When Catholics say that the Old Testament is composed of protocanonical (first canon) and deuterocanonical (second canon) books, they are essentially making the same distinction as that of the early Church, only using different terms. The early Fathers spoke of "those that are canonized" as the books accepted by Christians and Jews and "those that are read" as the books accepted only by Christians. The "apocrypha" were books that were neither read nor accepted as Scripture by Christians or Jews.

The Fathers who used this three-fold division consistently placed the deuterocanon in the second division and treated its books as inspired Scripture that is capable of confirming doctrine. Their usage shows that the first and second categories were, more or less, subdivisions within the same inspired corpus. It can also be said that none of the early Church Fathers, up until this point in history (the late fourth century) ever assigned the deuterocanon to the category of apocrypha. In fact, they often explicitly said that the deuterocanon was distinct from apocrypha—that is, until a monk living in a cave in Bethlehem decided to pronounce that it was not.[274]

6

Crossing the "Apocrypha" Line

Although the deuterocanon may not have found its way into the "canonical" category of some lists, no early Father ever rejected it as apocrypha until four centuries after the time of Christ, with St. Jerome.

Had Jerome been an ordinary Christian, his opinion would have been just one eccentric voice among others who, like Theodore of Mopsuestia, created their own list of what they believed Sacred Scripture to be. But Jerome was different. Unlike all the early Fathers who preceded him, Jerome was commissioned by the pope to produce a fresh Latin translation of Scripture. This commission and Jerome's fiery determination to win an argument sowed the seeds of confusion about the deuterocanon for centuries to come.

Jerome (340–420)

Born in Stridon in Dalmatia, Jerome was baptized around the age of twenty. Interested in theological and biblical studies, he entered a school in Tier and later transferred to the famed school of Aquileia where he befriended Rufinus. East to Antioch, he studied under (the then-orthodox) Apollinaris. After becoming a priest and a monk, he traveled to Constantinople and eventually stopped in Rome a few years before the death of Pope Damasus I (d. 384). With his irascible demeanor and insatiable appetite for controversy, Jerome quickly made enemies in Rome and was essentially forced to leave. Returning to the East, he settled in a monastery in Bethlehem, where he spent the rest of his life.

Jerome's greatest contribution to the Church is his work in biblical studies. His mastery of Latin, Greek, Hebrew, and Aramaic is unique for his time. By the fifth century, the common Latin translation of the Greek Septuagint in service for centuries, known as the Old Latin version, had become corrupted beyond revision. It was said that there were as many variations in the text as there were manuscripts. A new translation was needed. Pope Damasus commissioned Jerome to undertake this work.

Jerome began translating what would be called the *Vulgate* from the Greek Septuagint just as Christian translators had done for centuries—indeed, from the days of the apostles.[275] He quickly became frustrated with this task, however, because he had to examine and collate various versions of the Septuagint in order to arrive at an original. By contrast, he had a Hebrew text available that seemed to have circulated a long time in only one standardized and stable version. Since the Septuagint itself is a translation of the Hebrew, he thought, why bother dragging in the Greek at all? Why not simply translate directly from the Hebrew? Jerome called this principle—that of placing the Hebrew Masoretic Text over and against all other versions—the principle of *Hebrew Verity*.

In principle, Jerome was right: the original, inspired Hebrew really is what ultimately needed to be translated. Unfortunately, Jerome made a critical error in his application of that principle. He thought that the Hebrew original had been preserved *only* in the single manuscript tradition, the Masoretic Text, and that the Greek Septuagint was nothing but a (faulty) translation of *that* text. In this Jerome was wrong. With the discovery of the Dead Sea Scrolls, we have been able to confirm what more traditional voices had insisted upon all along—that parts of the Septuagint preserve remnants of a more ancient Hebrew textual tradition that is now lost. Though the Masoretic Text is undoubtedly a very good and authentic witness to other more ancient texts, it underwent a process of development before reaching its final form during the middle of the second Christian century. What Jerome unwittingly did was to pit one authentic textual tradition (the Masoretic Text) against all other authentic texts.

Jerome's adoption of Hebrew Verity carries with it an important corollary for the canon.[276] If the Masoretic Text were identical to the inspired Hebrew original, then any books not included within this text (such as the deuterocanonical books) could not be inspired authentic Scripture and must therefore be spurious. This corollary Jerome ultimately accepted, though it put him at odds with the whole of the early Church. Jerome became the first Western Father to deny the inspiration of the deuterocanon and the first of the early Church Fathers to designate them as apocrypha.[277] The Catholic biblical scholar Francis Gigot goes even further, calling Jerome "the *sole* Father on record *as quoting* sometimes the deuterocanonical books with a restriction concerning their canonical character."[278]

The canon that Jerome proposed for Christians to adopt was an innovation—and he knew it. He knew that it would provoke a maelstrom of criticism from all over the ancient world; yet like Julius Africanus before him he was convinced that he, by means of Hebrew Verity, had stumbled upon a truth that had eluded the entire Christian world up to that point. As a preemptive strike against his critics, Jerome wrote a series of prefaces to the various books of his newly completed Vulgate, then sent copies of the books to influential friends. These friends, in turn, circulated the translation, along with his critical prefaces, among the Christian public.[279]

The first preface to appear was the *Preface to Samuel and Chronicles,* known as the *Helmeted Prologue*, because Jerome wanted it to serve as an armored defensive against his critics. Of all Jerome's prefaces this is the most pointed, and it contains the strongest denial of the inspired and canonical status of the deuterocanon:

> This preface to the scriptures may serve as a "helmeted" introduction to all the books which *we now turn from Hebrew into Latin*, so that we may be assured that *what is not found in our list must be placed amongst the apocryphal writings.* Wisdom . . . the book of . . . Sirach, and Judith, and Tobias, and the Shepherd are not in the canon.[280]

Likewise, in the *Preface to the Book of Proverbs,* Jerome writes,

> We have the authentic book of Jesus Son of Sirach, and another pseudepigraphic work, entitled the Wisdom of Solomon. I found the first in Hebrew, with the title "Parables" not Ecclesiasticus, as in Latin versions . . . The second finds no place in Hebrew texts, and its style is redolent of Greek eloquence: a number of ancient writers assert that it is a work of Philo Judaeus. Therefore, just as the Church reads Judith, Tobit, and the books of Maccabees, but does not admit them to the canon of Scripture; so let the Church read these two volumes, for the edification of the people, but not to support the authority of ecclesiastical doctrines.[281]

Jerome forcefully asserts the principle of Hebrew Verity in the *Preface to Ezra* when he says,

> What is not received by them [the Hebrews] and what is not of the twenty-four ancients is to be repulsed far from one.[282]

Jerome's *Preface to the Book of Esther* reduces the deuterocanonical sections of that book to "ragged patches of words."

Jerome's most disparaging remarks are found in his *Letter to Laeta* 107, 12, in which he advises,

> Let her shun all apocrypha, and if ever she should read them, not for confirmation of dogmas, but out of reverence for the words, let her know that they are not of those who appear in the titles, and that there are many false things intermingled in them, and that one has need of great prudence to seek the gold in the slime.[283]

Although Jerome permits the daughter-in-law of Paula to read these books "out of reverence for the words," she should do so with caution because they contain false things mixed in them. His analogy of gold being mixed in slime is perhaps the most irreverent expression used against the deuterocanon since Julius Africanus's dispute with Origen.

Jerome's outright rejection of the deuterocanon as apocrypha was a decisive break from the belief of the primitive Church.[284] This fact is recognized not only by Catholics but also by Protestant historians. Indeed, the Protestant historian H.H. Howorth spoke of it as an inconvenient and undisputable fact:

> [I]n addition to the mischief he did by his ungoverned rhetoric in his quarrels with other theologians, he [Jerome] did a much greater mischief by giving the sanction of his great fame as a scholar to a theory on the canon, which, whatever its merits, *was not that of the primitive Church*. What I ventured to say was, for the most part, *of common and elementary knowledge*; but it needs to be continually emphasized in view of the still prevailing theories about the canon in many high quarters.[285]

The laws of physics teach that for every action there is an equal and opposite reaction. A similar principle also has applications to Church history. Whenever an individual attempts to foist an innovation contrary to the common accepted practice, there is usually a reaction. Jerome's case is no exception. Jerome expected opposition, and he got it: not only in personal correspondences but also in formal conciliar decrees.[286]

One of Jerome's most bitter opponents was his once-best-friend-turned-adversary, Rufinus. In Rufinus's *Apology Against Jerome* and in Jerome's *Apology Against Rufinus*, the topic of Hebrew Verity (and by extension Jerome's adoption of the Jewish shorter canon) was discussed at length. Rufinus writes,

> There has been from the first in the churches of God, and especially in that of Jerusalem, a plentiful supply of men who being born Jews have become Christians; and their perfect acquaintance with both languages and their sufficient knowledge of the law is shewn by their administration of the pontifical office. In all this abundance of learned men, has there been one who has dared to make havoc of the divine record handed down to the churches by the apostles and the deposit of the Holy Spirit?[287]

Some controversialists argue that the deuterocanon was accepted in the ancient Church only because Christians were ignorant of Hebrew and relied on the Greek Septuagint for Scripture. It is argued that had the early Church understood Hebrew and been able to converse with the rabbis of their day, they would have learned the truth about the canon. What they forget is what Rufinus reminds Jerome: there *always was* a steady stream of Hebrew-speaking converts coming into the Church. They knew both Hebrew and Jewish traditions. Yet none of them, according to Rufinus, had ever attempted to alter the Christian canon. Rufinus claims, much like his master Origen against Africanus, that the scriptures are a deposit left by the apostles for Christ's bride: the Church. It is inconceivable that the apostles failed in their duty by not providing for the Church a true and undoubted collection of Scripture. Rufinus summarizes this argument dramatically:

> These men [the apostles] who bid us not attend to Jewish fables and genealogies . . . is it conceivable that they could not foresee through the Spirit that a time would come, after nearly four hundred years, when the Church would find out that the apostles had not delivered to them the truth of the Old Testament, and would send an embassy [Jerome] to those whom the apostles spoke of as the circumcision, begging and beseeching them to dole out to them some small portion of the truth which was in their possession: and that the Church would through this embassy confess that she had been for all those 400 years in error; that she had indeed been called by the apostles . . . to be the bride of Christ, but that they had not decked her with a necklace of genuine jewels; that she had fondly thought that they were precious stones, but now had found out that those were not true gems which the apostles had put upon her, so that she felt ashamed to go forth in public decked in false instead of true jewels, and that she therefore begged that they would send her Barabbas . . . so that in conjunction with one man chosen from among her own people, he might restore to her the true ornaments with which the apostles had failed to furnish her.[288]

Jerome's innovation tampered with the deposit of faith. A person's own intellectual prowess, however great, is not capable of determining what is the word of God and what is not.[289] The Church does not make Scripture. Instead, the bride of Christ passively receives the written word of God from Christ and his apostles as part of the original deposit of faith. Rufinus and Origen argue that to suggest that those books that have been received by the Church are wrong would ultimately mean that Christ and his apostles had failed in their duty of supplying the true and unadulterated word of God to the churches, and that our trust in divine Providence is misplaced.

Despite his tenacity, Jerome did bend a bit in the face of the daunting opposition to his views. He agreed to translate a couple of deuterocanonical books for the Vulgate, stating in his *Preface to Tobit* that he did this, "judging it better to displease the Pharisees, in order to grant the requests of the bishops."

According to an ancient adage, no man is an island, not even a monk secluded in a Bethlehem monastery. Through personal contact and written correspondences, Jerome still had to live and interact with the people around him. On more than a few occasions, Jerome accommodates his writing style to the conventions of a Christian world.[290] In this sense, Jerome becomes an involuntary witness in favor of the deuterocanon.[291] As A.E. Breen writes,

> We have no wish to minimize Jerome's opposition to the deuterocanonical books. At times, it was pronounced and violent. But he could, at most, only be termed a violent doubter. He never was calm and constant in his rejection of those books. The fact that, in such strange opposition, he was at variance with all his contemporaries, made him waver, and we find more quotations from deuterocanonical

> Scripture in Jerome than in any other writer yet quoted. Oft when opposed by his adversaries for his scriptural views he vented his resentment upon the books themselves. Then, when asked by a friend, he would calmly discuss the merits of the same writings.[292]

Jerome's use of the deuterocanon is mostly negative. He calls the deuterocanonical sections of Daniel a fable and flatly denies that Tobit is part of the canon,[293] although elsewhere he cites it without qualification.[294] The book of Baruch is omitted in his *Prologue to Jeremiah*, "setting at naught the rage of his calumniators."[295] However, Jerome adopts the popular convention in his *Letter to Oceanus* by quoting Baruch as a voice made by "the trumpets of the prophets."[296] Sirach is both rejected and quoted as Scripture,[297] although it is formally quoted[298] and occasionally used without qualification.[299] Wisdom is also occasionally formally quoted.[300] Jerome even attributes the passages from Wisdom to the Holy Spirit.[301] Maccabees is used without distinction.[302] Jerome at times alludes to the deuterocanonical sections of Daniel in his letters.[303] Deuterocanonical passages from Esther are likewise quoted.[304] Jerome prefaces a quote from Judith with the words "if anyone is of opinion that it should be received as canonical."[305] Elsewhere, he lists Judith as one of the virtuous women of Sacred Scripture.[306] Despite his vicious opposition to the deuterocanon (especially in his prefaces), Jerome was compelled by the consensus of his peers to use the same books in the manner they were customarily used.

Augustine of Hippo (354–430)

Born in the North African town of Tagaste, Augustine was the offspring of a mixed marriage: his mother Monica was a Christian, and his father was a pagan who converted to Christianity before his death. Although raised a Christian, Augustine became a member of a heretical sect known as the Manicheans. Through the influence of Ambrose of Milan, however, he came back to the Faith. He later became a priest and, at the age of thirty-four, bishop of Hippo in North Africa. Augustine quickly won notoriety for his holiness and his keen theological mind. He is a figure revered by both Catholics and Protestants.

Augustine was well familiar with the topic of the canon. Heretical sects throughout history often tampered with the canon of Scripture in order to give better support to their views, and both the Manicheans and the semi-Pelagians expressed doubts concerning the canonicity of several books in the Old and the New Testaments.[307] Augustine addressed the issue of the canon on many occasions, although his most detailed and systematic explanation is found in his treatise, *On Christian Doctrine*, where he writes,

> Now, in regard to the canonical scriptures, he must follow the judgment of the greater number of Catholic churches; and among these, of course, a high place must be given to such as have been thought worthy to be the seat of an apostle and to receive epistles. Accordingly, among the canonical scriptures he will judge according to the following standard: to prefer those that are received by all the Catholic churches to those which some do not receive. Among those, again, which are not received by all, he will prefer such as have the sanction of the greater number and those of greater authority, to such as are held by the smaller number and those of less authority. If, however, he shall find that some books are held by the greater number of churches, and others by the churches of

> greater authority (though this is not a very likely thing to happen), I think that in such a case the authority on the two sides is to be looked upon as equal.[308]

Like Rufinus and Origen before him, Augustine recognized Church usage as the indicator of canonicity. For Augustine, the canon was established by the apostles and handed by them to the churches via the succession of bishops to be read as divine Scripture. Therefore, those churches that were established by an apostle are given special emphasis or authoritative weight.[309] Augustine continues,

> Now the whole canon of Scripture on which we say this judgment is to be exercised, is contained in the following books: five books of Moses, that is, Genesis, [Exodus, Leviticus, Numbers, Deuteronomy; Joshua; Judges; Ruth; four books of Kings, and two of Chronicles] . . . The books now mentioned are history, which contains a connected narrative of the times, and follows the order of the events. There are other books which seem to follow no regular order, and are connected neither with the order of the preceding books nor with one another, such as [Job, Tobias, Esther, Judith, two books of Maccabees, and the two of Ezra]. . . . Next are the prophets, in which there is one book of the psalms of David; and three books of Solomon, viz., Proverbs, Song of Solomon, and Ecclesiastes. For two books, one called Wisdom and the other Ecclesiasticus, are ascribed to Solomon from a certain resemblance of style, but the most likely opinion is that they were written by Jesus the son of Sirach. Still they are to be reckoned among the prophetical books, since they have attained recognition as being authoritative. The remainder are the books which are strictly called the prophets . . . [Hosea, Joel, Amos,

> Obadiah, Jonah, Micah, Nahum, Habakkuk Zephaniah, Haggai, Zechariah, Malachi; then there are the four greater prophets, Isaiah, Jeremiah, Daniel, Ezekiel]. The authority of the Old Testament is contained within the limits of these forty-four books.[310]

The same thought is expressed more succinctly in his *Apology Against Faustus the Manichean*, in which Augustine writes,

> [I]f you acknowledge the supreme authority of Scripture, you should recognize that authority which from the time of Christ himself, through the ministry of his apostles, and through a regular succession of bishops in the seats of the apostles, has been preserved to our own day throughout the whole world, with a reputation known to all."[311]

Augustine's point is important. The Church does not *make* or *construct* the canon. Instead, it authoritatively passes on what the apostles prescribed to be read publicly in the Church as divine Scripture. By this practice, the Church makes manifest which books were entrusted to it by the apostles.[312] Therefore, for Augustine, the canon of Scripture is a verifiable, historical, and definable entity.

Just as Jerome stated with great clarity that his rejection of the deuterocanon was because of his commitment to the principle of Hebrew Verity, Augustine, with equal clarity, bases his knowledge of the canon on historical grounds: the canon is manifested through the Church's ancient and constant use of these books as divine writings.

Often Augustine's position on the canon is mischaracterized in writing and on the internet as being founded on less-solid ground. For example, it is sometimes claimed that

Augustine accepted the deuterocanonical books because he believed that the Greek Septuagint was an inspired translation, and so the saint assumed that the deuterocanon must be inspired Scripture.

It's difficult to see how Augustine could have believed this, since neither the Septuagint nor its supposed inspiration is mentioned in his discussion of the canon in the paragraphs quoted above.[313] Indeed, Augustine elsewhere defends the book of Wisdom against the semi-Pelagian heretics by appealing not to the inspiration of the Septuagint, but to the ancient practice and acceptance of the Church:

> [T]he judgment of the book of Wisdom ought not to be repudiated, since for so long a course of years that book has deserved to be read in the Church of Christ from the station of the readers of the Church of Christ, and to be heard by all Christians, from bishops downwards, even to the lowest lay believers, penitents, and catechumens, with the veneration paid to divine authority. For assuredly, if, from those who have been before me in commenting on the divine scriptures, I should bring forward a defense of this judgment, which we are now called upon to defend more carefully and copiously than usual against the new error of the Pelagians . . . But if any wish to be instructed in the opinions of those who have handled the subject, it behooves them to prefer to all commentators the book of Wisdom . . . because illustrious commentators, even in the times nearest to the apostles, preferred it to themselves, seeing that when they made use of it for a testimony they believed that they were making use of nothing but a divine testimony . . . And the book of Wisdom, which for such a series of years has deserved to be read in Christ's Church, and in which this is read, ought

> not to suffer injustice because it withstands those who are mistaken on behalf of men's merit.[314]

Here again Augustine makes his stand against the semi-Pelagians, stating that Wisdom ought not be rejected since it has been read as divine authoritative Scripture in the Church of Christ from the very beginning. There is no appeal to the inspiration of the Septuagint here. Nor is there an appeal to the Septuagint when he explains why the deuterocanon ought to be accepted even though the rabbis do not,

> He [Solomon] also is found to have prophesied in his books, of which three are received as of canonical authority, Proverbs, Ecclesiastes, and the Song of Solomon. But it has been customary to ascribe to Solomon other two, of which one is called Wisdom, the other Ecclesiasticus, on account of some resemblance of style, but the more learned have no doubt that they are not his; *yet of old the Church, especially the Western, received them into authority*, in the one of which, called the Wisdom of Solomon, the passion of Christ is most openly prophesied . . . But in Ecclesiasticus the future faith of the nations is predicted in this manner . . . We see this prophecy in the form of a wish and prayer fulfilled through Jesus Christ. But the things which are not written in the canon of the Jews cannot be quoted against their contradictions with so great validity.[315]

Once again, there is no mention of the inspiration of the Septuagint. Augustine accepted the deuterocanon because the Church from ancient times had accepted it. Remember, he is speaking of the practice being already considered ancient at the end of the fourth century! True, the saint acknowledges that because the rabbis don't accept these books they cannot be used to confirm doctrine against their "contradictions," but this had been well known for centuries.

Another mischaracterization is the claim that Augustine definitively explains his acceptance of the deuterocanon through an off-handed comment in *The City of God*. Commenting on the books of Maccabees, Augustine wrote,

> These are held to be canonical, not by the Jews, but by the Church, on account of the extreme and wonderful sufferings of certain martyrs.[316]

Since this is the only passage quoted, it appears as if it is the sum total of Augustine's rationale for accepting the deuterocanon. Maccabees is canonical because it contains a wonderful martyrology! Invariably, a quip is also added that the same rationale could be used to show that *Foxe's Book of Martyrs* is also canonical Scripture. As we have seen, this is a gross mischaracterization of Augustine's view. Augustine accepted Maccabees and the rest of the Christian canon because the Church from the earliest times accepted it as inspired Scripture. But why did Augustine say that Maccabees was accepted because of the wonderful sufferings it records? He appears to be speculating about why the first Christians accepted it. Hebrews 11:35 references the suffering of the Maccabees. Maybe he is inferring that this is the reason why it was first accepted.

Augustine's acceptance of the deuterocanon as inspired Scripture is acknowledged by all. There is little need to demonstrate it now. He quotes the book of Wisdom as one of the "many passages of holy Scripture."[317] Its words are that of "a prophet."[318] Augustine states that Wisdom contains a prophecy about what will happen on Judgment Day.[319] It is used as a prooftext along with the Psalms.[320] In regard to the lengthy paragraph quoted above against the semi-Pelagians, Catholic theologian Charles Costello rightly observes,

> St. Augustine not only states that these early Fathers regarded the book of Wisdom as one of the divine scriptures, but also testifies, and gives proof that they used its authority in support of Catholic teaching. He singles out St. Cyprian as one of the Fathers before him, who had used the book of Wisdom in support of Catholic doctrine. And an examination of St. Cyprian's writings reveals that he used it frequently in support of Catholic teaching. . . . Had St. Augustine desired, he could have mentioned by name other early Fathers who had used the book of Wisdom as a divine testimony in confirmation of their teachings.[321]

Augustine calls Sirach "holy Scripture"[322] and states plainly that the book contains the words of a prophet.[323] He also refers to Baruch as "the prophet"[324] and describes the story of Susanna as coming from Scripture.[325] Augustine speaks of Tobit in the same manner[326] and elsewhere refers to it as "holy Tobit."[327] In regard to the books of the Maccabees as Scripture and the mother of the Maccabean martyrs possessing the same Holy Spirit who authored the New Testament,[328] he twice quotes 2 Maccabees as a prooftext.[329] Elsewhere, he quotes Maccabees as a passage from the "holy scriptures."[330]

Augustine's positive viewpoint was later enshrined in the decrees of the Councils of Hippo Regius (393) and Carthage III (397) in which he participated.

The Church normally doesn't define a doctrine unless a truth of the Faith has been denied or undermined. Up until now, the early Church Fathers may have had differing views about how the deuterocanon fits within the body of

Sacred Scripture, but none of them (except for Julius Africanus) actually denied that these books were inspired Scripture. It wasn't until St. Jerome rejected the deuterocanon and broadcasted his opinion throughout the Latin-speaking Church through his prefaces in the Vulgate that clarification was needed. This clarification came by way of a series of solemn pronouncements on the authentic Christian canon.

The Councils of Hippo (393) and Carthage III (397)

The crisis raised by Jerome's actions was confined largely to the Latin-speaking West, since his views had circulated through his prefaces in the Latin Vulgate. It is not surprising, then, that the correction came from the West. It is these North African councils that "appear to have been the first church councils to make a formal pronouncement on the canon."[331]

The first council known with certainty to have defined the canon is the Council of Hippo Regius (October 8, 393). The same canon was reaffirmed four years later in the Third Council of Carthage (August 28, 397), which stated,

> [It has been decided] that nothing except the canonical scriptures should be read in the Church under the name of the divine scriptures. But the canonical scriptures are [lists the protocanon and deuterocanon]. Moreover, of the New Testament . . . [it has been decided] that the Church beyond the sea may be consulted regarding the confirmation of that canon; also that it be permitted to read the sufferings of the martyrs, when their anniversary days are celebrated.[332]

The Protestant theologian F.F. Bruce states that the formal pronouncements of these African councils "did not impose any innovation on the churches; they simply endorsed what had become the general consensus of the churches of the West and of the greater part of the East."[333] Jerome's insistence that Christians abandon the deuterocanon was the innovation.

Although these North African councils were local, this in no way detracts from their witness as to the inspiration of the deuterocanon. Their decisions reflected the common usage of the Church and were later reaffirmed by popes and other local councils.[334]

Codex Claromontanus (D^p, 06, δ 1026) (c. 400)

The *Codex Claromontanus* is a Greek/Latin manuscript dated to the early fifth century, containing a list of the books of Scripture that includes Wisdom, Judith, Tobit, along with 1, 2, and 4 Maccabees.

Pope Innocent I (378–417)

Innocent's pontificate was marked by conflicts within the Church in which he nobly fought for orthodoxy. The only extant writings come to us in the form of correspondences, one of which concerns the canon.

Exsuperius, the bishop of Toulouse, was a personal friend of St. Jerome. In fact, Jerome had dedicated his *Commentary on Zechariah* to Exsuperius in 406.[335] Perhaps having encountered Jerome's opinion on the canon, Exsuperius had become confused on the subject and sought a better answer from a more authoritative voice.[336] On February 20, 405, Pope Innocent I responded to Exsuperius's question on the canon:

> A brief addition shows what books really are received in the canon. These are the desiderata of which you wished

> to be informed verbally . . . [lists the protocanon and deuterocanon of the Old and New Testaments].[337]

Innocent's canonical list mirrors the so-called Decree of Damasus (the Council of Rome) as well as the decrees of the Councils of Hippo and Carthage. Innocent I's letter corrects Jerome's mistaken theories and re-affirms the traditional Christian canon in contradistinction to his novel opinions.

The Council of Carthage IV (419)

Another important African council that spoke to the canon occurred in 419. As the Protestant theologian Henry R. Percival notes,

> Councils were nowhere more frequently called in the primitive times than in Africa. In the year 418–19, all canons formerly made in sixteen councils held at Carthage, one at Milevis, one at Hippo, that were approved of, were read, and received a new sanction from a great number of bishops, then met in synod at Carthage. This collection is the Code of the African Church, which was always in greatest repute in all churches next after the Code of the Universal Church.[338]

Having Faustinus, bishop of Pontentia, present on the pope's behalf, this council held in Carthage issued what is perhaps the most solemn affirmation of the canon. Here is what the council said:

> It is decreed that nothing but the canonical Scripture may be read under the name of divine scriptures. The canonical scriptures are the following . . . [lists the protocanon

> and deuterocanon of the Old and New Testaments]. This decree shall be made known to our brother and fellow priest Boniface, the bishop of Rome, or even to the other bishops for its confirmation; for we have received from the Fathers, that thus should be read in the Church.[339]

The African councils are sometimes treated lightly because they were "only" local councils. But the African Code was different. As Percival notes, "There seems no doubt that the collection substantially as we know it was the code accepted by the Council of Trullo, the canons of which received a *quasi-ecumenical authority* from the subsequent general imprimatur given them by the Seventh Ecumenical Council, the Second of Nice."[340]

Beyond Carthage

The acceptance of the deuterocanon was widespread and uncontroversial. It is included in the Ethiopian Scripture[341] and the Armenian version of Scripture.[342] John Cassian (360–426) accepted it as inspired Scripture,[343] as did Theodoret of Cyrus (393–466),[344] Vincent of Lerins (d. c. 450),[345] Pseudo-Dionysius Areopagita (c. 500),[346] and Pope Anastasius II.[347]

A document falsely attributed to Athanasius known as the *Synopsis of Sacred Scripture* (*c.* 490) essentially repeats Athanasius's list in his *Thirty-Ninth Festal Letter.*[348] A collection of ancient ecclesiastical decrees, known as the *Apostolic Canons* (late fourth or early fifth century) also appeared around this time. It includes a rather odd list of Scripture, accepting the protocanonical books (including Esther), three books of Maccabees, and possibly also the deuterocanonical book of Judith.[349] Sirach is appended to the list as a recommended book. The so-called *Decree of Gelasius* (fifth century) should also be noted.[350] It lists the "true divine Scripture" that is "universally received" by the Church. The list includes the deuterocanon.

Jerome Against the World

As we have noted, there seems to be a principle in history that major action provokes an opposite reaction. Jerome's innovative idea that the deuterocanon is apocryphal was met by a series of decrees that reaffirmed the historic Christian Old Testament. Although they were local councils, the incorporation of the canon into the African Code gave their decisions what Henry Percival called "quasi-ecumenical authority." Another solemn affirmation came in a papal response to the friend and patron of St. Jerome, Exsuperius, the bishop of Toulouse. Exsuperius petitioned the pope for answers on a number of different issues, including which books were canonical. Innocent I's response simply echoed that of the African councils.

If the Church solemnly spoke against Jerome's rejection, how did the idea that the deuterocanon is apocryphal continue? As we said at the outset, had Jerome been a mere theologian his views would have ended at his death and become just another strange individual's speculation about what Scripture ought to be. But Jerome wasn't an ordinary theologian. He was commissioned to make a new Latin translation of the Bible. Jerome used this opportunity to strike out at his potential critics in regard to his use of Hebrew Verity and his views on the canon. As a result, Jerome's opinion continued to circulate throughout the Latin West unhindered, and its influence grew with each new copy of the Vulgate. Jerome's opinion lived on centuries after his death.

Jerome's innovation on the canon and the publication of the Vulgate also came at the outset of a long, tremulous period of the Church. The barbarian hoards had already begun attacking the Roman empire, tensions grew between Christians in the East and West, and Christianity was being put to the test on a number of different fronts. Faced with these challenges, Christian literary activity came to focus more on the preservation of knowledge, especially the views of the early Church Fathers, than on speculative development.

7

The Age of Preservation

Jerome's rejection of the deuterocanon was vanquished only for a time. His Vulgate grew in popularity—so much so that by the sixth century it had replaced the old Latin translation as *the* biblical text for anyone who could read. This growth in the popularity and the authority of the Vulgate cast a glow of credibility onto Jerome's accompanying prefaces because of their proximity to the sacred text.

From the sixth century through the tenth, Christian writers as a rule accepted the deuterocanon as divine Scripture. Those of scholarly acumen recognized that Jerome, the greatest biblical scholar of antiquity, held a different view on the canon, and they were forced to wrestle with how the two views could be reconciled. Others simply quoted Jerome when the occasion called for it, but used the deuterocanon as inspired Scripture. Slowly, however, as the Vulgate became *the* Bible translation in the West, a few Christian writers appear to have adopted Jerome's view wholesale.

The Earliest Complete Christian Bibles

The earliest complete Christian bibles to survive the ages come from the fourth and fifth centuries. The three most important of these are known as the *Great Codices*.

In layman's terms, a codex (pl. codices) is a collection of several books written and compiled in leaf form and bound together, as opposed to the scroll, which contains only a few writings on one continuous roll of paper. The codex offered ancient Christianity the ability to include several books in a single volume. Varying in size and usage, the codex has been used by Christians since the first century. Three scriptural codices stand out in quality and antiquity; these—Aleph, A, and B—are referred to as the Great Codices. These codices are quite large and constructed primarily for public reading in a church;[351] this means that, unlike a single manuscript, they express the collective mind of an entire body of Christians spread over a vast period of time, rather than the opinions of any single author, however learned. The earliest of the Great Codices was likely copied at the beginning of the fourth century. The others date from the fifth and sixth centuries, but likely reflect the views of an earlier period.[352]

The following chart is a summary of the contents of early and important codices.[353] The order of the books has been rearranged to aid the modern reader in comparing the contents of one codex to that of another. The titles and nomenclature of various books have also been modernized for the same purpose. The disputed books are in italics, and the blank spaces represent those books that are absent from a given codex.

The Great Codices

B Vaticanus	**A Alexandrinus**	**(Aleph) Sinaiticus**	**C[354] Ephraemi Rescriptus**	**N + V[355]**
Fourth Century	Fifth Century	Fourth Century	Fifth Century	Eighth Century
Genesis	Genesis	Genesis		
Exodus	Exodus			
Leviticus	Leviticus			Leviticus
Numbers	Numbers	Numbers		Numbers

Dueteronomy	Dueteronomy			Dueteronomy
Joshua	Joshua			Joshua
Ruth	Ruth			Ruth
1–4 Kings[356]		1–4 Kings		1–4 Kings
1–2 Chronicles		1–2 Chronicles		1–2 Chronicles
Ezra–Nehemiah	Ezra–Nehemiah	Ezra–Nehemiah		Ezra–Nehemiah
Psalms	Psalms	Psalms		
Proverbs	Proverbs	Proverbs	Proverbs	Proverbs
Eccl/Song/Job	Eccl/Song/Job	Eccl/Song/Job	Eccl/Song/Job	Eccl/Song/Job
Wisdom	*Wisdom*	*Wisdom*	*Wisdom*	*Wisdom*
Sirach	*Sirach*	*Sirach*	*Sirach*	*Sirach*
Esther	Esther	Esther		Esther
Judith	*Judith*	*Judith*		*Judith*
Tobit	*Tobit*	*Tobit*		*Tobit*
12 Minor Prophets	12 Minor Prophets	12 Minor Prophets (incomplete)		12 Minor Prophets
Isaiah & Jeremiah	Isaiah & Jeremiah	Isaiah & Jeremiah		Isaiah & Jeremiah
Baruch	*Baruch*			*Baruch*
Lamentations	Lamentations	Lamentations		Lamentations
Ezekiel	Ezekiel			Ezekiel
Daniel	Daniel			Daniel
Epistle of Jeremiah	Epistle of Jeremiah			
	1, 2, 3, 4 Maccabees	*1, 4 Maccabees*		*1, 2, 3, 4 Maccabees*
	Psalms of Solomon[357]			

Notice that none of the Great Codices restricts itself to the shorter Hebrew canon. Instead, all five include some, many, or all of the disputed books. Significantly, Wisdom, Sirach, Tobit, and Judith are represented in *all three* of the Great Codices. Baruch and 1 Maccabees are present in two of the three. Only 2 Maccabees found acceptance in but one of the three Great Codices.[358] Although we do not find complete agreement here (several protocanonical books are also missing from some of the codices), there is a substantial concurrence among these texts in favor of the larger canon.

Because the books have been reordered, there is an additional matter of importance that the chart above does not illustrate: namely, that the books of the deuterocanon are thoroughly intermixed among the others in all five of these codices. None of them separates the deuterocanonical books or differentiates among them in any way, indicating that the compilers understood these sections to be authentic parts of the same inspired corpus.

Leontius of Byzantium (c. 485–543)

Born in Constantinople, Leontius became a monk and at one time flirted with the Nestorian heresy, only to return to orthodoxy and become a firm supporter of the Council of Ephesus. He spent some time in Jerusalem, engaged in debates, and returned back to Constantinople.

Leontius sometimes makes the list of those who opposed the deuterocanon. But what he put in the list doesn't tell the whole story, as Breen notes:

> It can be said of him [Leontius], as of Cyril [of Jerusalem], that exclusion from canonicity was not with him exclusion from divinity. With them the divine books of the

> Old Testament were arranged in two classes: canonical and non-canonical. They used the latter as divine scriptures without according them the pre-eminence of canonicity. Leontius used in several places quotations from deuterocanonical works as divine Scripture.[359]

Leontius's usage of the deuterocanon makes his own opinion clear. For example, he explicitly quotes three of the deuterocanonical books as Scripture.[360] He also uses the book of Wisdom to confirm the doctrine of the consubstantiality of the Son.[351] We can surmise from this that Leontius held the deuterocanon to be divinely inspired Scripture capable of confirming doctrine and that his list reflects the tripartite division of Scripture, where books excluded from the "canonical" category can still be considered inspired Scripture (what we today would call "canonical Scripture").

Pope Gregory I (the Great) (540–604)

Gregory came from a wealthy Christian family in Italy. He excelled in grammar, rhetoric, and dialectic and became prefect of the city of Rome. At the age of thirty, he resigned his post, became a monk, and was named ambassador to the court of Byzantium. He stayed in Constantinople for six years before being recalled to his monastery in Rome around the year 585 or 586. Not long after his return, Gregory published a set of lectures based on the book of Job and known as the *Magna Moralia.* When Pope Pelagius II died in 590, Gregory was elected his successor. His pontificate lasted fourteen years until his own death in 604. Gregory the Great's accomplishments are far too numerous to be mentioned here, but this short summary will suffice for our purposes.

Gregory is invariably named as an authoritative figure who rejected the deuterocanon. Some even go as far as to say that his alleged rejection represents a definitive (even infallible) papal pronouncement that was later contradicted when the Catholic Church accepted the deuterocanon!

What's astounding is that the entire claim of Pope Gregory's formal rejection of the deuterocanon is based on a single qualified statement concerning 1 Maccabees. Here are Gregory's words:

> [W]e are not acting irregularly, if from the books, though not canonical, yet brought out for the edification of the Church, we bring forth testimony. Thus Eleazar in the battle smote and brought down an elephant, but fell under the very beast that he killed.[362]

Note first that Gregory is not rejecting the deuterocanon as a whole; in fact, he does not even reject 1 Maccabees. What he is actually doing is anticipating questions on the subject (acknowledging the widespread influence of Jerome's ideas) and pausing to establish that the example he will offer is still valid, even for those who accept Jerome's point of view.[363] Catholic apologist Arthur Sippo expresses it this way:

> So St. Gregory . . . accepted the moderate view that the deuteros were "ecclesiastical." But notice that he is not apologizing for using 1 Maccabees. He is not saying that it is of no value but rather that he felt the necessity of using this book despite doubts about its canonicity. This is very significant. The inspired character of 1 Maccabees showed through despite the doubting of mere men.[364]

As for Gregory's personal view of the deuterocanon, we only have to look at the rest of his works. In them he clearly sees the deuterocanonical books as indistinguishable from the rest of Scripture. Tobit, for example, is quoted without any qualification.[365] There are about twenty-eight instances where Gregory quotes Sirach along with the protocanonical books of Scripture without distinction or qualification. He also counts Sirach as the work of Solomon. For this reason, Gregory often introduces quotes from Sirach as the sayings of a "wise man" and the "voice of wisdom."[366] Fifteen times he quotes the deuterocanon with the solemn introduction "It is written." The book of Wisdom is quoted without qualification about twenty-eight times and with the formula "It is written" some sixteen times. Gregory quotes from every book of the deuterocanon except Judith and Baruch.[367]

Does the single, isolated qualification of Maccabees by Pope St. Gregory constitute an infallible papal pronouncement? It's hard even to pose this question with a straight face. The answer is decidedly "no." To argue such a thing is to betray a profound ignorance about how the pope's teaching authority works.

First of all, in order to teach with papal authority a man must actually *be* pope—and there is considerable doubt as to whether Gregory had yet been elected when the above quotation was penned. As Sippo notes,

> [T]he *Moralia* [or *Commentary on Job*] was started in 578 while St. Gregory was in Constantinople and he completed the last section (Book XXXV) in 595. According to Rev. James Barmby, D.D. . . . it was "in a great measure written during his residence in Constantinople." St. Gregory was pope from 590 to 604. Hence this work was started twelve years before he was pope and was mostly

> composed before he assumed that office. In no way could this be considered an official magisterial document. It is a work of private speculation and has no authority beyond the scholarship used in its composition.[368]

Secondly, even if the dates are wrong and Gregory did happen to have written this book during his pontificate, the passage in question still could not be held to constitute an infallible statement. The pope speaks infallibly when he acts in his official capacity as chief teacher of the universal Church, not every single time he opens his mouth. In order for his teachings to be infallible, in other words, he must actually *be teaching*. He must (in the words of the First Vatican Council) be making a definitive judgment on a matter of faith or morals. Yet here, Gregory is only acknowledging that some people may not agree with his appeal to 1 Maccabees. Gregory's statement says nothing about making the views of these critics binding upon the whole Church. Any claim, therefore, that Gregory infallibly rejected the book of 1 Maccabees is grasping at straws.

Primasius, Bishop of Hadrumetum (527–565)

In his *Commentary on the Book of Revelation*, Primasius wrote,

> The twenty-four elders are the books of the Old Testament which we receive of that number as possessing canonical authority.[369]

The twenty-four books would correspond to the books of the rabbinic (Protestant) canon. However, this interpretation of Revelation is Jerome's, not Primasius's. In his *Helmeted Prologue*, Jerome wrote that we

> should thus have twenty-four books of the old law. And these the Apocalypse of John represents by the twenty-four elders, who adore the Lamb, and with downcast looks offer their crowns.

Primasius is the first in a long line of Christian writers who quote Jerome's opinion on the canon but continued to use the historic Christian canon. We know he did because he calls Baruch "Sacred Scripture" that predicted the Incarnation of the Lord.[370] Had Primasius followed Jerome's canon, he would have known that Jerome had forcefully rejected Baruch in his *Preface to the Book of Jeremiah.*

Dionysius Exiguus (the Little) (d. 544)

The date of Dionysius's birth is unknown, but it is fairly certain that he died around the year 544. He was a historian and friend of Cassiodorus (see below). In his *Codex Canonum Ecclesiasticarum,* Dionysius includes the canons of the Council of Carthage, which affirmed the deuterocanon.[371]

Junilius Africanus (d. c. 551)

Junilius Africanus (not to be confused with Julius Africanus) offers an unusual listing of the canon. In his *De Partis Divina Legis*, Junilius divides and subdivides the books of Scripture into various degrees of authority. According to his rendering, the historical books of "perfect authority" are the Pentateuch, Joshua, Judges, Ruth, Kings, four Gospels, and Acts. The books of "intermediate authority" are Chronicles, Job, Judith, Esther, and Maccabees. Junilius notes of this second class,

> They are not included among the canonical scriptures because they were received among the Hebrews only in the secondary rank, as Jerome and others testify.[372]

The prophetic books of "perfect authority" are the Psalms, the sixteen prophets, Proverbs, and Ecclesiastes. The book of Revelation is doubted in the East. The second "intermediate" category contains the Song of Solomon and the book of Wisdom. Of the didactic books there are Sirach, the fourteen epistles of Paul, 1 Peter, and 1 John. In the second category are James, 2 Peter, Jude, and 2 and 3 John.

Junilius's strange list is notable in that it is the first attempt to understand the canon of Scripture in terms of utility.[373] The apostle Paul wrote, "All Scripture is inspired by God and profitable for teaching, for reproof, for correction, for training in righteousness."[374] Yet although all Scripture is equally inspired, not every book is equally profitable or useful in confirming doctrine. The book of Genesis, for example, is as inspired as Esther because the Holy Spirit is the primary author of both, but Genesis is certainly more *useful* for teaching, reproof, and training than Esther. Junilius confuses utility with inspiration; therefore, for him there are different categories of Scripture. Junilius's list is clearly the product of his own theological speculations and represents nothing more than a historical curiosity.

Flavius Magnus Aurelius Cassiodorus (490–583)

Cassiodorus's life is divided into his political career and his life as a monk. Several works of his have survived. One of these, the famous *De Institutione Divinarum Litterarum,* addresses the contents of the Old Testament canon. Written between 543 and 555, *De Institutione* was intended as an introduction to

Scripture for the brothers at his monastery and a guide to the study of Scripture. It contains three canonical lists: Jerome's *Helmeted Prologue* (the rabbinic canon); Augustine's list in *On Christian Doctrine* (the Catholic canon); and the books of the Vulgate (the Catholic canon). Cassiodorus presents these lists without commenting on how they differ.

Isidore of Seville (c. 560–636)

Born in Cartagena, Spain, Isidore was educated at the Cathedral School in Seville where he mastered Latin, Greek, and Hebrew. He became bishop of Seville and was instrumental in rebuilding a new culture that had been destabilized by the invasion of the Goths. He also played a key role in the Council of Seville and the two Councils of Toledo. The *Catholic Encyclopedia* states,

> Isidore was the last of the ancient Christian philosophers, as he was the last of the great Latin Fathers. He was undoubtedly the most learned man of his age and exercised a far-reaching and immeasurable influence on the educational life of the Middle Ages.[375]

Isidore is sometimes wrongly appealed to as accepting the shorter rabbinic canon. His comments in his work *Etymologies* is usually the focal point of these appeals:

> The Hebrews, on the authority of Ezra, receive twenty-two books of the Old Testament.[376]

But Isidore was only recounting what rabbinic Judaism accepts as Scripture. What is sometimes missed is what Isidore writes later in the same passage:

> There is a fourth order with us of those books of the Old Testament, which are not in the Hebrew canon. The first of these is Wisdom; the second Ecclesiasticus; the third, Tobias; the fourth, Judith; the fifth and sixth, the Maccabees . . . the Church of Christ honors them and promulgates them *as divine books.*[377]

Being conversant with the Hebrew language, Isidore knew the rabbinic tradition of limiting Scripture to twenty-two books. Nevertheless, he acknowledges the deuterocanon as *divine books* and that it constitutes a fourth division within the Old Testament.

Another list in his work, *De Ecclesiasticis Officiis,* likewise confirms the deuterocanon:

> These are the seventy-two *canonical* books, and on this account Moses elected the elders, who should prophesy; for this cause, the Lord Jesus sent seventy-two disciples to preach.[378]

Isidore's views on the deuterocanon are very clearly stated in his *Prologue to the Old Testament:*

> Of these (the historical books), the Hebrews do not receive Tobias, Judith, and Maccabees, but *the Church ranks them among the canonical scriptures.* Then follow also those two great books—books of holy teaching, Wisdom and Ecclesiasticus; which, although they are said to be written by Jesus the son of Sirach, nevertheless, on account of the similarity of diction, are called of Solomon. And these are acknowledged to have, in the Church, *equal authority with the other canonical scriptures.*[379]

Isidore is an excellent example of how a writer acknowledges the rabbinic canon without rejecting the deuterocanon. He is merely passing on information for the benefit of his readers and not suggesting that that position is correct.

Other Witnesses to the Historic Canon

During the fifth and sixth centuries, several important churches in the southeastern part of the empire rejected the Christology of the Councils of Ephesus and Chalcedon and broke away from the main body of Christianity. Even in this separated condition, however, they retained the books of the deuterocanon as authentic parts of the Old Testament. These groups would include the Chaldean Nestorians, Jacobites, Copts, and Monophysites.[380] Even Islam, which arose in the seventh century, went farther and rejected the divinity of Christ altogether (though retaining him as a very important prophet); yet even several Muslim jurists quote from the deuterocanon, sometimes ascribing it to the books of Moses.[381]

We can also add Paul of Tella (c. 616) whose *Syro-Hexaplar,* a six-columned document used to compare various versions or translations of Scripture, includes the deuterocanonical books of Wisdom, Sirach, and Baruch. Eugenius II (the younger) (d. 647) who put Isidore's canonical list (which included the deuterocanon) to Latin verse,[382] and Ildephonsus (Archbishop of Toledo, ca. 600–667) includes Augustine's canon in his *Treatise on Baptism.*[383]

The Sixty Books (post-650)

The *Sixty Books,* found among the manuscripts of Anastasius of Sinai's *Questions and Responses,* is an ancient manuscript written by an unknown author.[384] It lists all of the books of the protocanon except Esther. Its New Testament listing fails to include the book of Revelation. The list distinguishes the sixty books from apocrypha, which include Esther and 3 and 4 Maccabees.

The Council of Trullo (Quinisext) (692)

The Council of Trullo or Quinisext met to pass the disciplinary canons that were lacking in the fifth and sixth ecumenical councils. As the anti-Catholic historian Philip Schaff notes, it adopted 102 canons ("canons" in this sense, means legal decrees), most of them taken from previous councils. It must be emphasized, however, that these decrees were not legally or ecumenically sanctioned. They were signed by the emperor, with a second place being left blank for the signature of the pope; but that place was never filled. The names of Paul of Constantinople, Peter of Alexandria, Anastasius of Jerusalem, George of Antioch, and other important prelates were added—211 Greek and Oriental bishops or their representatives in all, of whom forty-three had been present at the Sixth Ecumenical Council. Yet no pope ever approved the canons of the Council of Trullo—though some attempt was later made to sanction as many of them as might be acceptable.

Trullo adopted the decrees of both the Councils of Carthage and Laodicea, including, perhaps, the spurious sixtieth canon as well. Unless the Trullian Fathers rejected Laodicea's sixtieth canon or found some way to harmonize the incompatible lists that would have resulted, their position on Scripture remains hopelessly at odds with itself. To make matters even more confusing, the Trullian council also sanctioned the eighty-fifth decree of the so-called *Apostolic Canons,* which accepts the *four* books of Maccabees.[385] The council also affirmed the teachings of several Church Fathers on the subject, of whom at least two (Gregory of Nazianzus and Amphilochius) omitted the deuterocanon from their lists. In short, Trullo's decrees are a confusing mixed bag from which no clear teaching on Scripture emerges. Sippo offers one possible way to understand these canons in a more coherent fashion:

> As to the "contradictions" . . . there was actually a total of five different listings of the canon of Scripture among the 102 canons at Quinisext. None of them are identical with each other. To counter the argument that they were contradictory to each other, Percival opined that the affirmation of these canons was "not specific but general." In other words, Quinisext was giving a general witness to the usage of the scriptures in the Early Church with these different canons. As in any law code, there are bound to be portions of that code that are obsolete, superseded, or overturned by judicial authority. Since the long canon has always predominated in the Eastern Church we can only surmise that Quinisext would have given pride of place to the canon of Scripture from Hippo/Carthage.[386]

The Protestant scholar Osterley, likewise, argues that Trullo accepted the deuterocanon because it gave primacy to the canons of the Council of Carthage.[387]

Bede (c. 673–735)

Born in Northumberland, England, Bede began his education in the monastery of St. Peter and Paul. By the age of thirteen he had become a priest and joined the religious leaders at the monastery. He is best known as a historian, especially for his *Ecclesiastical History of the English People.* Bede was a devoted reader and commentator on Scripture. He wrote,

> From the time of my admission to the priesthood to my present fifty-ninth year, I have endeavored for my own use and that of my brethren, to make brief notes upon the holy Scripture, either out of the works of the venerable Fathers or in conformity with their meaning and interpretation.[388]

Two passages are sometimes offered as evidence that Bede rejected the disputed books. The first passage is in his *De Temporum Ratione,* written about 703. It reads,

> Thus far divine Scripture contains the series of events. The subsequent history of the Jews is exhibited in the book of Maccabees, and in the writings of Josephus and Africanus, who continue the subsequent history down to the time of the Romans.[389]

The work *De Temporum Ratione*, recounts history from creation down to Bede's own time. Bede's concern is not to determine the limits of the canon of the Old Testament but to explain what sources are available to cover this particular period in the history of the Jews. As Breen explains,

> We believe, therefore, that in distinguishing Maccabees from the other historical books of divine Scripture, he merely wishes to point out that it does not alone continue the series of historical events from Ezra to the era of the Romans. Up to the time of Ezra, indeed, not all historical events were written, but enough was written to form a continuous chain of chief events, and no other writings

> contain the events of those times except the Holy Books, which follow each other in a certain historical series. But after Ezra a great lacuna occurs in the history of the Jews down to the time of the Romans, which is only partly bridged over by the combined data of Maccabees, Africanus, and Josephus . . . Hence Bede could not say that the divine Scripture contained the series of events down to the Roman epoch. He, therefore, drew a distinction between Maccabees and the preceding historical books, not from the nature of the books, but from the fact that the scriptural history of the Jews became broken at Ezra, and the fragment of it which existed in Maccabees had to be supplemented by the two cited authors.[390]

Bede's comments then are similar to those of Josephus in that writer's work *Against Apion.* At the beginning of this book we saw how Josephus also saw the period from creation to Ezra as a continuous historical narrative, which he deemed to be written by an exact succession of prophets. As a historian, Bede's continuous narrative also breaks down after Ezra and is picked up again by Maccabees, the New Testament, and other books. This does not mean, however, that Bede rejected the deuterocanon. On the contrary, the rest of *De Temporum Ratione* and Bede's other works are filled with quotes from all of the deuterocanonical books, often introducing them with solemn formulas commonly restricted to Scripture. He even wrote a *Commentary on the Book of Tobit,* which he understood to be an allegory concerning Christ and his Church.[391] It is true that, like Primasius before him, Bede adopts Jerome's interpretation of the twenty-four elders in Revelation; but the clear acceptance of the deuterocanon in his other works demonstrates that Bede could not have adopted Jerome's views on the canon.[392]

John Damascene (John of Damascus) (676–730)

In his youth, Damascene excelled in the areas of science and theology, eventually becoming the chief councilor of Damascus. Later, he felt called to the religious life and entered the monastery in St. Sabas near Jerusalem. As an ordained priest, he fought against the heresy of iconoclasm.[393] The Synod of Constantinople denounced him in 754, but some thirty-five years later his opposition to iconoclasm was vindicated by the Second General Council of Nicaea. With John Damascene the patristic age comes to a close in the East.

Damascene too accepted the old symbolic theory that there must be twenty-two books of the Old Testament to correspond with the twenty-two letters of the Hebrew alphabet.[384] He states that there are also Wisdom and Sirach that are "excellent and useful, but are not numbered, nor were they placed in the ark."[395] Being "placed in the ark" refers to the law that was placed in the Ark of the Covenant by the Jews. Epiphanius uses the same odd image when he reproduces the rabbinic canon.[396] Damascene, however, is trying to reproduce those books that are accepted by rabbinic tradition.

Nevertheless, John quotes Wisdom 3:1, in the same work, explicitly as divine Scripture.[397] He also quotes Baruch as holy Scripture along with the Psalms without qualification.[398] Baruch, Zechariah, and Micah are also quoted as prophecies about the Incarnation.[399] Second Maccabees was used to support the doctrine of God's omniscience.[400]

Alcuin (735–804)

Alcuin was the head of the cathedral school of York before being commissioned by Charlemagne, in 781, to organize his palace school. Like Bede before him, he was a collector of the writings of the Fathers and other important documents. Alcuin was also commissioned to restore Jerome's original Vulgate, which had gradually been corrupted by copyists' errors. The product of Alcuin's work became known as the *Charlemagne Bible.* In it, he put to verse the "holy books of the old law," that includes the deuterocanon.[401] *The Codex Paulinus (Carolinus)* and *Codex Statinus (Vallicellianus)* (sixth and seventh century) contain Alcuin's text, and both include the deuterocanon (*Codex Paulinus* omits Baruch).

Even though Alcuin lists the deuterocanon as Scripture, he is sometimes included among those who are said to have rejected the deuterocanon. The reason for this comes by way of a single qualified statement about Sirach in *Against Elipandus.*

Elipandus quoted Sirach 36:15 in favor of the Christological heresy of Adoptionism. Alcuin replied,

> In the books of Jesus, the son of Sirach, the aforesaid sentence is read, of which book blessed Jerome and Isidore positively testify that it is placed among the apocryphal, that is to say, the doubtful books.[402]

Alcuin's statement is odd to say the least. We've seen that Jerome didn't consider the deuterocanon doubtful; he rejected it outright as apocrypha. Moreover, Isidore didn't consider the deuterocanon doubtful; he believed it to be nothing less than divinely inspired Scripture. It seems that either Alcuin badly misinterpreted both Fathers or he is asserting a middle position between these two opposing views. This middle position would place Elipandus's quotation in doubt, but it doesn't go as far as to dismiss Sirach as spurious. If this is so, Alcuin may be counted the first of several writers who will attempt to reconcile Jerome's opinion on the canon with the rest of the Church.

But what did Alcuin really believe about Sirach? Did *he* see it as doubtful? In another treatise, *De Virtutibus et Vitiis*, Alcuin writes,

> The saying is read in *the divinely inspired scriptures*: "Son, delay not to be converted to the Lord; because you know not what the coming day may bring forth" [Sir. 5:8] . . . These are the words of God, not mine.[403]

It's difficult to think of a more forthright positive statement about the inspiration of Sirach. The "doubts" about Sirach expressed in *Against Elipandus* most certainly weren't his own.

Theodulf of Orleans (760–821)

Theodulf was the bishop of Orleans and a contemporary of Alcuin. He amended the text of the Vulgate, using Hebrew texts as well as the Septuagint. Theodulf's version includes all of the deuterocanon.

The Ecumenical Council of Nicaea II (787)

Convoked to deal with the Iconoclast heresy that had gripped the East, the council assembled somewhere between 330 and 367 bishops and produced decrees containing authoritative quotes from the books of Wisdom and Sirach.[404]

Codex Amiatinus (A) (Eighth Century)

This codex belonged to the monastery of Amiata, from which is receives it name. At one time, it was thought to be one of the more pristine manuscripts of the Vulgate and was used in the Sixtus edition of the Bible (1590). Scholars now place its origin not in Italy but in northern England during the early eighth century. It was given to Pope Gregory II in 716, and it very likely represents the Scripture brought into England by the missionaries of Pope Gregory the Great.[405] This codex contains all of the deuterocanon with the exception of Baruch. The codex also contains Jerome's prefaces, including his *Helmeted Prologue.*

Nicephorus (758–829)

Nicephorus was the patriarch of Constantinople and a staunch defender of the use of sacred images. He represented the empress at the Council of Nicaea II (see above) and played a key role in the condemnation of the Iconoclast heresy.

Nicephorus produced a catalogue of scriptural books categorized by their degree of certainty. He begins his list of the Old Testament with the shorter canon of twenty-two books, including Baruch and omitting Esther, and followed by a list of the New Testament books.

His second category he called *antilegomena*, which means "those spoken against." This list contains the books of Maccabees, Wisdom, Sirach, the Psalms of Solomon, Esther, Judith, Susanna, and Tobias, followed by the New Testament antilegomena. The book of Revelation is included among this second group. Nicephorus concludes by listing the apocrypha.[406] Nicephorus's catalogue did not consign the deuterocanon to the apocrypha, but it does list some of them as being doubted.

Like others before him, Nicephorus uses the deuterocanon in an authoritative manner. Sirach and Wisdom he quotes right along with protocanonical books, entirely without qualification or distinction.[407] Baruch is said to be the voice of the prophet.[408] Wisdom is quoted with the introduction "It is written."[409] And Nicephorus believed that Wisdom 2:12–23 was a prophecy of our Lord's death.[410]

Rhabanus Maurus (780–856)

Born in Falda in 788 to a prominent family, Rhabanus was raised in a monastery and studied under Alcuin in Tours. When he returned to his home, he was elected abbot of the monastery. In 847 he was elected archbishop of Mayence and became renowned as a zealous guardian of the Faith.

In his book *De Instituteione Clericorum*, Rhabanus essentially reproduces the canon of Isidore of Seville, enumerating seventy-two books as canonical scriptures.[411] Rhabanus Maurus also produced commentaries on the books of Wisdom, Sirach, Judith, and 1 and 2 Maccabees.

Walafrid Strabo (808–894)

Surnamed Strabo, meaning "the squint-eyed," Walafrid was reared in a monastery under Rhabanus Maurus. He eventually became dean of St. Gall and later abbot of Reichenou in Constance. One of his best-known works is the *Glossia Ordinaria of Sacram Scripturam* (or the *Glossia* for short). The *Glossia* is essentially a series of notes written in the margins of the Bible to help illuminate a given text for the reader. These notations are primarily taken from the works of the early Church Fathers. Being placed in close proximity to the sacred text, these notations gained a certain amount of prestige and authority. The *Glossia* became highly influential during the late or high Middle Ages.

Walafrid's selection of works is important for our discussion: he has provided evidence both for and against the acceptance of the books in question. In favor of the deuterocanon, his *Glossia* adopts extracts from Rhabanus Maurus's commentaries on the books of Wisdom, Sirach, Judith, and 1 and 2 Maccabees. He also uses Bede's *Commentary on the Book of Tobit*.[412]

There is no question, however, that the *Glossia* uncritically accepts Jerome as its primary source. For example, it begins with Jerome's *Letter to Paulinum*, and it includes his other prefaces for individual books such as his *Preface to Judith*.[413] The same is true with Esther.[414] Since Jerome didn't translate the book of Wisdom, Strabo repeats a few comments Jerome made in his *Preface to the Books of Solomon*.[415] The *Glossia*, however, does not contain any introductory remarks from Jerome for the book of Sirach.[416] Walafrid Strabo's incorporation of Jerome's prefaces undoubtedly contributed to the spread of his doubts about the deuterocanon in the Middle Ages.

Pope Nicholas I (d. 867)

Considered by some as one of the greatest popes of the Middle Ages, Nicholas ascended to the papal throne during one of the darkest periods in Church history. Charlemagne's empire was on the verge of collapse, and Christian morality was lukewarm among the faithful and even worse among certain worldly clerics. Nicholas also faced the illegitimate appointment of Photius to the powerful patriarchal see of Constantinople. Nicholas met all these challenges and prevented matters from escalating.

In his *Letter to the Bishops of Gaul*, Pope Nicholas I wrote that the *Decree of Pope Innocent I* (which reiterated the larger canon of Carthage and Hippo) was part of *the universal law of the Church*.[417]

Photius (c. 815–891)

When it looked as if matters could not be worse for Christianity, Photius made them worse. Not only did hostile forces threaten the Church from without, schism and rebellion were boiling up from within. When Photius, a very learned man of science and dialectics in Constantinople, was illegitimately elected patriarch of Constantinople, Pope Nicholas I refused to accept him. He rallied the Church against Photius, who, in turn, "excommunicated" the pope. These actions brought about the first East-West schism.

In regard to the canon of Scripture, Photius's *Syntagma Canonum* shows that he adopted the decisions of Trullo, which had accepted the eighty-fifth canon of the *Apostolic Canons*, the sixtieth canon of Laodicea, and the twenty-fourth canon of Carthage.[418] Both Protestant and Catholic scholars count him as a positive witness for the inclusion of the deuterocanon.[419] Photius's views confirm Nicholas I's statement that the deuterocanon was part of the *universal* law of the Church.

The Council of Constantinople IV (869–870)

At the Eighth Ecumenical Council, Constantinople IV was requested by Emperor Basil to reinstate Patriarch Ignatius and to depose Photius. About sixty-five bishops attended the council.[420] Within the decrees of Constantinople IV is a quotation from Sirach 11:7, referred to explicitly as "divine Scripture."[421]

Codices Toletanus (T) and Cavensis

Dating from the ninth and tenth centuries, these two Latin manuscripts come from Spain and both include the entire deuterocanon.[422]

Notker Balbulus (840–912)

Virtually nothing is known about Notker, author of *On the Interpretation of Divine Scripture*. He is given the surname Balbulus, which means "the stammerer." He died in the monastery of St. Gall in Ireland.

In his book Notker comments on the Pentateuch, Joshua, Judges, Samuel, and the books of Kings and the Prophets. Turning his attention to the book of Wisdom, Notker writes,

> I have found no author's exposition, we accept some testimonies (therefrom) explained in relation to other books. The book is totally rejected by the Hebrews, and is by Christians considered uncertain, nevertheless, *since on account of the utility of its doctrine*, our forefathers were accustomed to read it, and the Jews have it not, it is called with us Ecclesiasticus. What you believe of this, it behooves you to believe also of the books of Jesus the son of Sirach, except that this latter is possessed and read by the Hebrews . . . The priest Bede wrote some things on Tobias and Ezra, more pleasing than necessary, since he has striven to convert simple history into an allegory. What shall I say of the books of Judith, Esther, and Paralipomenon [Chronicles]? By whom, or how shall they be explained, since their contents are not intended for authority, but only as a memorial of wonderful things? This you may also suspect of the books of Maccabees.[423]

Notker's strange canon seems to have been the product of his own religious imagination; certainly it cannot be shown to have been used by any other writer or group of Christians. It seems that for him usefulness equals authority. He accepts Wisdom because he finds it useful; the same seems to hold true for Sirach. Tobit he finds devoid of spiritual meaning, a mere secular history. However, Ezra, Esther, Chronicles, and perhaps Maccabees, he says, were not intended for "authority" but only "a memorial of wonderful things." Chronicles is not authoritative? Obviously, Notker's comments reflect his own personal taste and speculation.

Bibles, Glosses, and Scholars

The earliest complete Christian bibles (the Great Codices) all included the deuterocanon. None of them restricted themselves to the canon found in Protestant bibles. Moreover, the deuterocanonical books within these codices were not segregated, qualified, or in any way distinguished from the protocanon. On the contrary, they were intermixed with the other books of Scripture. The same is true for the Latin codices mentioned in this chapter. These bibles reflect what we have seen so far in our survey of the early Church Fathers, who (with very rare exceptions) quoted the deuterocanonical books alongside the protocanonical books without distinction or qualification.[424]

The presence of the deuterocanon within these early Christian bibles provides us with a partial answer to the main question in this book: did the Council of Trent add books to the Bible, or did Protestantism remove them?

Clearly, the Great Codices and the Latin codices witness to the fact that the deuterocanon was an integral feature within every early Christian Bible, just as it was present in every early Protestant Bible. However, these ancient bibles didn't gather the deuterocanon into an appendix marked "Apocrypha" or include a declaration that these books could not be used to confirm doctrine, as was done in early Protestant bibles. Although the earliest Protestant bibles departed from the practice of the earliest Christian bibles, later

Protestant bibles depart even more significantly by excluding the deuterocanon entirely from its covers. On the other hand, by retaining the deuterocanon intermixed with the protocanon Catholic bibles mirror the practice of the most ancient Greek and Latin bibles. We will speak more to this issue later.

8

"As Jerome Saith . . ."

The last half of the first Christian millennium was a very difficult period for the Church. The barbarian invasions, the rise of Islam, meddling by secular powers, heresies, and the Great Schism racked Christian civilization to the core. During this tumultuous period, Christian scholars' main concern was the preservation of knowledge—especially codifying and propagating the texts of Scripture and the writings of the Fathers.

During this time, acceptance of the deuterocanon was the rule; the few isolated doubts that did surface were either unique personal convictions or else the echoes of earlier writers quoted for the benefit of posterity. The Councils of Carthage, Hippo, and Trullo (Quinisext) and the *Decree of Pope Gelasius* and Innocent I had reaffirmed the historic Christian canon, and by the end of the ninth century, Pope Nicholas I could speak of Innocent I's canonical list as *the universal law in the Church.* It is the larger canon, not that of Jerome, that had wide, substantial support.[425]

From the turn of the first Christian millennium until the high Middle Ages, the Church experienced a renewed vigor and development in the study of Scripture and theology. These studies often involved the systemization and crystallization of the teachings of the Fathers into a coherent whole. This renewed vigor of synthesis and analysis was a great benefit for the Church, but it also carried with it some unintended consequences. Under a growing humanism, fed by the rediscovery of classical literature, some medieval scholars attempted to reconcile beliefs that were not really reconcilable. Such was the case with the canon of Scripture. The isolated doubts we have seen scattered sparsely through our story so far began to be synthesized into a cohesive body of thought, and divisions that did not formerly exist began to arise. Terminology changed as well. Terms that were loosely defined in antiquity became well-defined and fixed, while other words were stretched to mean practically anything.

The reinvigoration of biblical studies in the Middle Ages also gave new life to the writings of Jerome, and, consequently, to his shortened canon. His Vulgate became not only popular but downright venerable, and his prefaces became the focus of uncritical study. Biblical novices studied these prefaces along with the sacred text, and the popularity of *Glossia Ordinaria* only served to amplify Jerome's critical remarks and integrate them into mainline biblical studies. As Gigot comments,

> If now we inquire into the causes of this persistent division between the ecclesiastical writings of the Middle Ages, we shall find that its main, *if not its exclusive, cause,* is the influence which the views of St. Jerome exercised upon the minds of many Doctors of that period . . . It is not therefore to be wondered at, if the view so unfavorable to the deuterocanonical books, which these prefaces contained, seemed tenable to many schoolmen, and were, in fact, held by them in the teeth of contrary practice in the Church, and of disciplinary decrees of the popes. Finally, as it was the fashion of the time to get rid of difficulties by means of subtle distinctions, several ecclesiastical writers . . . [tried to] reconcile the statements of St. Jerome, in his prefaces, with the papal decrees and the practice of the Church.[426]

This chapter will chronicle the growing tension between Jerome and the common practice of the Church. Some writers will try to reconcile Jerome with the Church; others will give Jerome the honor of quoting him while still maintaining the historic use of the deuterocanon; and a few will go as far as to accept Jerome entirely.

Alfrick (d. 1009)

Alfrick was a monk in the Benedictine Abbey of Abingdon, England. He became bishop of Wilton, England in 990 and archbishop of Canterbury five years later. Alfrick had to combat the devastating results of one of the barbarian invasions of England.

In a treatise called *On the Old and New Testament,* Alfrick writes of Sirach and Wisdom as being included in the Bible among the works of Solomon because of their similarity in style to Proverbs and Ecclesiastes. Likewise, 1 and 2 Maccabees, Tobit, Esther, and Judith he also reckons as authentic parts of Sacred Scripture.[427]

Burchard of Worms (d. 1025)[428]
Ivo (Ives) of Chartres (c. 1040–1116)[429]
Gratian (d. 1155)[430]

Both Burchard of Worms and Ivo of Chartres received the so-called *Decree of Gelasius* as authentic and an authoritative sanction of the deuterocanon. Their works, along with Gratian's, later formed the basis for Church discipline in their era.

Stephen Harding (1109–1133)

Harding and the other monks at Citeaux made a recension

of the Vulgate in 1109. They relied on many manuscripts and consulted several learned Jews on the Hebrew text. The corrected Latin text they produced included the deuterocanon.

Gislebert (Gilbert Crispin) (979–1117)

In a fictional dialogue between a Christian and a Jew, Gislebert defends the prophetic integrity of Baruch, arguing that the prophet Jeremiah dictated its contents.[431]

Honorius of Autun (1120)

In his work *Gemma Animae,* Honorius establishes the order of the books of Scripture that are to be read in the Divine Office. With the exception of Baruch, all of the deuterocanon is included. Baruch was found in the readings from the book of Jeremiah.[432]

Aegidius (c. 1180)

This deacon of Paris composed a list of Scripture in Latin verse that includes all the deuterocanon.

Hugh of St. Victor (1096–1141)

Hugh was a canon regular of St. Victor at Paris, becoming one of the most influential theologians in that city. His impact on the revival of biblical studies in the Middle Ages should not be underestimated.

Hugh rejected the deuterocanon as part of the canon of Scripture, though he acknowledged that the Church read it. This view can be seen in his preface to *De Scripturis et Scriptoribus Sacris*, in which he writes,

> [After enumerating the books of the protocanon] All, therefore, make twenty-two. There are besides certain other books, as the Wisdom of Solomon, the books of Jesus the son of Sirach, the book of Judith, Tobit and the Maccabees, which are read, but are not written in the canon.[433]

After listing the New Testament canon and the writings of the Fathers (including Jerome), Hugh continues,

> But these writings of the Fathers are not computed in the text of the divine scriptures, just as we have said that there are books which are not embodied in the canon of the Old Testament, and yet are read, as the Wisdom of Solomon and other books. The text, therefore, of holy Scripture, as one body, is principally made up of thirty books. Of these twenty-two books are comprised in the Old Testament.[434]

He expresses a similar view in his preface to the book *De Sacrementis*.[435]

Hugh of St. Victor's opinion about the deuterocanon, as the Protestant theologian F.F. Bruce notes, was dependent on St. Jerome.[436] The popularity of Hugh's works contributed greatly to the wholesale adoption of Jerome's views on the canon during the Middle Ages."[437]

Rupert of Deutz (1075–1130)

A well-known Benedictine monk from the Abbey of Deutz near Cologne, Germany, Rupert also rejected the deuterocanon. He claimed that the book of Wisdom is not "of the canon."[438] He also omits Baruch and the deuterocanonical sections of Esther in his commentaries.

Like Hugh of St. Victor, Rupert's views are taken from Jerome. We can see Jerome's influence most clearly in Rupert's work *De Divinis Officiis* (*On the Divine Office*) where he repeats Jerome's claim that Judith and Tobit were adopted on the authority of the Council of Nicaea.[439]

Despite his dependence on Jerome, Rupert still includes the deuterocanonical books in his Divine Office.

Peter of Cluny (1092–1156)

Peter of Cluny (also known as "Peter the Venerable") became the abbot general there in 1121 and spent most of his life combating heresy in France. Some believe that Peter also opposed the deuterocanon. Their foundation for this opinion is found in a passage from his treatise *Against Peter of Bruys,* in which he writes,

> There remain besides these authentic books of holy Scripture six other books which are not to be passed over in silence, viz., Wisdom, the book of Jesus son of Sirach, Tobias, Judith and the two books of Maccabees. Although these do not reach the sublime dignity of the preceding, nevertheless, on account of their *laudable and very necessary doctrine, they have merited to be received by the Church.* There is no need that I should labor in commending these to you. For if you value the Church in any wise, *you will receive something, at least a little, on her authority.* But if (as Christ said to Moses of the Jews) you will not believe Christ's Church how will you believe my words?[440]

The context of this letter is important. Peter of Bruys and his followers accepted only the Gospels as authentic Scripture. Peter implored them to accept the whole of Scripture, including the deuterocanon, because of its ancient and undoubted acceptance by the universal Church. In other words, he believed that the deuterocanon could be entered into debate and serve as a proof for doctrine. His statement that the deuterocanon does not attain to the same "sublime dignity" as earlier books cannot be taken as a denial of authority or inspiration; we know this because Peter's usage elsewhere demonstrates that he did accept these books as Scripture.[441]

Peter of Riga (1140–1209)

A contemporary of Aegidius, Peter of Riga also composed a list of the books of Scripture that included all of the deuterocanon intermixed with the other books of the Old Testament, without distinction or qualification.

Rudolf of Flavigny (1064/1065–c. 1155)

Rudolf divides Scripture into four categories: historical, prophetic, proverbs, and simple doctrine. He includes the books of Sirach and Wisdom among the protocanonical books of simple doctrine. He qualifies the authority of Tobit, Judith, and Maccabees by writing, "although read for the instruction of the Church, [they] have not perfect authority."[442]

Peter Comestor (1100–1178)

Peter was known for his prodigious reading and has been called the "Master of History." In his *Preface to the Book of Joshua*, Peter provides a list of the books of Scripture:

> Job, David, three books of Solomon, Daniel, Paralipomenon [Chronicles], Ezra, Esther, Sapientia [Wisdom],

> Ecclesiasticus [Sirach], Judith, Tobias, Maccabees are called the *hagiographa* (al. apocrypha) because their author is unknown; but since there is no doubt of their truth, they are received by the Church.[443]

Here we see Peter wrestle with Jerome's designation of the deuterocanon as apocrypha. In order to reconcile Jerome with the practice of the Church, he parenthetically equates the division of Scripture known as the writings (or *hagiographa*) with "apocrypha." Since apocrypha means "hidden," he states that these books are apocrypha because their authors are unknown. Being of uncertain origin, their truthfulness is vouchsafed by their reception by the Church.

Elsewhere, Peter makes a similar and more disastrous attempt to reconcile Jerome in his work *Historia Scholastica*. In a reference to a deuterocanonical section of Daniel, he writes,

> There follows the history of Susanna, which the Hebrew [text] does not contain in the book of Daniel. It calls it a fable, not that it denies the history, but because it is falsely stated there that the priests were stoned whom Jeremiah testifies to have been burned; and because we fabled it to have been written by Daniel, whereas it was written by a certain Greek.[444]

Jerome himself is quite plain in this matter; he twice calls the deuterocanonical sections of Daniel "a fable"[445]—meaning, without any doubt, that he considers them to be fictional, fantastic, or mythological. Peter, however, unable to bear the sight of his hero at direct loggerheads with the official Church, chooses to imagine that Jerome was commenting upon some alleged claim that Daniel himself authored the passages in question. It is remarkable to see how highly prized Jerome's reputation was that an otherwise orthodox writer would go to such lengths to bring him in line with the rest of Christianity.

Jean Beleth (1135–1182)

This noted theologian of Paris edited the order of readings for the Divine Office in his *Rationale Divinorum Officiorum*. In it he followed the same order as Honorius of Autun, noted above, which includes the deuterocanon.

Anonymous Writer (Mid-Twelfth Century)

An anonymous writer of the twelfth century (likely a monk) bears witnesses to the received canon of his day in these words:

> [After enumerating the protocanonical books] . . . Besides the aforesaid there are five books which are called by the Hebrews apocryphal, that is to say hidden and doubtful, but the Church honors these and receives them. The first is Wisdom: the second Ecclesiasticus [Sirach]; the third, Tobias, the fourth Judith, the fifth, Maccabees.[446]

John of Salisbury (1120–1180)

A native of England, John was appointed to the papal court by Henry II. He later returned to England and was advanced through various offices by St. Thomas Becket. After Becket's martyrdom, John was appointed the bishop of Chartres.

John of Salisbury is rightly counted among those who rejected the deuterocanon. He writes,

> Since, therefore, concerning the number of the books, I read many and different opinions of the Fathers, *following Jerome*, a

> Doctor of the Catholic Church, *whom I hold most approved in establishing the foundations of Scripture*, I firmly believe that, as there are twenty-two Hebrew letters, thus there are twenty-two books of the Old Testament, arranged in three orders . . . and *these are found in the prologue of the book of Kings which Jerome called the* Galeatum Principium *of all Scripture* . . . But the book of Wisdom, Ecclesiasticus, Judith, Tobias, and Pastor, as the same Father asserts, are not in the canon, neither is the book of Maccabees, which is divided in two.[447]

John of Salisbury clearly depends on Jerome and his *Helmeted Prologue*.

Peter of Blois (1130–1203)

Peter of Blois was a statesman and theologian who studied in Tours, Bologna, and Paris. He became chancellor of the archbishop of Canterbury and archdeacon of Bath in 1176. Following Isidore's fourfold division of the Old Testament books, Peter writes,

> These books [the deuterocanon] the Jews place apart among the apocrypha; but the Church of Christ honors them among the divine books and promulgates them.[448]

Peter, therefore, accepted the deuterocanon as inspired Scripture.

The Fourth Lateran Council (1213–1215)

An impressive number of patriarchs, metropolitans, bishops, abbots, and priors attended this important Church council.[449] Section 70 of the Council's remains contains two quotes from the book of Sirach with the solemn introduction "It is written."[450]

Albert the Great (1206–1280)

Also called the "Universal Doctor" (*Doctor Universalis*), this Dominican was known for his unparalleled erudition. A young Thomas Aquinas studied under him; particularly by means of this tutorage, Albert had an enormous influence over the theology of his day.

Albert never addresses the issue of the canon per se, but his usage indicates that he understood the deuterocanon to be Scripture. Albert defends the inclusion of Baruch as Scripture against Jerome's contentions. In his works, he uses the entire deuterocanon in a manner indistinguishable from the other books of Scripture. Albert's acceptance of the deuterocanon is not contested.

Bonaventure (1217–1274)

Another Doctor of the Church, Bonaventure was the cardinal-bishop of Albano and the minister general of the Friars Minor. His writings and teachings were quite influential in later theology and Christian philosophy.

Bonaventure provides a list of twenty-six books of Scripture, which includes the deuterocanon. Elsewhere, he happens to have picked the book of Wisdom to explain various types of causality, and in so doing, provided us with a particularly succinct statement of his opinion of it:

> The efficient cause of the book is threefold: God who inspired it, Solomon who produced it, and Philo who compiled it.[441]

Clearly, we must count the Seraphic Doctor among those who held the deuterocanon to be inspired Scripture.

Alexander Neckam (1157–1217)

Professor of the famed University of Paris, Alexander wrote a commentary that focused on difficult passages of Scripture. In it, he plainly accepts the deuterocanon as the inspired word of God.[452]

Robert Grosseteste (1235–1253)

Robert Grosseteste was bishop of Lincoln, England. He quotes the books of Maccabees, Wisdom, and Sirach as Scripture in his letters.

Hugh of St. Cher (c. 1200–1263)

Hugh joined the Dominican order and later became a teacher in the school at Sorbonne. Eventually he was made a cardinal. Like several before him, Hugh penned a list of the books of Scripture in Latin verse. After enumerating the protocanon, he included the deuterocanon under the title "apocrypha." However, as with Peter Comestor, that term he redefined to mean "hagiographa," Hugh writes in another place:

> The palace of the king is made up of four things: the foundation is the law: the walls are the prophets and the epistles: the roof is the Gospels, and the ornaments are the hagiographa and the apocrypha.[443]

In the preface to his *Commentary on Sirach*, Hugh states that the books of the deuterocanon are accepted only for moral instruction and not for the confirmation of dogma.

Hugh of St. Cher clearly adopts Jerome's abridged canon and attempts to reconcile it with ordinary Church usage. Like others we have seen, Hugh neither adheres completely to Jerome nor rejects his views outright—because, though he is willing to label them apocrypha, Hugh still considers the deuterocanon to be Scripture *in some sense.*

Thomas Aquinas (c. 1224–1274)

In terms of influence on Christian theology, arguably no individual since Augustine has had as much of an impact as the Angelic Doctor. St. Thomas was a prodigious writer, but scholars need not go beyond his most famous work to learn that he accepted the disputed books as nothing less than the word of God. In his monumental *Summa Theologiae*, Thomas uses the books of the deuterocanon as authoritative sources throughout.[454]

One such passage that is worthy of attention is Aquinas's use of the book of Judith in the article *Whether every lie is a sin?* Aquinas defends the book of Judith against the accusation (later employed by those who opposed the deuterocanon) that it propagates a moral error by showing God commending Judith's lie to Holofernes. Thomas answers,

> Some, however, are commended *in the scriptures*, not on account of perfect virtue, but for a certain virtuous disposition, seeing that it was owing to some praiseworthy sentiment that they were moved to do certain undue things. It is thus that Judith is praised, not for lying to Holofernes, but for her desire to save the people, to which end she exposed herself to danger. And yet one might also say that her words contain truth in some mystical sense.[455]

Thomas's works manifest that he did accept the deuterocanon as Scripture in its fullest sense.

Robert Helot (1290–1340)

This English Dominican theologian follows Augustine's canonical list in his work *On Christian Doctrine* as noted in his lectures on the book of Wisdom:

> St. Augustine expressly declares in his Christian doctrine (II.9) that the book of Wisdom should be enumerated in the sacred scriptures; for, enumerating the books of the canon of the Bible, he says thus of Wisdom and Ecclesiasticus: "Wisdom and Ecclesiasticus, since they have merited to be received in authority, are reckoned among the prophetic books." *Wherefore, it is evident that the book is counted among the canonical scriptures in the Church*, though the contrary is held by the Jews . . . and therefore, although by the Jews rejected, the books are of great authority among the faithful.[456]

Thomas Netter (Thomas Waldensis) (1375–1430)

An English Carmelite theologian, Thomas Netter was educated at Oxford. His writings were very popular in his time and commonly touched upon questions of Scripture. Netter opposed Wycliffe and argued that the Church had the authority to establish the canon.[457] He believed the question of the canon had already been authoritatively settled by the so-called *Decree of Gelasius*, which espoused the deuterocanon.

The Council of Vienne (1311–1312)

This was a local council that met to address the problems

with the Order of Knights Templar and various ecclesiastical abuses and practices. It is thought that something between 114 and 300 bishops attended this council.

Like the councils before it, Vienne authoritatively quotes the deuterocanonical books in its decrees.[458]

Nicholas of Lyra (1270–1349)

This Parisian theologian and famed convert from Judaism rejected the deuterocanon. The reason for Nicholas's adoption of the shorter canon is easily discernible—the influence of Jerome. In his *Commentary on Ezra*, Nicholas writes,

> I intend, for the present, to pass over the books of Tobias, Judith, and Maccabees, although they are historical; because they are not in the canon of the Jews or Christians. *Jerome, indeed, says they are reckoned among the apocrypha.*[459]

Like those writers before and after him who opposed the deuterocanon, Nicholas of Lyra is content to rest upon the authority of Jerome.

Andrew Horne (c. 1345)

This English lawyer's writings betray certain doubts about the authority of the deuterocanon. Arguing that all law is based upon Scripture, Horne finds only the canonical books authoritative:

> Besides these there are other books in the Old Testament, although they are not authorized as canonicals, as Tobit, Judith, Maccabees, Ecclesiasticus [Sirach].[460]

Although Horne did not believe the deuterocanon should be used as fundamental texts for law, he did, nevertheless, note that they are part of the Old Testament, if only because of utility.

William of Occam (1285–1347)

An English philosopher and member of the Gray Friars, William was excommunicated by Pope John XXII for his support of Louis of Bavaria's stand against the pope. However, historians believe that he was reconciled to the Church before his death in 1347. William is, perhaps, most famous for the "Occam's razor" analogy and his contribution toward the philosophical school of Nominalism, which was influential in the universities during the time of Luther.

Occam acknowledged that the Church read the deuterocanon but denied that it was canonical because it cannot be used to confirm doctrine. He derived this view from the writings of Jerome and, perhaps, Gregory the Great.[461]

Clement VI (1342–1352)

Pope Clement VI's papal bull declaring the Jubilee, *Unigentius Dei Filius*, on January 25, 1343, quotes Wisdom 7:14.[462]

John Wycliffe (1324–1384)

Venerated by many Protestants as a forerunner of the Reformation, Wycliffe composed two manuscripts translating the scriptures into English. According to the Protestant biblical scholar B.F. Westcott, the first manuscript contained a translation of the entire deuterocanon, along with Jerome's prefaces, noting that within them "he [Jerome] affirms the exclusive authority of the Hebrew canon."[463] A second revision by the Protestant English theologian John Purvey (c. 1354–c. 1414) provides a summary of Jerome's *Helmeted Prologue*, in which he essentially and uncritically reiterates Jerome's views in his preface.[464] It is worthy of note that despite Purvey's preface, the deuterocanon was still included in this edition of Wycliffe's Old Testament, intermixed with the protocanonical books.

Although Wycliffe reproduced Jerome's doubts in the prefaces to his translation, he was definitely not on the same page with Martin Luther and subsequent Protestants. Although it may be disconcerting for some Protestants to hear, the man known as the "Morning Star of the Reformation" used the deuterocanon as Scripture and even appealed to it to confirm doctrine! As the Anglican scholar Daubney points out,

> Even John Wycliffe himself does not seem to have held very different views on this subject. In his *Sermons* he quotes Wisdom and Ecclesiasticus very freely, Tobit but rarely. In his *De Ente Predicamentali* he refers to Ecclesiasticus [Sirach] 3:11 as "*scriptura*" and 18:1 is cited with "*ut dictitur.*" But perhaps his strongest assertion is in *Quaestiones Logicae et Philosophicae*, where he clinches his argument by saying, "*Ista conclusio etiam patet auctoritate scripturae,*" Ecclesiasticus [Sirach] 18:1. In his *De Eucharistia* he guards against idolatry in the Mass by Baruch 6:1, 56; and in his *Opus Evangelicum*, ch. xxviii, he quotes 2 Maccabees 19, against the pope. This practice of Wycliffe's of confuting popery from the apocryphal books, in view of later developments on either side is not without its humorous aspect. In his *Paternoster* he refers to Tobit 6:17 with apparently full acceptance. He also wrote a *Practical Exposition of the Song of the Three Men in the Furnace*, Daniel 3:51 sqq.[465]

Wycliffe can be added to the list of medieval scholars who parroted Jerome's prefaces in one work but continued to use the deuterocanon as inspired Scripture, capable of confirming doctrine, everywhere else.

John of Ragusa (1380–c. 1443)

A Dominican professor at the Sorbonne and president of the ill-fated Council of Basel in 1450, John of Ragusa stated in the strongest terms the acceptance of the deuterocanon by the Church during that council. He writes,

> Moreover, it is manifest that there are many books in the Bible, which are not held in authority with the Jews, but are by them reckoned apocryphal, which nevertheless, by us are held in the same veneration and authority as the others, and our acceptance of them rests on nothing but the tradition and acceptance of the whole Catholic Church, which is not lawful perniciously to contradict.[466]

John's statement on the equality of the deuterocanon with the protocanon is a point that some during his time missed. Nevertheless, he clearly states that his belief was based solely upon the acceptance and the constant teaching of the universal Church. His words about the unlawfulness of contradicting this universal acceptance echoed those of Pope Nicholas I's *Letter to the Bishops in Gaul* some 500 years earlier.

Ragusa's sentiments found their voice in the Council of Florence and, subsequently, were accepted by the Council of Trent.

It is often said that there was a continuous "scholarly tradition" of rejecting the deuterocanon from Jerome to the Middle Ages. This chapter shows that the claim is not exactly true.

Everyone knew of Jerome's prefaces, but not everyone accepted his position entirely. Most scholars[467] were fully on board with the decrees of Carthage and Hippo. A few attempted to reconcile Jerome with the Church by redefining "apocrypha" or by quoting Jerome but still used the deuterocanon as inspired Scripture. Only a few quoted *and followed* Jerome entirely (Hugh of St. Victor, John of Salisbury, Nicholas of Lyra, William of Occam). Do four scholars over a period of 400 years make up a "scholarly tradition"? If there is a scholarly tradition, it is in favor of the deuterocanon.

9

Florence, Trent, and the Renaissance

Jerome's growing influence among Christian writers grew to astronomical heights during the Renaissance, especially during the 1400s and 1500s. This period of enthusiasm for ancient Greek culture carried with it a renewed interest in the study of ancient languages, such as Greek and Hebrew.

By this time, Jerome's Vulgate was venerated as *the* Latin translation for the West. One would think that it would be pushed to the side by the new enthusiasm for all things ancient, but the opposite occurred. Jerome wrote extensively about the Hebrew language, and he was a master of Greek as well. The new enthusiasm of the Renaissance and the humanist movement served only to magnify Jerome's prestige and influence. Jerome became the last word in biblical studies, and for some he became the last word on the canon as well.

In this chapter, we will see the growth of the *Jeromists*—those who set Jerome above all other biblical authorities—and we will also take a close look at the Council of Trent and its decree on the canon. Many see Trent's decree on the canon as the product of a biased overreaction to Luther, as the Protestant apologist Norman Geisler explains:

> At the Roman Catholic Council of Trent the infallible proclamation was made accepting the Apocrypha as part

> of the inspired word of God. Unfortunately, the proclamation came . . . in an obvious polemic against Protestantism. Furthermore, the official infallible addition of books that support prayer for the dead is highly suspect, coming as it did only a few years after Luther protested against this very doctrine.[468]

Are there grounds for such suspicion? None at all. A reaction never precedes the thing it is reacting to; the deuterocanon had already been affirmed as Scripture by an ecumenical council 104 years before Trent's declaration and seventy-seven years before Luther publically rejected the deuterocanon at the Council of Florence.

The Council of Florence (1439–1445)

Beginning as the ill-fated Council of Basel, this council was moved to Florence on January 10, 1439, when an opportunity for reconciliation between West and East presented itself. The reunion of the two estranged halves of the Church occurred, however temporarily, on July 6, 1439 with the approval of a *Decree on Reunion with the Greeks.* Other decrees were issued concerning reunion with the Syrian, Armenian, and Coptic churches, and eventually with the Bosnians, the Syrians, Chaldeans, and Maronites of Cyprus as well. On February 24, 1443, the council was moved to Rome, where it finally closed on August 7, 1445. Unlike prior conciliar decrees, the decisions made by the Council of Florence were not given as legal canons, but were issued in the form of papal bulls.

One such bull was *On the Unification of the Jacobites,* issued on February 4, 1442. Promulgated by Pope Eugene IV and adopted as part of the Council of Florence, this decree listed the books of Sacred Scripture:

> Most strongly it [the Church] believes, professes, and declares . . . one and the same God as the author of the Old and New Testament, that is, of the law and the prophets, and the gospel, since the saints of both testaments have spoken with the inspiration of the same Holy Spirit, whose books, which are contained under the following titles it accepts and venerates: the five books of Moses . . . Josue, Judges, Ruth, four books of Kings, two books of Chronicles, Ezra, Nehemias, Tobias, Judith, Esther, Job, the Psalms of David, Proverbs, Ecclesiastes, Canticle of Canticles, Wisdom, Ecclesiasticus, Isaiah, Jeremiah with Baruch, Ezechiel, Daniel, twelve prophets . . . and the books of Maccabees.[469]

Note that this is the first time any ecumenical council had promulgated a list of inspired scriptures and raised the issue of the canon to this level of solemnity.[470] Florence did not qualify its acceptance of the deuterocanon, nor did it place it into a separate category. The protocanonical and deuterocanonical books are intermixed without distinction, as they were in the past.[471] The wording of this decree is also important. The council states that *all* the books of the Old and New Testaments, including the deuterocanon, are inspired by the Holy Spirit and are to be accepted and venerated.

Florence also employs the deuterocanon elsewhere in an authoritative manner. For example, Sirach 18:23 is quoted as Scripture in session 21. Wisdom 10:19 is quoted with the formula "It is written" in session 3. Tobit 12:20, Susanna (Daniel 13:9), and Wisdom 5:21 are quoted elsewhere by the council without qualification.[472]

This raises the question: how can Trent's canon (already reaffirmed over a hundred years earlier at Florence) be a reaction to Luther? Geisler offers this explanation:

> Even before Luther, the Council of Florence (1442) had proclaimed the Apocrypha inspired, which helped bolster the doctrine of purgatory that had already blossomed in Roman Catholicism. However, the manifestations of this belief in the sale of indulgences came to full bloom in Luther's day, and Trent's infallible pronouncement of the Apocrypha was a clear polemic against Luther's teaching.[473]

Geisler's solution is little more than a conspiracy theory, since there is no connection between the Florentine canon and purgatory. Florence is unique in that it dealt with a series of separate issues, usually in the form of papal bulls that were adopted by the council. Therefore, its decrees are somewhat compartmentalized. The *Decree for the Greeks* (the bull *Laetenur Coeli*, July 6, 1439) addressed purgatory among other issues.[474] The decree on the canon, however, dealt with an entirely different issue, namely the reunion with the Jacobites (*Cantata Domino*, February 4, 1442). There's nothing to link the *Decree for the Greeks* to the canon or the decree for the Jacobites to purgatory. Both accepted the deuterocanon and to some extent purgatory.[475]

In our Information Age, it is tempting to assume that after Florence promulgated its list all confusion stopped and strict uniformity on the canon became the norm. Unfortunately, in Church history such conformity rarely happens immediately. It takes time for the various declarations, symbols, and decrees to disseminate. Moreover, those whose views are condemned by a council often repackage their heretical views so as to give the impression that they have changed their positions. The lack of effectiveness of a council does not reflect on its authority. The most important and authoritative councils of the Church took decades (even centuries) to bring about unity; the great Council of Nicaea of 325, for instance, accepted by both Catholic and Protestant alike, was contradicted by important figures *within the Church* for decades afterward.[476] In this respect, Florence was no different. Its decrees seemed to have circulated more swiftly in the East than they did in the West.[477]Consequently, the decrees at Florence had little impact once the Eastern churches rejected its decrees on reunion.[478]

Alphonsus Tostatus (1400–1455)

Rarely is an examination of one man's views more confused and contradictory than the attempt to get to the bottom of Alphonsus Tostatus's understanding of the canon. In his *Prologue to the Book of Kings* (*Prologus Galaetus*), for instance, Tostatus writes,

> It is said that the book of Wisdom is not in the canon, because the Jews expunged it thence; in the beginning they received it, but after they had laid hands on Jesus and slain him, remembering the evident testimonies concerning him in the same book . . . taking counsel, lest we should impute to them the evident sacrilege, they cut the book off from the prophetic volumes, and interdicted its reading. *But we on the Church's authority receive the book among the authentic scriptures, and read it at stated times in the Church.* Again the book of Jesus, the son of Sirach, is not in the Jewish canon and although the Jews never received it into the canon of scriptures, *the Church receives it and reads it.* . . . These things are true according to the Jews; but with us it is otherwise, for the book of Judith is received among the authentic scriptures, for the reason that the Church approved it at the Council of Nice, and received it in her divine liturgy, as she reads the other authentic books.[479]

These positive comments seem clear enough and rather more straightforward than many we have examined. Yet when the same author comments upon Jerome's first *Preface to the Books of Chronicles*, we read the following:

> There is a difference between them [the deuterocanonical books] and the canonical books that are called authentic; and validly argue against both Jews and Christian to prove truth; but from the apocryphal books we may receive doctrine, because they contain holy doctrine, wherefore they are called at times hagiographa; but their authority is not sufficient to adduce in argument against anyone, nor to prove things to which are in doubt, and in this they are inferior to the canonical and authentic books . . . None of these apocryphal books, even though it be included among the other books of the Bible, and read in the Church, is of such authority that the Church may from it prove doctrine and in this regard the Church does not receive them, and thus is to be understood the declaration of Jerome, that the Church receives not the apocrypha.[480]

As should be abundantly clear by now, the Church most definitely did use these books in the confirmation of doctrine and always had. Even individual scholars who seem, at times, to affirm otherwise, slip continually back into the habit of confirming doctrine by means of the deuterocanon. Furthermore, Jerome himself is not shy about rejecting these books outright; he calls them apocrypha, useful, perhaps, *"for the edification of the people, but not to support the authority of ecclesiastical doctrines."* Tostatus's words, therefore, utterly fail to be faithful to either Jerome or the Church. He also complicates matters further by his inconsistent use of terminology. For example, earlier Tostatus denied the title of "authentic" Scripture to the deuterocanonical books, yet in the second quotation, he frankly declares that the Church accepts Wisdom "among the authentic Scripture."[481]

As to why Tostatus believed the deuterocanon to be incapable of establishing doctrine, consider this from his *Prologue on the Gospels*:

> The Church knows not whether writers inspired by the Holy Ghost wrote these [the disputed] books . . . When, therefore, there is doubt concerning the writers of certain books, whether they were inspired by the Holy Ghost, their authority is taken away, and the Church does not place them in the canon of Scripture. Furthermore, regarding these books, the Church is not certain whether or not heretics have not added to, or taken from that which was written by their proper authors. The Church, therefore, receives such books, permitting every one of the faithful to read them; the Church also reads them in her offices on account of the many devout things which are contained in them; but she obliges no one to believe that is contained therein, as is the case with the books of Wisdom, Ecclesiasticus, Maccabees, Judith, and Tobias. For though these books are received by Christians, and proof derived from them in some degree may have weight, because the Church retains those books, yet they are not effectual to prove those things that are in doubt against heretics and Jews, as Jerome says in his prologue upon Judith.[482]

Tostatus's devotion to the opinions of Jerome had led him to deny the inspiration of the deuterocanon, a point that is attested-to over and over again by the Fathers of the early

Church. He also seems to divide Scripture along lines of utility, equating the intrinsic nature of a book (whether or not the Holy Spirit was its primary author) with its extrinsic usefulness. Because the deuterocanon has "some degree" of authoritative weight only in the Church, and because the canonical books are authoritative both in the Church and with the Jews, the inspiration of the deuterocanon is in some manner inferior to the canonical books.

Antoninus (1389–1459)

In spite of the Council of Florence, Antoninus, the archbishop of Florence, also remained faithful to Jerome. Antoninus writes,

> The Church receives these books as true, and venerates them as useful, moral treatises, though, in the discussion of those things which are of faith, not conclusive in argument . . . Wherefore, perhaps, they have such authority as have the sayings of holy Doctors approved by the Church.[483]

As Breen points out, Antoninus seems to have had only a vague recollection of Florence's *Decree on the Reunion of the Jacobites and Armenians.*[484] Antoninus claims that his opinion comes from St. Thomas Aquinas, but as we have seen in our survey, this is not the case. Instead, Antoninus's views were dependent upon Jerome.[485]

Denis of Chartreux (Denis the Carthusian) (1404–1471)

Denis of Chartreux believed that the Church received the deuterocanon as true, but not canonical writings. He considered the deuterocanonical portions of Esther to be divine Scripture.[486]

Franciscus Ximenes de Cisneros (1436–1517)

The high office of Franciscus Ximenes de Cisneros, better known simply as Cardinal Ximenes, earned him a small fortune near the end of his life, and the cardinal used his wealth to found a school for the arts and sciences and had it built in an old Roman town called Complutum. Ximenes's endowments enabled this upstart university to become well known; by the end of its first year, it had nearly 3,000 students. The crowning achievement of Ximenes's career was the publication of a polyglot Bible: formatted in such a way as to provide various texts and translations in parallel columns:

> Ximenes's role in the making of the Polyglot was that of general supervisor. His main contribution was to secure Hebrew manuscripts for use in it. Under him, a host of editors put the Polyglot together, including three Hebraists who were converts from Judaism: Alphonso of Alcala, Paul Coronel of Salamanca, and Alphonso de Zamora.[487]

Ximenes*'s Complutensian Polyglot (Biblia Computensia* as it became known) places the Vulgate as its center of focus. The New Testament has two columns, the Vulgate and a Greek text. The Old Testament of the Vulgate is flanked by the Septuagint and the Masoretic Text (the Pentateuch also included the *Targum Onkelos*).

The introductory preface explains to the reader the nature of the work, and includes an explanation as to why some Old Testament books (the deuterocanon) only have a double translation (the Vulgate and the Septuagint) without the third Hebrew column. The author refers to the deuterocanon using the words of Jerome from his *Helmeted Prologue*:

> The books . . . which are without the canon, which the Church receives rather for the edification of the people than the establishment of ecclesiastical doctrines are only given in Greek, but in a double translation.[488]

This quote from Jerome is not at all out of place with the rest of the Polyglot, which reproduces Jerome's *Letter to Paulus* and his prefaces to the Pentateuch, Joshua, the book of Kings, Paralipomenon (Chronicles), Ezra, Tobit, Judith, Esther, Psalms, Ecclesiastes, the books of Solomon, Jeremiah, Ezekiel, etc. . . . In other words, the Polyglot contains the whole Vulgate complete with Jerome's prefaces.

What truly made the Polyglot groundbreaking wasn't its reproduction of Jerome's work, but that it was the first Bible printed in Hebrew, Greek, and Aramaic text. It also sported a Hebrew and Aramaic dictionary in the back. For this reason, it enjoyed the support of Pope Leo X, who supplied several manuscripts for the project.

It is likely that Ximenes adopted Jerome's views on Hebrew Verity because he himself references, in two of the prefaces, the Masoretic Text as being the truth (*veritas*).[489] Be that as it may, there is no doubt as to Jerome's influence on the Polyglot. Indeed, its uncritical and positive acceptance of Jerome's remarks further served to promote the saint's influence among scholars of the age.

Erasmus (1466–1536)

Erasmus is perhaps the best-known figure in the humanist movement of Luther's day. Erasmus also attempted to reconcile Church usage with Jerome. The three quotes below are samples of how Erasmus wrestled with these views:

> For the rest . . . it is not yet agreed in what spirit the Church now holds in public use books which the ancients with great consent reckoned among the apocrypha. Whatever the authority of the Church has approved I embrace simply as a Christian man ought to do . . . Yet it is of great moment to know in what spirit the Church approves anything. For allowing that it assigns equal authority of the Hebrew canon and the four Gospels, it assuredly does not with Judith, Tobit, and Wisdom to have the same weight as the Pentateuch.[490]

After enumerating the protocanon minus Esther, Erasmus writes,

> [T]hat Wisdom, Ecclesiasticus [Sirach], Tobit, Judith, Esther, and the additions of Daniel have been received into ecclesiastical use. Whether, however, the Church receives them as possessing the same authority as the others the spirit of the Church must know.[491]

> That it is not unreasonable to establish different degrees of authority among the holy books, as St. Augustine has done. The books of the first rank are those concerning which there has never existed a doubt with the ancients. Certainly, Isaiah has more weight than Judith.[492]

Erasmus is puzzled as to the exact status of the deuterocanon. He confuses the utility of Scripture with its inspiration. The book of Genesis and the book of Esther are not equally useful in confirming doctrine. However, the Holy

Spirit is still the primary author of both books. Therefore, they are equally inspired and authoritative, even though they may not be equally useful.

Thomas de Vio (Cajetan) (1469–1534)

Rarely does an anti-Catholic work fail to mention Thomas de Vio, better known as Cardinal Cajetan. Cajetan was a papal legate to Germany and an official intermediary between Martin Luther and Rome. He was tapped as legate because he was one of the finest and strictest Thomistic scholars of his day. Although Cajetan's study of Thomas Aquinas made him a suitable candidate to dialogue with Martin Luther over his theological innovations, it was also a deadly weakness. So singular was Cajetan's focus on Aquinas that he lacked the flexibility to grapple with the unorthodox complexities of Luther's theology. This inflexibility can be seen in Cajetan's first meeting with the Reformer. Catholic historian Warren Carroll recounts,

> In explaining why these propositions [Luther's views on indulgences and the sacraments] were heretical, Cajetan, a great authority on St. Thomas Aquinas, relied on the Angelic Doctor, whom Luther despised, for much of his argumentation. . . . [Cajetan] was so incensed by Luther's provocative manner and diatribes against St. Thomas Aquinas, to whom he was devoted, that most uncharacteristically he began shouting at him. Luther replied even more loudly (the man did not live who could out shout Martin Luther) and finally Cajetan dismissed him with: "Go, and do not return unless you are ready to recant!"[493]

Aquinas was *the* last word in Cajetan's theology. When it came to biblical studies, however, Jerome was his master.

Cajetan's devotion to these two great theologians is admirable, but it should have had limits. No theologian, however great and knowledgeable, is immune from error. Even the two great Doctors of the Church, Jerome and Aquinas, occasionally made mistakes. They are subject to correction. Cajetan's unbalanced devotion to Jerome can be seen in his rather bizarre statements in his *Commentary on the Book of Esther:*

> The Church receives such books [the deuterocanon], permitting the faithful to read them; the Church also reads them in her offices, on account of the many devout things which they contain. But the Church obliges no one necessarily to believe what is contained therein, which is the case with the books of Wisdom, Ecclesiasticus [Sirach], Maccabees, Judith, and Tobit. For though these books are received by Christians, and proof derived from them may, in some way or other, have weight, because the Church retains those books; yet they are not effectual for proving those things which are in doubt, against heretics or Jews. We here terminate our commentaries (on the books of Judith, Tobit, and the Maccabees), which are reckoned by Jerome without the canonical books, and are placed among the apocrypha, together with Wisdom and Ecclesiasticus, as appears in his *Prologus Galeatus* [*Helmeted Prologue*]. Nor should you be disturbed, O novice, if you should anywhere find those books reckoned among the canonical books, either in the holy councils, or in the holy Doctors. *For the words of the councils, as well as of the Doctors, are to be submitted to the correction of Jerome; and according to his judgment to the bishops Chromatius and Heliodorus,* those books (and if there be any similar ones in the canon of the Bible) are not canonical, that is, they are not those which are given as a rule for the confirmation of

> the Faith. They may, however, be called canonical (that is, given as a rule) for the edification of the faithful; since [they are] received and authorized in the canon of the Bible for this purpose.[494]

In one paragraph, Cajetan places Jerome above every pope, every council, and every Christian teacher. He admits that the Church receives the deuterocanon and calls it canonical, and he admits that the deuterocanon does carry some weight in doctrinal proofs, albeit not enough to persuade heretics and Jews.[495] The most fascinating aspect of this commentary is to see the lengths to which this otherwise sober theologian will go to reconcile Jerome with the official Church. Even Cajetan's own language becomes twisted when he writes that the deuterocanon is in the "canon of the Bible," but later he claims that it is "not canonical." Did Cajetan really mean to make a distinction between canonical-canonical books and canonical non-canonical books? The confusion in Cajetan's otherwise clear thinking serves to illustrate how the discussion of the canon had degraded by the time of the Protestant Reformation.

The Synod of Sens (February 3–October 9, 1528)

The local council of Sens met to reaffirm the teachings of the Faith that were being denied by Protestants. They held that the *Decree of Pope Gelasius*, the Third Council of Carthage, and Pope Innocent I had already settled the question of the canon, so they decreed that anyone who did not accept these ancient teachings was to be denounced as a heretic and schismatic.[496] The synod's decree, however, had little effect on the maelstrom of opinions and viewpoints of this age. Consequently, the need for a general council appeared all too obvious. Unfortunately, because of political, social, and logistical difficulties, that council would not be convened until December of 1545.

The Council of Trent (1545–1563; Decree, February 11, 1546)

The Council of Trent decided early on to address questions of Scripture and Sacred Tradition because both were prerequisites to all discussions of doctrine.[497] Trent's action in the defining of the canon lies at the heart of the Catholic/Protestant controversy. Did the Council of Trent *add* books to the Bible, or did Protestants *remove* them?

To answer this question, researchers should to start with the decree itself. On April 8, 1546, the fourth session of the Council of Trent issued a dogmatic decree titled *The Sacred Books and the Traditions of the Apostles.* It touched upon doctrine (e.g. the canon) and upon discipline as well (e.g. the acceptance of the Vulgate). The council fathers declared,

> The sacred and holy ecumenical and general Synod of Trent . . . following the examples of the orthodox Fathers, receives and holds in veneration with an equal affection of piety and reverence all the books both of the Old and of the New Testament, since one God is the author of both, and also the traditions themselves, those that appertain both to faith and to morals, as having been dictated either by Christ's own word of mouth, or by the Holy Spirit, and preserved in the Catholic Church by a continuous succession. And so that no doubt may arise in anyone's mind as to which are the books that are accepted by this Synod, it has decreed that a list of the sacred books be added to this decree.

> Books of the Old Testament: [lists all of the protocanonical and deuterocanonical books] . . . Books of the New Testament [lists all of the protocanonical and deuterocanonical books of the New Testament] . . . If anyone, however, should not accept the said books as sacred and canonical, entire with all their parts, as they were wont to be read in the Catholic Church, and as they are contained in the old Latin Vulgate edition, and if both knowingly and deliberately he should condemn the aforesaid traditions let him be anathema. Let all, therefore, understand in what order and in what manner the said synod, after having laid the foundation of the confession of faith, will proceed, and what testimonies and authorities it will mainly use in confirming dogmas, and in restoring morals in the Church.[498]

How did the council fathers arrive at this canon? Did they add books to the canon in a reactionary move against the Protestants? The deliberations of the council provide the key that unlocks the answer.

Deliberations of the Council of Trent

The council held three official sessions before issuing its decree on the canon. The first officially opened the council; the second laid down various points of procedure and issued the statement of faith called the *Symbolum Fidei*.[499] The third adopted a plan to divide the body into three particular congregations for the purpose of readying questions to be discussed during the meeting of the general congregations (in which all the bishops would participate).

The first general congregation (February 8) discussed whether a decree on the canon of Scripture was actually needed; after all, Cardinal Pacheco argued, the Church Fathers and previous councils had already addressed the issue. It was suggested that Trent merely collect and confirm these decrees without any additional deliberation. This idea won the approval of several of the council members.[500] Others considered any discussion of the canon superfluous, being under the impression that Lutherans and Catholics held similar views on the topic. The majority, however, wished to consider the issue and voted to do so.

In the first particular congregation (February 11), it was asked if the canon of Scripture ought to be received as "pure and simple" (*pure et simpliciter*), or whether there should be some preliminary discussion of the objections raised against it, "not as if the question itself were in doubt, but in order that the synod should be able to give an account of itself to any believer whatsoever."[501] It was decided "to receive the books simply and entirely as the Church had done in other councils, and especially in the Council of Florence."[502] That night, the cardinal legates wrote that all three particular congregations had agreed on the acceptance of the books of Scripture pure and simple, "as was done by many of the ancient Fathers, by the Third Provincial Council of Carthage, by that of Pope Gelasius, by Innocent I, and lastly by the Council of Florence."[503] The letter also proposed that a group of theologians should be brought together, outside of the council, to answer objections raised against certain books. Two council fathers, Pietro Bertano and Girolamo Seripando, proposed that a distinction be made between the deuterocanon and the protocanon, as Jerome had called for in the *Helmeted Prologue*. This proposal was offered to the congregation, but failed to win acceptance.[504] Breen notes,

> So here, it is not evident just what distinction this man wished to induce. But in every case, his proposition was

> useless. If he wished merely to say that the import of some divine books is more important in Christian doctrine than others, the truth is understood by all Christians, and needs no definition. The council was not about to define that Maccabees was as valuable to use as Matthew. But if he wished to say that the relation which God bore to any book was less than inspiration as we have defined it, the proposition is false. The council simply extended proper inspiration to all the books, and left the question of their respect dogmatic and more values intact.[505]

The second general congregation met on February 12. Cardinal del Monte opened by presenting the findings of all three particular congregations: the sacred books were to be accepted just as they had been in former councils, especially Florence. By the end of this general session, the adoption of these decrees seemed, to del Monte, to have gained the assent of all but one of the council fathers.[506]

The third general congregation (February 15) offered three questions for final approval by the entire congregation. The first question asked if the Council of Trent should approve all the books which had been approved at Florence. The second question asked whether a distinction should be made in regard to the authority of one book over another. The third question was whether the arguments of the adversaries should be discussed, examined, and solved. The council had already resolved to affirm the canon as given the former councils, especially Florence, and that the canon should be given pure and simple without any additional distinctions.

The third question occupied much discussion. Some thought it would be beneficial both to the faithful and those who opposed the deuterocanon to address their objections. Others believed that this would only invite more dispute and take away from the authority of the decree. But in the end, it was agreed that if objections needed to be answered, it ought to be done by consulting theologians and not as part of the decree.

The next issue was whether the decree should include an *anathema*. The anathema is a term used to assign a canonical penalty against any Catholic who holds a given proposition that is contrary to the Faith. It is used both to underscore the importance of a given teaching and the spiritual danger it placed one in by rejecting it.[507]

We have already seen in this chapter how the prestige of Jerome had caused some of his devotees to place him as the norm that sets all norms in all things biblical. A corrective was definitely needed.

Cardinal Pacheco proposed the inclusion of an anathema, stating that it would remove all doubt as to the authority of the canonical lists of the past. Cardinal Cajetan (Thomas de Vio) is mentioned as "one of our own people who was not ashamed to dispute the authority of many of our books and reject them as apocryphal."[508] The inclusion of an anathema was carried with twenty-four votes in favor, fifteen votes against.[509]

The inclusion of the anathema brought the canon given by previous councils into sharper relief and brought about uniformity in practice within the Church. As the *Catholic Encyclopedia* (1908) describes it,

> The Tridentine decrees from which the above list is extracted was the first infallible *and effectually* promulgated pronouncement on the canon, addressed to the Church universal.[510]

Unfortunately, the point about Trent being the first infallible *and effectual* pronouncement has been misconstrued to mean that previous councils (Hippo, Carthage, Florence) lacked dogmatic weight.[511] Although the Tridentine decree may be the most solemn pronouncement on the canon, the previous conciliar decisions and papal decrees were already considered part of the universal law of the Church.[512]

Did Trent Add Books to the Bible?

The beautiful thing about Church bureaucracy is that it leaves a paper trail. The official *Acts of Trent* along with the unofficial diaries, letters, and so on give us an insight into the inner workings of the council. The "inside information" that we have seen ought to convince even the most hardened skeptic that Trent didn't *add* books to the Bible. Rightly or wrongly, this body acted in a manner entirely conservative, basing its decisions on precedent alone. Even its refusal to provide a defense of the deuterocanon or to allow further discussion was based upon conservative principles; after all, why provide a fresh apology for something that had been settled for centuries? The desire of the council was to avoid tampering with the canon in any way—to offer, rather, a simple "rubber stamp" upon the judgments of previous authorities (especially that of the Council of Florence).[513] Despite the suggestions of a few concise Fathers, Trent's conservatism won out, and the canon was published pure and simple: a plain, unadorned reiteration of the traditional position. Did Trent *add* books to the Bible? The answer is decidedly no.

For the sake of completion, we will close this chapter by looking at two post-Tridentine sources that touch upon the canon, namely the patriarch of Constantinople, Cyril Lucar, and the First Vatican Council.

Cyril Lucar (Cyril Lucaris) (1572–1637)

The Eastern Orthodox churches also flirted with the Protestant canon for a time. Cyril Lucar was patriarch of Alexandria (1602–1620) and later Constantinople (1620–1637). He was attracted to Calvinist Europe and sent many young priests to the West to study. Cyril had also made overtures of friendship to the Anglican Church as well as to the Lutherans. He even donated the *Codex Alexandrinus* to King Charles I. In 1627, Lucar published a treatise called *The Confession of Faith,* which rejected the deuterocanon as apocrypha.[514] Metrophanes Critopulus, a friend of Lucar, in his *Confession of the Catholic and Apostolic Eastern Church,* followed his friend's opinion by claiming that the Church of Christ had never received the deuterocanon as authentic Scripture.[515] These books were widely circulated throughout the East.[516] In 1638, the Patriarch Parthenius convened a council in Constantinople. The two patriarchs and the 120 Eastern bishops present at this council issued a letter to the providential synod of Jerusalem (Jassy), condemning the views of Cyril Lucas as heretical. This letter affirmed that the deuterocanon had always been accepted in the East, despite isolated doubts.[517]

Vatican Council I (1870)

The First Vatican Council reaffirmed Trent's decree on the canon:

> And, indeed, these books of the Old and New Testaments, whole with all their parts, just as they were enumerated in the decree of the same council, are contained in the old Vulgate Latin edition, and are to be accepted as sacred and canonical. But the Church holds these books

> as sacred and canonical, *not because, having been put together by human industry alone, they were approved by its authority; nor because they contain revelation without error; but because, having been written by the inspiration of the Holy Spirit,* they have God as their author and, as such, they have been handed down to the Church itself.[518]

This decree of the First Vatican Council is certainly helpful in clearing up a few misconceptions. It had long been an anti-Catholic bugaboo, for example, that the Catholic Church believes itself to have *made* or *created* the canon of Scripture—a misrepresentation that has been circulating within Protestantism since the beginning of the Reformation. It is true that the Church preserved these books and promulgated them as a canon, but Vatican I rejects the idea that they are *made* canonical by being declared such by the Church. The Catholic Church teaches that the canonical books are canonical because they were written by the inspiration of the Holy Spirit and, in God's providential care, were entrusted to the Church.

The Holy Spirit inspired a certain number of books. Christ and his inspired apostles handed those books on to the Church. Whenever doubters and innovators have tried to alter this sacred deposit, the Church has promulgated a catalogue of those books that have always been accepted as inspired. The Church is not somehow above Scripture; instead, the Church is Scripture's duly authorized custodian.

10

Why Protestant Bibles Are Smaller

If the Council of Trent didn't add the deuterocanon to the Bible, as its deliberations show, why do Protestant bibles exclude these books?

This wasn't always the case. Before 1599, nearly all Protestant bibles included the deuterocanonical books; between the years 1526 and 1631, Protestant bibles with the deuterocanon were the rule and not the exception.[519] It was not until the middle of the seventeenth century that the tide began to turn toward smaller bibles for Protestants. By 1831, the books of the deuterocanon, along with their cross-references, were almost entirely expunged from Protestant translations. This eradication has been so complete that few Protestants today are aware that such editions of Scripture ever existed. This process of eradicating the deuterocanon began with Martin Luther.

Martin Luther (1483–1546)

Luther is the father of the Protestant Reformation. He grew up in a Catholic family and became a priest and monk of the Augustinian order. It was during this time that he became embroiled in a controversy over the issue of indulgences, which led to the publication of his Ninety-Five Theses in 1517. The publication of the theses is generally seen as the beginning of the Protestant Reformation.

Luther was very much a child of his age. He too was caught up in the enthusiasm for studying the ancient languages, exposing him to the exaggerated importance of Jerome.[520] This background led to his German translation of Sacred Scripture, which we will speak about later.

Catholic apologists sometimes claim that Martin Luther *removed* the deuterocanonical books from Scripture. This is not entirely true. Luther's *German* Translation of the scriptures included the deuterocanon. In fact, the completion of Luther's German Bible was delayed because an illness prevented him from finishing the section containing those books! And since Luther's Bible (with its "Apocrypha" section that contained the deuterocanon) became a paradigm for subsequent Protestant translations, most of these bibles also included them as well. It is, therefore, incorrect to say that Luther removed the deuterocanon. He did, however, introduce certain innovations into his translation that led eventually to smaller Protestant bibles—innovations that were the culmination of a process of development within Luther's theology.

If Protestantism rejected the deuterocanon, then we ought to see somewhere early in Protestant history a transition from the initial acceptance of the deuterocanon to its rejection. This transition occurs during the early years before Martin Luther officially broke off from the Church.

Resolutions on the Disputation Concerning the Power of Indulgences (1518)[521]

If there is a single date for the beginning of the Protestant Reformation, it is October 31, 1517. On this day Martin Luther posted his Ninety-Five Theses, marking his first public and formal dispute with the Church. The theses were a list of propositions to be debated, but Luther never had a public debate on them. Therefore, Luther became convinced that he needed to compose a writing that would explain and defend them to the public.[522] The resulting work was the *Resolutions* [or *Explanations*] *of the Disputation Concerning the Power of Indulgences.* According to the Lutheran historian Bernard Lohse, this work was Luther's first true Reformation writing.[523]

Luther's defense of the Ninety-Five Theses begins, as with most disputations of the time, with a *protestatio* or a declaration of principles upon which the work will argue. Luther begins his *protestatio* for the *Resolutions* with the following declaration:

> First, I testify that I desire to say or maintain *absolutely nothing* except, first of all, what is *in the holy scriptures and can be maintained from them.*[524]

This is important because Luther quotes from the deuterocanon in this work. For example, he offers in the first paragraph of thesis 17 the following scriptural authority:

> [A]ccording to which it says, "Although the righteous fall, he shall not be cast headlong, for the Lord is the stay of his hand" [Ps. 37:24]. *And also,* "Precious in the sight of the Lord is the death of his saints" [Ps. 116:15], *and again,* "If the just man shall be snatched by death, he shall be at rest" [Wis. 4:7]. Both the just and the unjust have found a reason for death . . . The just man, on the other hand, who is tired of this life, desires especially to be released, and so his desire is granted to him.[525]

Luther also appeals to Sirach as a proof in his defense of thesis 35:

> I prove my argument in the following manner: every doctrine of Christ is an exhortation to penitence and points to the fact that men should turn from the devil, the sooner the

> better. As Ecclesiasticus says, "Do not delay in turning to the Lord" [Sir. 5:8]. And the Lord himself says . . . [quotes Matt. 25:13]. The apostle Paul says . . . [quotes Heb. 4:11], and the apostle Peter says . . . [quotes 2 Pet. 3:11–12].[526]

From Luther's *Protestatio* and his use of Wisdom and Sirach, he must have understood the deuterocanon to be Scripture that can be adduced in debate as proof of a doctrine. If the *Resolutions* were the only text we had where Luther did this, we may be tempted to assume that it was merely a case of carelessness on Luther's part. However, we find a similar text in his response to the master of the papal palace, Silvester Maccoloni.

Response to Silvester Prierias Dialogue Concerning the Power of the Pope (1518)[527]

After Luther's publication of the Ninety-Five Theses, word was sent to Rome to prohibit Luther from preaching against indulgences. In February, Pope Leo X handed the matter over to the head of Luther's order and a formal response was given by Silvester Maccolini da Prierio, better known today by the Latin Sylvester Prierias. In June 1518, Prierias issued *A Dialogue against Martin Luther's Presumptuous Theses Concerning the Power of Pope.*[528]

As in the *Resolutions,* Luther begins his reply with a short *protestatio*, in which he says,

> First is that of St. Paul: test all things; hold what is good; and Galatians 1: if an angel from heaven should preach to you other than what you have received, let him [or it] be anathema. Second is that of St. Augustine to Jerome: I have learned to give honor *alone* to those books *which are called canonical*, and I firmly believe that no Scripture of

> them errs. However, as for the rest, however much doctrine and sanctity they contain, I do not likewise believe them to be true."[529]

There are a few features worth noting. First, Luther quotes St. Augustine about giving honor alone to the canonical books. Augustine, as we have seen, taught that the deuterocanon was fully canonical. Second, Luther's *protestatio* stakes out as his authority *the canonical Scripture* for his response to Prierias. In this regard, Protestant theologian Henry Howorth notes,

> Luther answered [Prierias] in the words of Augustine that the only authority he could accept in the matter was the canonical scriptures. What Luther actually meant at this time by the phrase *eis libris, qui canonici appellantur* is not quite clear, for we now find him . . . [quoting] Tobias . . . in each case apparently as authoritative.[530]

If Luther states at the outset that he would give honor *only to canonical Scripture* and he cites Tobit 3:24 [Vulgate] in the same work, would it not be reasonable to assume that Luther, at this point in his career, still believed Tobit to be canonical Scripture? The *protestatio* in both the *Resolutions* and the *Response to Prierias,* along with Luther's appeals to deuterocanonical books of Sirach, Wisdom, and Tobit as proofs in these disputes, certainly speaks in favor of this position. We can add one more example to the list.

The Heidelberg Disputation (1518)

In April 1518, Luther engaged in one of his most famous public debates—what became known as the *Heidelberg Disputation*—

in which he discloses his *theology of the cross*. The *Disputation* centered around twenty-nine theological theses and twelve philosophical theses and led to two important outcomes. First, Luther had won over Martin Bucer, who would later become an influential leader within the Protestant movement. Second, the disputation encouraged the Catholic theologian Johann Maier von Eck to challenge Luther to a debate in the city of Leipzig.

In the ninth theological thesis of the *Heidelberg Disputation*, Luther once again adduces a deuterocanonical book as a scriptural proof:

> For in such a way God is constantly deprived of the glory which is due him and which is transferred to other things, since one should strive with all diligence to give him the glory—the sooner the better. For this reason the Bible advises us, "Do not delay being converted to the Lord" [Sir. 5:8].[531]

There is a flaw in the translation given above that is very illuminating. Luther didn't write, "For this reason *the Bible* [Latin, *biblia*] advises us." He wrote, "For this reason *the Scripture* [Latin, *Scriptura*] advises us."[532] Why did the English translator translate *Scriptura* as "Bible" instead of "Scripture"? The footnote says, "This quotation is from Sirach 5:8. The Vulgate Bible contained the apocryphal books."[533] In other words, the translator wishes the reader to believe that Luther was not appealing to Sirach as "Scripture," but simply as a book that he happened to find in his Bible. Elsewhere, though, the translator correctly translates *Scriptura* as "Scripture."[534] Clearly the translator saw that that Luther's citation of Sirach as Scripture in this *Disputation* was at odds with Luther's later position on the deuterocanon.

Luther appears to have changed his policy concerning the admissibility of the deuterocanon in debate and its ability to confirm doctrine in his next controversy.

The Second Leipzig Disputation (1519)

If there was one person who was not afraid to go toe-to-toe with the fiery Luther in public debate it was Johann Maier von Eck (1486–1543). In 1519, Eck agreed to a series of debates with Andreas Karlstadt (1486–1541) and Luther in the electoral palace in Leipzig. The most famous of these debates took place on July 4 of that year, when Luther denied the infallibility of councils and popes and asserted that the ultimate authority is Scripture alone.[535]

The second disputation was on several different subjects. On the subject of purgatory, Eck appealed to 2 Maccabees 12:45:

> But if he was looking to the splendid reward that is laid up for those who fall asleep in godliness, it was a holy and pious thought. Therefore he made atonement for the dead, that they might be delivered from their sin.

On July 8, 1519, Luther responded by refusing to allow Maccabees to be admitted into argument, stating,

> There is no proof of purgatory in any portion of Sacred Scripture *which can enter into the argument and serve as a proof*; for the book of Maccabees not being in the canon, is *of weight with the faithful*, but avails nothing with the obstinate.[536]

Luther's response is sometimes overstated. Luther did not deny that Maccabees had authority. It had (authoritative?) weight *with the faithful*, but, according to Luther, it lacked sufficient weight to move him from his convictions. This denial of canonical status was something new. As the Anglican scholar H.H. Howorth notes,

> This was undoubtedly a very important *new departure*. It is quite true that the book in question was not in the Jewish canon, and that consequently St. Jerome excluded it from *his* canon, but there could be no doubt about *its continuous acceptance by the Church Catholic as canonical from the earliest times*, nor that it was expressly included in the lists of canonical books issued by the three African councils of Hippo in 393 and of Carthage in 397 and 419, which were under the immediate influence of Augustine, and which constitute the earliest corporate pronouncement on the subject made by the Western Church.[537]

Luther's appeal to the rabbinic canon opened the field for Eck to advance. He immediately countered by insisting that Maccabees had always been a part of the Christian canon, though the Jews had, admittedly, rejected it. At this point, Luther had no other option but to appeal to the authority of Jerome.[538] Howorth comments,

> Luther, however, clearly seems to have thought that this disingenuous special pleading a way not a sufficient support to his case, for it in effect meant setting up Jerome as an infallible pope to revise the decision of the Church upon such a critical matter as the legitimate canonicity of the two Maccabean books, upon which it had corporately always held the same view . . . He therefore goes on to affirm another reason that shows at how early a period in his career he had really broken with the Church as the ultimate rule of faith and set up a pontifical authority of his own. He says

> he knows that the Church had accepted this book, but the Church could not give a greater authority and strength to a book than it already possessed by its own virtue.[539]

Luther's statement is, of course, true—and it later became a formal doctrine of the Catholic Church.[540] The Church does not invest a book with any special power; rather, it affirms and promulgates that which it had received as divine scriptures from the apostles.[541] But Luther was skipping a step: by what process does one learn which books possess this authority by nature and which ones do not?

In this sense, Howorth's observation is correct. The rabbis have their canon. Other heretical Christian sects have theirs. There were many "Gospels" and other writings purporting to be Scripture circulating in antiquity. Jerome has no more competency to determine which books are Scripture than Luther, Eck, or any individual or sect. The true canon is that which was received by the Church from the apostles and made manifest through practice.[542]

Canon Within a Canon

Luther's comments in the second disputation reflect a unique perspective that he held on canonicity. As already noted, he did not deny that Maccabees had *weight*, but only that it did not have sufficient weight to prevail over and against his convictions. For Luther, the canon represented a spectrum of authority with each book being more or less canonical depending on its degree of *apostolicity*. What is apostolicity for Luther? As Luther understood the term, apostolicity was the degree to which a book preached the gospel as Luther understood it.[543] Put another way, a book was considered *apostolic* only to the degree that Luther heard his theology clearly confirmed in it.[544]

The apostolicity or canonicity of several books (e.g., Esther, 2 Maccabees, James, Jude, and Revelation) was thus called into question.[545] This denial of canonicity did not necessarily exclude a book from the Bible. Instead, Luther posed a sort of canon within the canon. Had Luther wished to use the criterion of whether a writing "preached Christ" to determine a new Christian canon, he would have tested the Jewish apocrypha (e.g., the book of Enoch, Jubilees, et al.) for their apostolicity/canonicity.[546]

Like the Marcionites, Ebionites, and Gnostics before him, Luther's theological convictions determined what constituted the canonical scriptures. The canon and canonicity had to be radically re-conceptualized to support his gospel.[547]

Deuterocanon Becomes "Apocrypha"

As strange as it sounds, Luther did not reject the deuterocanon outright after the second Leipzig disputation. He continued to use the deuterocanon in his writings in a way very similar to how he used it before the debate. The difference being that before the disputation, Luther cited deuterocanonical books in debate as scriptural proof of doctrine. During the disputation, however, Luther denied canonicity of these books, that they can be adduced in debate, and that they can serve to confirm doctrine. This contradicts his earlier usage and, as Howorth noted earlier, it also contradicts the consistent practice of Christians from the beginning.[548]

Luther's German Translation

Luther's German translation of the Bible introduced more than one radical innovation. With rare exceptions, Christian bibles before Luther had not only included the deuterocanon, but intermixed these books with the rest of the books of the Old Testament.[549] Even John Wycliffe, considered by Protestants to be a role model of Bible translators, followed this practice. Luther's Bible broke with this traditional practice. Instead, he reordered the books of the Old Testament chronologically, removing the deuterocanonical books from their former place in the story of salvation and giving them the appearance of being extraneous to the word of God.[550] Luther's second novelty was the gathering of the deuterocanonical books into an appendix at the end of the Old Testament and marking them *Apocrypha*.

The title page of this new appendix is prefaced by this explanatory remark:

> Apocrypha—that is, books which are not held equal to the holy scriptures and yet are profitable and good to read.[551]

We must not read too much into this title *Apocrypha*; as we have seen, the meaning of the term had become quite fluid and confused by Luther's time. Some writers used it to mean "spurious writings of merely human origin"; others had no difficulty using it for books they themselves considered canonical Scripture![552] What did Luther mean by it?

Luther certainly did not believe, nor could he believe, that the deuterocanon was equal to the protocanon; but the fact that he saw these books still, in some sense, as part of the Old Testament is evidenced by the colophon he places after his "Apocrypha" in the appendix: "The end of the books of the Old Testament."[553]

Although segregated and devalued, the deuterocanon still remained part of Luther's Old Testament corpus.

Luther's prefaces to the various books of his Bible reflect his "canon in a canon" vision of assessing each book differently. Indeed, Luther's criticisms were not restricted to the Old Testament deuterocanon, but included the New Testament deuterocanon as well.[554]

Luther's actions speak to the fact that his innovation really was an innovation. Consider these points: if the deuterocanon never was really considered Scripture, why bother to qualify it as not being equal to Scripture? Why not just remove these books altogether? The answer is that such a move would have proved too radical, since Christian bibles had always included the deuterocanon. Instead, Luther reformatted the Bible. The resulting edition was still unlike any Bible ever seen before,[555] and it paved the way for more radical steps to be taken in the future.

Continental Protestantism

Although Luther's Protestant contemporaries quickly adopted his bold attitude toward the deuterocanon, they soon abandoned his shaky rationale for doing so. Indeed, sixteenth-century justifications for the deuterocanon's demotion varied widely (though the appeal to the "infallible" authority of Jerome was widespread).

Joseias Osiander, a Lutheran evangelist, finished a new edition of Jerome's Vulgate in Latin with certain corrections from the Hebrew. It was published in December 1522, the same month that Luther's New Testament appeared. Osiander strictly follows Jerome and adopts his canon. He makes, however, a curious admission concerning the book of Maccabees, which Luther flatly rejected as non-canonical. He comments that 1 and 2 Maccabees, "although not in the Hebrew canon, *were classed by the Church among divine histories.*"[556]

Swiss Bibles

Like Luther, Oecolampadius (1482–1531), a representative of the German churches in Switzerland, placed the deuterocanon on a level below that of Scripture. He shared Luther's view on the degrees of canonicity. In his *Letter to the Waldenses*, Oecolampadius writes,

> We do not the despise Judith, Tobit, Baruch, the last two books of Esdras, the three books of Maccabees, the last two chapters of Daniel, and we do not allow them divine authority, equal with those others [of the Hebrew canon]. In the New Testament we receive four Gospels, with the Acts of the Apostles, and fourteen epistles of St. Paul, and seven Catholic epistles, together with the Apocalypse; although we do not compare the Apocalypse, the epistles of James, and Jude, and 2 Peter and 2, 3, John with the rest.[557]

The Alsatian Zwinglite Leo Jud produced a translation of Scripture known as the Zurich Bible (1531). The deuterocanon is found in an appendix titled *Apocryphi*, which Jud includes so that those who read those books and like them will not complain about their absence. However, he claims to have followed the Fathers in not including the deuterocanon among holy Scripture: "[Y]et they [the deuterocanonical books] contain much which in no way contradicts the biblical writings, faith and love, and some things which are founded in God's word."[558]

Completed in 1531, three years before the publication of Luther's Bible, the Zurich Bible matches Luther's translation in contents and order. Another preface of the Zurich Bible, commonly ascribed to Zwingli, states that the Apocrypha are not highly esteemed, being less clear and accurate that the protocanon, although the books contain much that is true and useful. Zwingli leaves it up to the reader to divide the good from the bad. Like Jud's preface, Zwingli's states that the Apocrypha have been included in the Zurich Bible "so that no one may complain of lacking anything, and each may find what is to his taste."[559]

Just as Luther could not "hear the gospel preached" in the books of the deuterocanon, Zwingli did not find their contents to be altogether clear. Doubtless, these distorted or blurred passages of Zwingli's correspond to those texts supporting Catholic doctrine. For example, when Catholics cited Baruch 3:4 to confirm the doctrine of purgatory, Zwingli, in the work *Concluding Discourses* (1523), retorted that Baruch contains legends and is not canonical. Yet in spite of such appeals by his opponents, Zwingli did not feel compelled to remove the deuterocanon from the Bible entirely; to him those books were Old Testament apocrypha—*like* the protos, in some sense, but without the same "clarity of Scripture."

In the 1543 edition of the Zurich Bible, the title of the *Apocryphi* appendix was changed to *Ecclesiastici Libri* ("Ecclesiastical Books" or "Church Books"). The preface states,

> Church books which the Church *always held to be holy books*, worthy for the pious to read. Yet they were not given equal authority with the canonical writings. Our forefathers wanted them to be read in the churches, but not drawn on to confirm the authority of faith (articles of faith). *So they were called apocrypha, a word which is not in every respect appropriate or suitable for them.* They had no validity among the Hebrews, but were brought to light again among the Greeks.[560]

The title *Ecclesiastical Books* no doubt comes from Rufinus. Jerome's opinion is still retained, albeit with reservations concerning his use of the term *apocrypha*. It is significant that the authors of this preface admit that the Fathers wanted the deuterocanon read in church, yet they still feel the need to add the old (and incoherent) caveat about not using them to confirm doctrine.[561]

John Calvin (1509–1564)

Before we examine Calvin's view of the canon we must first examine the work of his cousin Olivetan, who produced the famous Olivetan Bible (1535).[562] Following Luther's German translation and the Zurich Bible, Olivetan placed the deuterocanon into an appendix marked *Apocrypha*. This edition contradicted the Zurich Bible, however, by stating that the apocrypha are not to be publicly read in church, but only privately and apart. Those books he segregated at the rear of the Bible to "make it clear which books give binding testimony, and which do not."[563] The preface specifically appeals to Jerome and Hebrew Verity as justification for their omission.

The 1540 edition of the Geneva Bible replaced Olivetan's preface with one from John Calvin. Here is what Calvin wrote regarding the disputed books:

> These books, called Apocrypha, have always been distinguished from the writings which were without difficulty called holy Scripture. For the Church Fathers wished to avoid the danger of mixing profane books with those which were certainly brought forth by the Holy Spirit. That is why they made a list, which they called a canon. The word means that everything which belongs to it was a firm rule to which one should hold. . . . It is true that the Apocrypha is not to be despised, insofar as it contains good and useful teaching. Yet there is good reason

> for what was given us by the Holy Spirit to have precedence over what has come from human beings. Thus all Christians, following what St. Jerome said, read the Apocrypha, and take from it teaching "for edification" [Eph. 4:12]. But in order to remind them that these writings cannot provide full assurance of their faith, it is to be noted that they do not contain any satisfying testimony.
>
> None of these books was in any way accepted by the Hebrews, and their original texts are not in Hebrew, but in Greek. It is correct that today, a great part of them are found in Hebrew. But it may be that they were [back] translated from the Greek. The safest thing is therefore to hold to what is extant in the language in which they are usually found.[564]

The preface suffers from numerous overstatements and blunders. For example, he states that the books of the "Apocrypha" have always been distinguished from Scripture "without difficulty." Anyone who has followed the historical overview presented so far knows that this is simply not the case, especially for the first four centuries of the Church. The deuterocanon was quoted explicitly as Scripture and used to confirm doctrine. The few who did make distinctions between the protocanon and the deuterocanon, as a rule, still used both as inspired Scripture capable of confirming doctrine. Even Jerome bends his own usage to that of his day. Furthermore, the same writers who expressed doubts about the deuterocanon often expressed similar doubts about some protocanonical books as well. Esther fares especially poorly in this regard. So what does the preface mean by "without difficulty"? The preface also insinuates that the early Fathers called the deuterocanon *apocrypha*. This is true in some cases only from the fifth century on. Before Jerome, the deuterocanon was *never* called apocrypha. In fact, it was often explicitly distinguished from it. The preface also states that the Hebrews never accepted the deuterocanonical books. As we have seen earlier, this is simply not the case.

Another error the preface commits is in the statement that the deuterocanon was originally written in Greek, not Hebrew. This is a rather big blunder because neither Jerome nor his sympathizers would say such a thing. Moreover, scholars around the time of the preface was written knew very well that the book of Sirach was originally composed in Hebrew.[565] Today, scholars know that all of the deuterocanon—with the exception of Wisdom and 2 Maccabees—was originally composed in Hebrew.

Antidote to the Council of Trent (1547)

Calvin's views on the deuterocanon are further explicated in a polemical tract titled *Antidote to the Council of Trent*. In his critique of the fourth session of Trent, Calvin warns that if the decree on the canon and Sacred Tradition were allowed to stand, it would spell the defeat of Protestantism.[566] Therefore, he sarcastically calls this session the "victorious and now, as it were, triumphal session."[567] Instead of refuting the council's decree point by point, however, Calvin vaguely and sporadically focuses his attention on the subject of the canon, preferring to spend most of his time attacking the deficiencies of the Vulgate. In his first pass on the canon, Calvin writes,

> Add to this, that they [the council fathers at Trent] provide themselves with *new supports* when they give full authority to the apocryphal books. Out of the second of the Maccabees they will prove purgatory and the worship of

> saints; out of Tobit satisfactions, exorcisms, and whatnot. From Ecclesiasticus they will borrow not a little. For from whence could they better draw their dregs? *I am not one of those*, however, who would *entirely disapprove the reading of those books*; but in giving them an authority which they *never before possessed*, what end was sought but just to have the use of spurious paint in coloring their errors?[568]

The author's reference to the Church providing "new supports" is surely more of a sneer than a statement of fact—and Calvin must have known it to be so. Catholic apologists (e.g., Herbon, Clichtovius, De Castro, and Bellarmine) had always appealed to these books in defense of the doctrines in question, beginning with Johann Eck's appeal to 2 Maccabees at the Leipzig Disputation of 1519. Moreover, Luther and Wycliffe themselves had both, at one time, used the deuterocanon to confirm doctrine. Later in the same tract, Calvin revisits the topic of the canon in a more detailed fashion:

> Of their admitting all the books promiscuously into the canon, I say nothing more than it goes against the consent of the primitive Church. *It is well known that Jerome states as the common opinion of earlier times*. And Rufinus, speaking of the matter as not at all controverted, declares with Jerome, that Ecclesiasticus, the Wisdom of Solomon, Tobit, Judith, and the history of the Maccabees, were called by the Fathers not canonical but ecclesiastical books, which might indeed be read to the people, but were not entitled to establish doctrine. *I am not, however, unaware that the same view on which the Fathers of Trent now insist was held in the Council of Carthage*. The same, too, was followed by Augustine in his *Treatise on Christian Doctrine*; but as he testifies that all of his age did not take the same view, *let us assume that*

> *the point was then undecided.* But if it were to be decided by arguments drawn from the case itself, many things beside the phraseology would shew that those books which the fathers of Trent raise so high must sink to a lower place. Not to mention other things, whoever it was that wrote the history of Maccabees expresses a wish, at the end, that he may have written well and congruously; but if not, he asks pardon. How very alien this acknowledgment from the majesty of the Holy Spirit![569]

These statements are almost the inverse image of what we have seen in our survey. Calvin holds Jerome's outlook to be the "common opinion of earlier times." Jerome himself, who introduced Hebrew Verity, knew that the truth was otherwise. Augustine affirms the deuterocanon as canonical Scripture in his *Treatise on Christian Doctrine*, and he bases his view on the near-universal acceptance of the deuterocanon as Sacred Scripture throughout antiquity. He also uses the same criteria for the protocanon of the Old and New Testaments as well. In Calvin's other work, *Institutes of the Christian Religion*, he quotes Augustine having a "lack of confidence" because "the Jews" did not hold Maccabees like they did the law (see below). In either case, this is hardly grounds for assuming that the question of the canon was then "undecided." Calvin fails to recognize that Jerome's opinion was based on his own theory of Hebrew Verity, whereas Augustine's canon was based on the *clear consensus of the early Church*, especially those churches with historical ties to the apostles. Nevertheless, Calvin *is* forced to concede that the canon of the Council of Trent did have historical (if not ecclesiastical) precedent since it followed the decrees of the Council of Carthage and the writings of Augustine. Sensing, perhaps, that his conclusion is not sufficient to overturn the decree of Trent, Calvin switches tactics from a historically based argument to one concerning the literary quality of Maccabees.

Institutes of the Christian Religion

A similar appeal is made in *Institutes of the Christian Religion,* in which Calvin writes,

> To the passage which they produce from the history of the Maccabees (1 Macc. 12:43), I will not deign to reply, lest I should seem to include that work among the canonical books. But Augustine holds it to be canonical. First, with what degree of confidence? "The Jews," says he, "do not hold the book of the Maccabees as they do the law, the prophets, and the Psalms . . . But it has been received by the Church not uselessly, if it be read or heard with soberness." Jerome, however, unhesitatingly affirms that it is of no authority in establishing doctrine; and from the ancient little book, *De Expositione Symboli,* which bears the name of Cyprian, it is plain that it was in no estimation in the ancient Church."[570]

Here again Calvin pits Augustine against Jerome (along with Rufinus, the author of the *Commentary on the Symbol of the Apostles*). His quote from Augustine is not from *On Christian Doctrine,* where Augustine lays out the biblical canon with certainty, but from a side-comment the saint made about Maccabees in the work *Contra Gaudentium* 31, 38:[571]

> And why do I here contend in vain? As if the author himself did not sufficiently show what degree of deference is to be paid him, when in the end he asks pardon for anything less properly expressed (2 Macc. 15:38). He who confesses

> that his writings stand in need of pardon, certainly proclaims that they are not oracles of the Holy Spirit.[572]

Here again he attacks 2 Maccabees because the author offers the work as his best effort. But the inspiration of a book is the product of the Holy Spirit; the literary quality is that of the author.

Elsewhere in the same work, Calvin addresses the role of the Church in promulgating a canon:

> Their dogma with regard to the power of approving Scripture I intentionally omit. For to subject the oracles of God in this way to the censure of men, and hold that they are sanctioned because they please men, is a blasphemy which deserves not to be mentioned. . . . They allege an old catalogue, which they call the canon, and say that it originated in a decision of the Church. But I again ask, in what council was that canon published? Here they must be dumb. Besides, I wish to know what they believe that canon to be. For I see that the ancients are little agreed with regard to it. If effect is to be given to what Jerome says (*Praef. in Lib. Salom.*), the Maccabees, Tobit, Ecclesiasticus, and the like must take their place in the apocryphal: but this they will not tolerate on any account.[573]

It may be true that some careless Catholic apologists have propounded a Church that *makes* a book scriptural by awarding its approval; this certainly is not the Church's own account of itself. Scripture became Scripture *as it was being written*, by virtue of the fact that God was acting as its primary author by the action of his Holy Spirit (2 Tim. 3:15). It can gain or lose nothing of this intrinsic quality by being either recognized by men, or forgotten by them. Yet recognition by men *is* important—not to the books themselves but to the men! Humanity needs an accurate account of which books have received God's inspiration and which books have not—a canon, in other words—and this is where the witness of the Church comes in. The Church is Christ's bride who bears witness to the divine inspiration of a given set of books, especially through their reading and proclamation in the sacred liturgy. So Calvin's attack here is a straw man; if anyone is "subjecting the oracles of God . . . to the censure of men" it is those who would allow the opinions of a lone scholar (Jerome is the only one named) to expunge a whole class of venerable books solely on the basis of his superior knowledge of the Hebrew language.

Calvin's Use of the Deuterocanon

Surprisingly, Calvin too used the deuterocanon early in his career in a manner quite unlike his followers of today. For example, he makes extensive use of the book of Wisdom in his treatment on the body and soul in his *Psychopannychia* (1542), only occasionally qualifying its authority. In Calvin's *Institutes* (1539), the author speaks of Wisdom and Sirach being works of Solomon, as did the early Fathers; however, he goes on quickly to discount this ascription because Sirach 15:14–17 teaches the "serious doctrinal error" of free will.[574] Most surprising of all is Calvin's use of Baruch and its subsequent corrections. Reformed theologian William Neuser writes,

> It is significant that Calvin, in the Institutes of 1536, refers to Baruch 3:12–14 and James 3:17 for the divine attributes: *sapientia, justitia, bonitas, misericordia, veritas, virtus ac vita.* Yet as early as the Institutes of 1539, this statement was no longer made. Similarly, in the section on prayer in

the first Institutes, Baruch 2:18–20 and 3:2 were quoted, in order to commend humble submission before God. In the introduction Calvin writes: *Alter vero propheta* (Bar. 2) *scribit.* Yet as early as the 1539 Institutes, Calvin corrects this: "Very true and very holy is another word which an unknown author (whoever he was) wrote, and which is attributed to the prophet Baruch." For Calvin, it remains true that the "scribe" Baruch in the book of Jeremiah is a "prophet," but he questions whether he is also the author of the book of Baruch. In the *Psychopannychia* (1542), some of the evidence is taken from this apocryphal book. To prove that God is the source of life, the "prophet" Baruch (3:14) is quoted. When the "prophet" Baruch 2:17 is used to explain Psalms 115:17: "the dead will not praise thee," it is in order to prove that "the dead" means the spiritually, not the physically dead. Yet in the second edition of 1545, the word *prophecy* (*prophetia*) is omitted: Calvin says simply *in libro Baruch.* However welcome Calvin may find this prooftext, he does not forget that Baruch is of the Apocrypha.[575]

Several citations from the books of Tobit, Wisdom, Sirach, Baruch, and the two books of Maccabees remain even in the later editions of the *Institutes*. Despite these oddities, Calvin's use of the deuterocanon is consistent with his rejection of their canonicity.

The Protestant Confessions

On February 11, 1546, the Council of Trent solemnly reaffirmed the traditional canon of the Old Testament. For their part, some Protestant communions also raised their canon to the level of dogma through various confessions of faith. These confessions are not universally accepted in Protestantism. For example, Lutherans have never raised the canon of Scripture to the level of dogma. Even today's Lutherans, who followed the more radical example set by their founder's German Bible, have not produced any binding declaration on the canon.

The following are excerpts on the subject of the canon from some of the more influential Protestant confessions.

The Belgic Confession (1561, revised 1619)

This is perhaps the oldest confession in Reformed Protestantism. Composed in the Lowlands (modern-day Belgium) by Guido de Bres, the Belgic Confession raises the canon of Scripture to the level of dogma. The fourth article produces a list of Old and New Testament books "for which there is no quarrel at all."[576] This list includes the Protestant Old Testament canon, and it goes on to explain why the authors accepted these books as canonical and authoritative:

> We receive all these books, and these only, as holy and canonical, for the regulation, foundation, and confirmation of our faith; believing, without any doubt, all things contained in them, not so much because the Church receives and approves them as such, but more especially because the Holy Ghost witnesses in our hearts that they are from God, whereof they carry the evidence in themselves. For the very blind are able to perceive that the things foretold in them are fulfilling.[577]

The sixth article continues,

> We distinguish these sacred books from the apocryphal, viz., [lists the deuterocanon, plus third and fourth Esdras and the Prayer of Manasses]. All which the Church may

> read and take instruction from, so far as they agree with the canonical books; but they are far from having such power and efficacy as that we may from their testimony confirm any point of faith or of the Christian religion; much less detract from the authority of the other sacred books.[578]

The French (Gallican) Confession (1559)

This confession was composed by the first national Protestant synod in Paris, which adopted many of the doctrines proposed by Calvin. In article three it addresses the status of the canon:

> We know these books [the protocanon] to be canonical, and the sure rule of our faith, not so much by the common accord and consent of the Church, as by the testimony and inward illumination of the Holy Spirit, which enables us to distinguish them from other ecclesiastical books upon which, however useful, we cannot found any articles of faith.[579]

Commenting on this confession, Neuser contends that Calvin's teaching about the inner testimony of the Holy Spirit was a reference to the Spirit's work of confirming the believer's faith in Scripture—not a test of canonicity. It is the French Confession, not Calvin's *Institutes,* that extended the "inner testimony" to include the discernment of which books function as the rule of faith and which ones do not.[580]

The Synod of Dort (1618–1619)

This Reformed synod also addressed the problem of the deuterocanon. Several of its members demanded that the synod insist upon the removal of the Apocrypha from the Geneva Bible.[581] Nevertheless, their motion failed to carry, and the approved version of Scripture endorsed by the synod included the so-called Apocrypha. However, the dissenting party did win a number of concessions. For example, Dort adopted the sixth article of the Belgic Confession, which strongly inveighed against the books in question. It also recommended that these books be printed in smaller type than the other books in order to make them conspicuous, and that derogatory notes be added to their margins. Dort also recommended that the appendix containing the deuterocanon be moved, from between the two testaments where Luther had placed them—the back of the Bible—creating an even greater physical distance from their former place within the corpus of the text. The Dutch Bible of 1637 carried out the dictates of the Synod of Dort, complete with a critical preface and notes in the margin explaining the points where these books were supposed to contradict the protocanon. It became *the* standard Bible for the Remonstrants as well as for the Reformed Church of Holland.[582]

Given this historical trajectory, it should not have been difficult to predict what would happen eventually. At the beginning, during his early confrontations with the pope, Luther seemed perfectly willing to use the deuterocanon to confirm doctrine. Later, when cornered in a debate, suddenly they lacked the authority to move him from his position. Recalling his days at Wittenberg under Reuchlin, he seized upon the doubts of Jerome, and the books become the Apocrypha from then on. Nevertheless, he hesitated to publish a Bible without them. Instead, he gathered them into an appendix at the end of his Old Testament—still part of the Bible somehow, but not really. The Synod of Dort took Luther's innovation one step further by segregating the ancient books even more and making other changes designed to cast doubt.

Sadly, a set of books that were once trumpeted by the Fathers as divine Scripture containing the words of the prophets has been reduced to jockeying for space in the part of the Bible usually reserved for maps and baptismal records! The next step, of course, was their total exclusion from Protestant bibles.

English Protestantism

The English Reformation differed considerably from that which took place on the European continent. All the different doctrinal and disciplinarian variations were kept under the one roof of the state-sponsored Church. King Henry VIII had rejected papal authority and set himself up as the head of the Church in England; yet Henry, quite unlike the Reformers on the continent, did not desire a radical break with the old Faith. He was, on the contrary, quite conservative in his theology and a persecutor of Lutheranism. Henry wished only to occupy himself the place in the English Church that had formerly been occupied by the pope. There were those, however, who wished to move this new, independent Church of England in a more distinctly Protestant direction. As time went on, this meant that the deuterocanon became a source of contention between those agitating for a more Protestant theology and those wishing to retain something more like the original Catholic faith of the English.

The story of how these books were accepted, then stigmatized, and eventually removed altogether is reflected in the succession of English bibles and in the official prayer books of the Anglican Church.

The Myles Coverdale Bible (1535)

Printed in Zurich in 1535, the English Myles Coverdale Bible continued the tradition of Luther and Calvin by placing the deuterocanon in a separate appendix. Coverdale followed much the same line as Zwingli's Zurich Bible: the deuterocanon could not be used to confirm doctrine because it did not enjoy the same doctrinal clarity as the protocanon, yet the books were good and profitable to read. In addition, Coverdale spoke of "dark sentences" in the deuterocanon that differed from the open and manifest truth of the protocanon (as if no one ever finds "dark sentences" in the Psalms or Ezekiel!).[583]

William Tyndale (1494–1536)

It is commonly believed that the honor of producing the first English translation of the New Testament belongs to William Tyndale (it may actually belong to Coverdale, but this has not been solidly established). Tyndale died before he could begin a translation of the Old Testament, but it is reasonably certain that his translation would have included the deuterocanon in an appendix between the Old and New Testaments.[584] An indication of his thoughts on the matter can be gained by his inclusion, in an appendix to the 1534 revision of his New Testament, of two readings from Sirach and Wisdom intended to be read during particular feast days.[588]

The Matthew Bible (1537)

This is a reworking of the Coverdale and Tynsdale translations. The deuterocanon is again placed in an appendix. The cautionary remarks are taken largely from Calvin's preface in the Olivetan Bible (1535).[586] Curiously, the 1539 and 1540 editions of the Matthew Bible changed the title of the appendix from *Apocrypha* to *Hagiographa*, a term historically reserved to denote a section of the canonical Old Testament.

The Taverner's Bible (1539)

This Bible was a reworking of the Matthew Bible, produced largely by Edmund Becke. The deuterocanon (along with 3 Maccabees) is placed in an appendix, combined with a preface explaining why these books were good to read but not to be considered inspired Scripture.

The Great Bible (1539)

Edited by Coverdale, using the Matthew Bible as a foundation, the Great Bible was commissioned by King Henry VIII through the auspices of then-archbishop of Canterbury Thomas Cranmer. It was intended to function as *the* authorized version of Scripture, and a copy of this Bible was to be supplied to every parish church. The Great Bible went through seven editions, all of which included the deuterocanon. The first edition (1539) sported Coverdale's preface. The Great Bible titled the deuterocanonical appendix *Apocrypha*, but as in some editions of the Matthew Bible the title was changed.[587] In later editions, the preface was titled "The volume of the books called the Hagiographa," or "The volume of the books called the Apocrypha, containing the books following," or "The fourth part of the Bible." This first authorized version of English Scripture, therefore, included the books of the deuterocanon—and in a manner recognizing them as, in some sense, a part of the Old Testament.

Geneva "Breeches" Bible (1560)

Famed for its rendering of Genesis 3:7 (Adam and Eve making "breeches" for themselves out of fig leaves), the 1560 Geneva Bible affixed a preface to its "Apocrypha," explaining the writings as "those books that were not to be received by common consent or to be read or expounded publicly in church. They could only prove doctrine inasmuch as they agree with the protocanon."[588]

Of how this common consent might be computed, there is no explanation. The statement, however, that these books were not "read or expounded publicly in church" can be easily established as completely false. We have already demonstrated that the deuterocanonical books were often, and from the earliest times, *prescribed* to be read in church.

These various English translations reflect the ebb and flow of Anglican thought on the deuterocanon. The authorized bibles often reflect something approaching a real acceptance of the deuterocanon as Scripture. Those translations depending upon foreign entities (e.g., the Zwingli and the Zurich bibles) usually took the opposite approach, reducing the deuterocanon to apocrypha—yet refusing, nevertheless, to eliminate such "merely human writing" from between the two covers of Scripture.

The change within the Church of England can be even more strikingly seen in the official articles of faith it promulgated.

The *Ten Articles* (1536), the Bishops' Book (1537), and the King's Book (1546)

In order to retain peace and unity in the English church, King Henry VIII imposed the *Ten Articles* as a compromise. Article one asserts that the Faith rested not only upon the "whole body and canon of the Bible" but upon the creeds as well. Article ten encourages prayers for the dead with the support of a prooftext taken from 2 Maccabees. In 1537, a committee set up by Archbishop Cranmer revised the *Ten Articles* but left this tenth essentially as it was in the original. The king disapproved of Cranmer's revision, however, and it never gained any authoritative sanction. In 1546, Henry VIII published *The Necessary Doctrine and Erudition of Any Christian Man*, which served as a statement of faith for the Church of England until Henry's death in 1547. It, too, included a statement on prayers for the souls departed, along with the same reference to 2 Maccabees. A series of new articles was drawn up during the reign of Edward VI, but was withdrawn after the accession of the Catholic Queen Mary in 1553. However, Cranmer had already issued a text of the *Forty-Two Articles* (1553). The later (and more famous) *Thirty-Nine Articles* was based largely upon this work.

The Thirty-Nine Articles (1562)

In 1562, the Church of England adopted the *Thirty-Nine Articles* to serve as a doctrinal measuring rod for Anglicanism.[589] The sixth article provides a list of the Old and New Testament books and closes with the following decree:

> In the name of holy Scripture, we do understand those canonical books of the Old and New Testaments, of whose authority was never any doubt in the Church. Of the names and number of the canonical books . . . [lists the Old Testament protocanon]. And the other books (as Hierome [Jerome] saith) the Church does read for example of life and instruction of manners; but yet does it not apply them to establish any doctrine. Such are these following [lists the deuterocanon, 3 and 4 Esdras, and the Prayer of Manasses]. All the books of the New Testament, as they are commonly received, we do receive and account them canonical."[590]

The sixth article's assertion that there never was any doubt concerning the authority of the protocanonical books reveals what F.F. Bruce calls "[a] certain naiveté." Individuals had expressed doubts about many of the protocanonical books. The sixth article's adoption of the Protestant canon not only contradicts how the deuterocanon was used throughout history, but also the thirty-fifth article, which reads,

> The second *Book of Homilies*, the several titles whereof we have joined under this article, does contain a godly and wholesome doctrine and necessary for these times, as doth the former *Book of Homilies* which were set forth in the time of Edward the Sixth: and therefore we judge them to be read in churches by the ministers diligently and distinctly, that they may be understanded [sic] of the people.[591]

The *Book of Homilies* was a set of lessons that were to be read in church during holy days. However, it used the deuterocanon in a manner that went beyond the restriction set forth in the sixth article, sometimes explicitly quoting it as divine Scripture. As the Anglican scholar William Daubney observes,

> In the index to Dr. Corrie's edition [of the *Homilies*] no less than seventy-five apocryphal texts are referred to as quoted in the *Homilies*. High honor is certainly paid to the Apocrypha in those Reformation sermons, almost beyond what at first sight the terms of the sixth article would seem to warrant. . . . In the homily against swearing, for example, a quotation from Ecclesiasticus is introduced by the words "Almighty God by the wise man says." In the homily against excess of apparel, Judith and the apocrypha portions of Esther are cited as "Scripture." Likewise, in the homily against idolatry,

> the canonical and uncanonical books are indiscriminately classed together under the common title of "the scriptures"; the doctrine of the "foolishness of images," it is said, is "expressed at large in the scriptures; viz., the Psalms, the book of Wisdom, the prophet Isaiah, Ezekiel and Baruch." The words found which preface a verse from Tobit, "The Holy Ghost does also teach in . . . Scripture, saying"; and in the next sentence a text is given from Ecclesiasticus, which is introduced as "confirming the same." But perhaps the strongest statement of all is that in the tenth homily, wherein we are exhorted to learn from the book of Wisdom, as being the "infallible and undeceivable word of God." . . . [A]nd in the last homily of all, that against rebellion, we still find ourselves referred to Wisdom as holy Scripture, and are still exhorted to hear Baruch as a prophet.[592]

The sixth article states that the deuterocanon cannot be used to establish doctrine, yet the thirty-fifth describes the *Book of Homilies* as containing "godly and wholesome doctrine," even though it uses the deuterocanon to establish these doctrines. Aware of this contradiction, Daubney suggests that the two articles can be reconciled if one understands the sixth article's reference to "any doctrine" to mean "any doctrine not already confirmed by the canonical scriptures." Daubney continues,

> Unless we take the words of the article in this sense, it seems impossible to reconcile it with the doctrinal use of the Apocrypha in the *Homilies* by the same authorities as those who put forth the articles.[593]

Daubney's cure is worse than the disease. If the deuterocanon is Scripture, as the *Book of Homilies* uses them, then according to Paul it ought to be profitable for teaching, correction, and training in righteousness (2 Tim. 2:15).[594] The apostle makes no distinction between Scripture that is profitable toward these ends and Scripture that is not. Moreover, who or what determines if a given doctrine is taught in the canonical books in order for the deuterocanon to confirm them?[595] Furthermore, if a doctrine is clearly taught in the canonical scriptures, why bother referring to the deuterocanon at all? In effect, Daubney's solution renders those books, which the *Book of Homilies* calls holy Scripture and the word of God, essentially worthless.

This contradiction within the *Thirty-Nine Articles* illustrates the theological tension that was present in much early Protestant theology with regard to the canon. Doctrinally, the deuterocanon could not be admitted to the same authority as the protocanon, yet a vast majority of the early Protestants, including the Reformers, would not dare remove these books because the simplest peasants knew they were part of the Bible. Therefore, early Protestantism propagated the deuterocanon while at the same time denying its authority.

The Westminster Confession (1646)

In 1643, the Long Parliament, which convened under Puritan influence, resolved that the liturgy and doctrines of the Church of England needed to be clarified. In 1644, it was proposed that a single confession, catechism, and directory of public worship would be imposed throughout the king's dominion. All work on editing and revising the *Thirty-Nine Articles* ceased, and in 1648, Parliament granted authority to work on new and independent confession that continued until the restoration of 1660. The *Westminster Confession* became that single confession of faith and enjoyed the unique distinction of being *the* confessional standard for the whole United Kingdom. Regarding the deuterocanon, the *Westminster Confession* states,

> The books commonly called apocrypha, not being of divine inspiration, are no part of the canon of Scripture; and therefore are of no authority in the Church of God, nor to be any otherwise approved, or made use of, than other human writing.[596]

The *Westminster Confession* introduces here a very subtle, but radical, departure from the past—a break from previous Protestant usage as much as Catholic. By stating plainly that the deuterocanon is *not* inspired and that it has no more authority than any "other human writing," the confession effectively condemns its inclusion between the covers of a Bible; it is no longer even an appendage to Scripture, as the Reformers would have it, but a mere collection of human opinion. Luther, Calvin, and Zwingli did not venture this far. Once considered the "fourth part of the Bible," consisting of holy and wholesome writings prescribed by the early Church to be read publicly, its writings were now no more authoritative than Bunyan's *Pilgrim's Progress*—if that. The loss of the deuterocanon from Protestant bibles can be traced, then, not to the Reformers themselves, but to that radical body of self-proclaimed Puritans who seized control of the English government under Oliver Cromwell.

The Puritan "Persecution"

Even after the *Thirty-Nine Articles*, after years of steady Protestantization under Cranmer and his successors, there were still some within the Church of England who believed the break with the old Faith had not gone far enough. For them, the English Church needed to be "purified"—by which they meant completely remade on a radically Calvinistic basis—removing all lingering "popish" teaching and practices. It was these Puritans who first began to pressure Church leadership to remove the deuterocanon from all English bibles, beginning what Frederic Kenyon once called "the Puritan persecution of the Apocrypha."[597]

Modern authors sometime assert that the move to exclude the deuterocanon from Protestant bibles was readily accepted without much discussion; this claim is far from true. The first attempts to do so met with stiff opposition, most notably from the Anglican Archbishop John Whitgift. For Whitgift, the thought of Protestant bibles being printed without the deuterocanon seemed unthinkable, almost revolutionary. Here is how the archbishop responded to a challenge by Puritan John Pentry to remove them:

> The Scripture here called apocrypha, abusively and improperly, are holy writings, void of error, part of the Bible, and so accounted of in the purest time of the Church and by the best writers; ever read in the Church of Christ, and shall never be forbidden by me, or by my consent.[598]
>
> Whoever separated the Apocrypha from the rest of the Bible from the beginning of Christianity to that day? . . . And shall we suffer this singularity in the Church of England, to the advantage of the adversary, offense of the godly, and contrary to all the world besides? . . . And therefore that such giddy heads as thought to deface them were to be bridled, and that it was a foul shame, and not to be suffered, that such speeches should be uttered against those books, as by some had been: enough to cause ignorant people to discredit the whole Bible.[599]

Pressure continued, and the Puritans eventually won a victory, with the exclusion of the deuterocanon from the 1599 edition of the Geneva Bible. The books were gone but, curiously enough, not their pages, which were left blank and unnumbered between the Old and New Testaments.

Why did the Puritans feel the need to exclude these books from the Scripture? After all, Luther's new format prevented them from being used to contradict Protestant theology. The Protestant scholar Goodspeed believes that their objection to the deuteros had less to do with scholarship and more to do with the grim or sensational character (as they perceived it) of certain passages within those books.[600] For whatever reason, the deuterocanon did not suit their tastes.

Eventually, the Puritans and other dissenters within the Church of England slowly began to emerge as a political and religious force. So much so that King James I called the *Hampton Court Conferences* (1604) to attempt, somewhat disingenuously, to appease these dissenting parties. Little was won for the dissenters, except to secure the king's permission to produce a new translation of Scripture. This version would be completed in 1611 and known as the King James Bible or the Authorized Version.[601]

The King James Version (1611)

Most people do not know that the original 1611 edition of the King James Version, and a few subsequent editions, included the deuterocanon in an appendix marked *Apocrypha*. As with previous versions, this appendix was sandwiched between the Old and New Testaments (though there was no preface). In later editions this appendix was removed, but the cross-references that linked the text to the deuterocanon remained for some time. Scholar Bruce M. Metzger believes that these cross-references were removed because the margins were too crowded.[602] However, the Protestant theologian Daubney explains that there was much more going on than cleaning up crowded margins:

> Plainly, the references to the Apocrypha told an inconvenient tale of the use which the Church intended should be made of it; so, either from dissenting influence without, or from prejudice within the Church, these references disappeared from the margin.[603]

All cross-references were removed, including the reference to the Maccabean martyrs in Hebrews 11:35–37 who were inexplicably expunged or, as Daubney puts it, "illicitly suppressed."[604] Given the exalted position this translation came to occupy within the English-speaking world, this action certainly did contribute to the ignorance of subsequent Protestant generations regarding the deuterocanon and the place it once held even in non-Catholic bibles.

The Almighty and the Almighty Dollar

Puritan pressure was not the only reason today's Protestant bibles today usually omit the deuterocanon; if it were, the books would surely have returned to their accustomed place once Puritan influence subsided. No, strange as it may seem, the widespread demise of the deuterocanon can be attributed to another influence as well—economics. Put simply, at a time when printing was laborious and expensive, smaller bibles were significantly cheaper to make. The prospect of higher profit margins undoubtedly wooed some printers into producing novelty bibles without the deuterocanon.[605]

At first, these smaller bibles were illicit. In 1615, George Abbott, the archbishop of Canterbury, went so far as to employ the power of the law to censure any publisher who did not produce the Bible in its entirety with the deuterocanon as prescribed by the *Thirty-Nine Articles*.[606] Nevertheless, economic incentives proved stronger than the threats of the archbishop, and editions without the deuterocanon were sporadically produced.[607] In a sense, these versions were unauthorized Authorized Versions.

Yet despite the growing number of Protestant bibles that omitted them, bibles that included the "Apocrypha" still remained the norm during this time. The books were too well known and too well integrated into European thought to be easily discarded. As Goodspeed notes,

> [W]hatever may be our personal opinions of the Apocrypha, it is a historical fact that they formed an integral part of the King James Version, and any Bible claiming to represent that version should either include the Apocrypha, or state that it is omitting them. Otherwise a false impression is created.[608]

Puritan influence continued long after the restoration under Charles II, and from then on the tide began to run decidedly against the deuterocanon.[609] Anti-apocryphal tracts and pamphlets began to circulate, and in 1740 some actually proposed that a law should be passed to force printers to remove the Apocrypha appendix from its place between the two Testaments.[610] This proposition and others like it had little effect other than to weaken the resolve of those Protestants who wished to include them. It was not until religious motivations and economic forces united in the early 1800s that Protestant bibles uniformly excluded the deuterocanon. Oddly enough, one of the chief factors in the demise of Protestant bibles containing the deuterocanon came through an agency that was originally designed to propagate the Bible everywhere.

11

The Deuterocanon in Exile

In the early 1700s, philanthropic groups convened to produce inexpensive copies of the Bible for the widest possible distribution throughout the world, especially among the poor. These societies enabled the ordinary man to own his own copy of Scripture at home or even to carry in it his pocket. The first of these societies was the Von Canstein Bible Society, founded in Germany in 1710. It produced and distributed Protestant bibles that contained the Apocrypha, following Luther's example in his original German translation. The society also produced stand-alone pocket editions of individual books of the Bible—a series that included an edition of the book of Sirach.[611]

In London in 1804, a similar group called the British and Foreign Bible Society (BFBS) was formed.[612] Because of its interdenominational, non-sectarian mission, the BFBS received broad-based support and enjoyed remarkable growth. Within a decade, the parent organization founded dozens of auxiliary Bible societies in England and in other European countries and provided financial and technical aid to other societies working along the same lines.

However, it was not long before the BFBS found itself embroiled in controversy. In 1813, several foreign societies began preparing to print bibles with the Apocrypha, as had been the custom with them since the time of Luther. The inclusion of the deuterocanon rubbed against the sensibilities of some BFBS members, who advocated that the parent organization cut funding to these foreign societies until they agreed to print their bibles in the same format as the British Society—that is, without the deuterocanon. Cutting the funds would have destroyed these fledging societies, but ultimately the board of the BFBS ruled that the printing of bibles in different formats would be permitted, because its by-laws had never explicitly prohibited the inclusion of the so-called Apocrypha. This pragmatic act of tolerance did not sit well with many Reformed Protestants, especially the Presbyterian preacher Robert Haldane, who began a speaking crusade against the BFBS's decision.[613] As the German historian Wilhelm Gundert recounts,

> [Haldane] taught a doctrine of verbal inspiration, applied exclusively to the canonical books of the Bible, and dismissed the Apocrypha as a human word. Like others convinced that God has given them a mission, he found it hard to understand that other Christians could have a different view. So he came back in 1819 from an evangelistic campaign in France to press the committee to reverse its resolution of 1813.[614]

The multiplicity of beliefs within Protestantism as to what constituted *the* Bible gradually became a serious obstacle for the BFBS. The foreign auxiliaries feared that they would be forced to print bibles in a format likely to alienate the very people they were trying to help. The Scottish societies, which had sympathetic members sitting on the BFBS's board, sided with Haldane and pressed for a tougher resolution that was eventually passed in 1822. This new resolution fully funded only Protestant societies that produced bibles lacking the deuterocanon. Foreign societies that wanted to continue producing bibles with the so-called Apocrypha would have to pay for the printing *of that section* with their own funds. Most were glad to do so.

Period of Tolerance

Compromises sometimes alienate the parties that they try to appease. In this case, on one side there were members who felt that the mission of the society was to promote the *widest possible distribution* of the Bible. If wider distribution meant contributing to the printing of bibles with the deuterocanon, then so be it.[615] It was also argued that no Protestant community had the right to dictate what constitutes the Bible to other Protestant communities.[616] On the other side, there were those who believed that the compromise had been a mistake to begin with and that *all* funding ought to be cut so as to discourage the printing of bibles containing the Apocrypha.

Finally, the uneasy peace was breached when the boards of the Edinburgh Bible Society and the Glasgow Bible Society resolved to withhold their support to the BFBS until all funding for such printing was cut.

The Edinburgh Crusade

The Scottish societies saw the mission of the British and Foreign Bible Society not merely to supply the Bible to those without it but as an evangelistic effort to spread the Protestant faith throughout the world. It sought to achieve the widest possible dissemination of bibles but only in a format that was conducive to their understanding of Protestantism. Their rationale may be examined in the committee statements of the Edinburgh Bible Society.

The statements record no effort on the part of the Scottish society to provide the *bona fides* of the shorter canon or to explain by what authority it sought to dictate to other Protestant communities what books are and are not canonical. The shorter canon was merely assumed to be true and self-evident. In the estimation of the committee, the mere presence of the so-called Apocrypha between the covers of a Bible either unduly elevated those books or degraded the character of the Bible as a whole.[617] The committee continued by listing various doctrines which the deuterocanon was held by them to confirm (e.g., intercession of saints, purgatory, that almsgiving atones for sins, that good works justify). These things are said to "strike at the root of some of the fundamental truths which God has revealed for the instruction and salvation of man."[618] Notice that the common thread uniting this grab bag of doctrines is that all of them had been warred upon by the Puritans and Scotch Calvinists—whereas mainstream Anglicanism allowed room for these teachings.[619]

The Edinburgh committee continued by candidly admitting something that many Protestant apologists today hotly deny: that the deuterocanonical writings actually present themselves as Scripture.

> Great indeed is the demerit of that book which contradicts the revealed will of God; but its demerit is unspeakably aggravated when . . . *it adds the blasphemous assumption of being itself a revelation of God's will.* Now such is the Apocrypha. *It pretends to a divine original.* Some, it is true, have denied this, and published their denial. *No one,* however, *who has read the Apocrypha can fail to perceive that the denial is founded in ignorance and inattention.* So plainly does it *affect to have the sanction of heaven*, that it actually apes *the phraseology of inspiration.* It contains messages to mankind which are *sometimes represented as proceeding immediately from God himself*, and sometimes

> as conveyed through the medium of angels. And frequently its declarations are introduced with that most awful and authoritative of all sanctions, "Thus says the Lord."[620]

If the deuterocanon *sounds like* Scripture and teaches Catholic doctrine, then it follows that those who read the Bible in its traditional format may become Catholic![621]

> Again, if they are Protestants among whom the Apocrypha is to be dispersed, it does not on that account lose its qualities of falsehood, absurdity, and blasphemy . . . we account it no sin to be instrumental in deliberately circulating that, which *endangers the souls of men and insults the honor of God*: And as sent to those who have been emancipated from the darkness and superstition of Popery [Catholic converts to Protestantism], it implies an endeavor on our part, not to perfect and perpetuate their emancipation, *but to continue them in the errors that still envelope their minds, or to send them back to the thralldom from which they had happily escaped.*[622]

The freedom to read Scripture in the format of the earliest Christian codices was deemed too dangerous for Protestants and potential Catholic converts. It was feared that those who did read these bibles in the traditional format would abandon Protestantism or that unsettled Catholics would decide against it. They believed the earlier dissemination of the Toulouse edition of Scripture confirmed this fear:

> With respect to the Protestants also, the circulation of the Apocrypha is inexpedient. Such of them in France . . . even though they were better informed on the subject . . . [They may] peruse it [the deuterocanon]

> with some portion of those reverent impressions with which they peruse the inspired books; and, of course, *not only to imbibe the erroneous notions which it inculcates, but to lose that exclusive submission to the word of God which is so dutiful and so becoming.* An example of this is to be found in Mr. Chabrand's correspondence relative to the Toulouse edition of the Bible. He objected to the addition of the Apocrypha because "there was danger of the Protestant confounding the apocryphal with the canonical books; *and of their being thus led to adopt some of the errors of Popery (particularly that of purgatory). . . ." This is the natural, and will be the frequent, effect of circulating the Bible containing the Apocrypha.*[623]

The committee statement also added,

> [T]hat practice judicious or wise, which, instead of confirming or improving the principles of those who have, in a Catholic country, embraced or been educated in the Protestant faith, *threatens to darken what had been made light, to corrupt what had been reformed*, and in any measure to *pave the way for backsliding or apostasy*? . . . But the evil of circulating the Apocrypha as a part of the Scripture volume is not limited to those Protestants who get the book to peruse; it is also injurious to the minds of Protestants, who *merely see or know that such a union and such a circulation are permitted.*[624]

According to the Edinburgh Bible Society, the only bibles safe to disseminate are those that have been sanitized from the presence of these "popish" books.[625] Clearly, it was too dangerous to leave it up to the individual reader to decide the merits or demerits of the deuterocanon. Not only does this statement arrogate an enormous amount of authority, it also calls into question the *Westminster Confession's* teaching on the perspicuity of Scripture:

> All things in Scripture are not alike plain in themselves, nor alike clear unto all: yet those things which are necessary to be known, believed, and observed for salvation are so clearly propounded, and opened in some place of Scripture or other, that not only the learned, but the unlearned, in a due use of the ordinary means, may attain unto a sufficient understanding of them.[626]

Would not the actions of the Edinburgh Bible Society circumvent the believer's innate ability to recognize the "falsehoods of popish errors" in these books? Does not the inner witness of the Holy Spirit enable the believer to distinguish truth from error? The committee statement argued that even the learned had difficulty separating the false from the true in the so-called Apocrypha; for the unlearned the task would be impossible.[627]

At least the members of the Edinburgh committee may be credited with frankness: they disliked the *doctrine* they found taught in the deuterocanon and wished, therefore, to have it censored. Plain and simple, without dragging in poor Jerome. This line of reasoning becomes especially clear in the following passage:

> [B]y sending them the Apocrypha, we are, in fact, abetting the Church of Rome in an impious attempt to establish the inspiration of that spurious document and seconding her efforts to compel those who acknowledge her spiritual dominion, to listen to its lying wonders as to the voice of the Almighty.[628]

Anti-Catholics often charge Trent with being reactionary and claim that the council added books to the Bible in an effort to subvert Protestantism. Is it not clear, however, that in this matter of the Edinburgh Bible Society, the very reverse is true? Here we find a Protestant Bible society waging a crusade rather than allowing an unedited Bible to be examined by the common folk. In a clear, candid, and passionate manner, the Edinburgh committee's notes advocate the removal of the deuterocanon *as a countermeasure against Rome*—and specifically against the Council of Trent:

> [I]t is *countenancing and supporting the Church of Rome in her system of imposition.* She, by her decree, has made that canonical which is uncanonical, and compelled the people to receive as the word of God what is only the word of man. And the London Committee, in name of the *British and Foreign Bible Society*, and of all who have contributed to its funds, *instead of resisting that act of spiritual despotism and delusion by which she props up her power, helps and encourages her to persist in it.* She can, perhaps, check the circulation and the perusal of the Bible, but she can tell the people at the same time, *and they will have too good reason to believe her*, that the Protestants themselves believe in the divinity of those passages which she brings from the Apocrypha to establish the doctrine of purgatory and of the saving merit of good works. And she will plead from what has been done, as far as Protestant authority can be of any weight, that her decrees can make any sayings or doctrines which she chooses to fix upon, tantamount to a revelation from heaven. And thirdly, when Protestants give the Apocrypha intermixed with the scriptures, they excite the contempt of the papists, instead of securing either

their respect or their gratitude. *The papists must conclude either that the Protestants are altogether indifferent to the canon of Scripture,* which would be discreditable both to their piety and their judgment, or that, believing the Apocrypha to be a mere human composition, *they yet are guilty of so much duplicity as to give under the form and appearance of having a divine original.*[629]

It is against the will of God that there be circulated for the word of God "the doctrines and commandments of men." The papists do circulate the Apocrypha as the word of God, and *we are their agents*, in fact, *if we furnish them with the means of doing so.* By contributing, therefore, "we become partakers of other men's sins."[630]

In the face of all such sophistry we recur again to the obligation under which we lie to do nothing against the truth, and everything for the truth, and to the unassailable position that the Apocrypha . . . impiously pretends to be a portion of God's holy word, and *is employed by the Church of Rome* to support the delusions of him "who opposes and exalts himself above all that is called God."[631]

[A]nd it is well that they have been so frankly avowed, because it makes us aware of the danger, and enables us to lift the voice of warning ere it be too late, for rescuing the Bible Society from that Apocryphal contamination which has so long and so inveterately cleaved to it, and which threatens to render it, while its present management continues, *not an instrument of Protestant benevolence, but an engine of popish error and superstition.*[632]

Despite repeated attempts by others to inform the Edinburgh Bible Society of how radical and unhistorical their demands were, it would not budge.[633]

Finishing the Problem

It would not budge because it believed its actions fulfilled the Protestant Reformers' wishes, i.e., the complete removal of the deuterocanon from the Bible:

> But we could call the attention of our readers, in a particular manner, to the fine opportunity afforded by the British and Foreign Bible Society, constituted as it is, for introducing a more exclusive, and decided, and general attachment to the pure canon of Scripture. It was a great step when the Apocrypha books were taken out of the Bible, and placed by themselves, with the apocryphal title. But it was only a step; and it still remained a desideratum to get quit of them, altogether, and to keep the pure word of God detached in every respect from their contaminating fellowship. This we believe to have been an object of anxious desire with many good and enlightened men at the time of the Reformation, though circumstances discouraged them from attempting to accomplish it.[634]

The first "great step" in eliminating the deuterocanon entirely was to remove the deuterocanon from its traditional place within Scripture and segregate it in an appendix "with the title Apocrypha." However, it was the "anxious desire with many good and enlightened men at the time of the Reformation" to "quit of them altogether." Edinburgh's insistence that the deuterocanon be eliminated from Protestant bibles was just carrying out their long-held desire.

In response to the continued Scottish threats to separate from the BFBS permanently and to continue a campaign against them, the British and Foreign Bible Society capitulated. In 1827, it adopted a resolution that no aid, financial or otherwise, would be given to any Bible society that produced bibles containing the Apocrypha. This would seem to have been the end of the matter; but the aftermath is worth recording as well.

Happily Ever After?

Evangelical accounts of this controversy are often written in a manner suggesting that all Protestants gratefully embraced the decision with relief.

F.F. Bruce, for instance, tells the story this way:

> When the British and Foreign Bible Society began to distribute exclusively editions lacking the Apocrypha, the Bible-buying public seemed quite content with such editions. That being so, other Bible publishers saw no reason why they should continue producing bibles with the Apocrypha.[635]

Similarly, Bruce M. Metzger summarizes the end of the Apocrypha controversy with:

> Several other Bible Societies, including the American Bible Society, which was founded at New York in 1816, followed the decision and practice of the London Society. As a consequence it was not long before commercial publishers, for obvious reasons of economy, likewise ceased including the apocryphal books in their editions of the Bible, and it soon became difficult to obtain ordinary editions of the Bible with the Apocrypha.[636]

In reality, the decision of the British and Foreign Bible Society was quite divisive and widened the existing rift between British and Continental Protestantism. Many European Bible societies (including those of Germany, Switzerland, France, the Netherlands, Sweden, and Denmark) broke with the BFBS over this Puritan-led coup and refused to distribute Protestant bibles without the deuterocanon. They were grateful for London's help in the past but were willing to go it alone if it meant keeping these books in the Bible. Howorth notes,

> The Lutheran authorities decided that they could have no part in such a movement and refused to countenance the issuing of mutilated bibles or to depart from Luther's example in such a critical matter, and they have since remained staunch to that decision.[637]

Nor did the decision succeed in mollifying the Scots for long; despite the BFBS's acquiescence to their demands, the Scottish societies eventually broke off and went their own ways.

The story of the suppression and removal of the deuterocanon by the British and Foreign Bible Society is rarely told, yet there are many interesting lessons to be learned from it: not least, that a deutero-free Bible was still seen to be, as late as 1827, a departure from traditional Christian practice—even as practiced by Protestants.

The Protestant Crusade in America

In the United States, though, the American Bible Society (founded in 1816) was more than willing to adopt the BFBS's decision. American Protestantism is deeply rooted in English Puritanism; therefore, bibles with the Apocrypha were not part of the Protestant American heritage. Likely, Lutherans and Catholics were the only sizable groups of Christians in America who used bibles containing the deuterocanon.

In the early nineteenth century, with American Protestantism in the midst of the Second Great Awakening, religious fervor was running high when the BFBS ruled against the Apocrypha. Unfortunately, this religious revival also carried with it a strong undertow of anti-Catholic sentiment. The combination of Protestant anti-Catholic sentiments and the propagation of bibles minus the deuterocanon led to some sad misunderstandings.

When Protestants offered copies of their bibles to Catholics, the Catholics predictably refused them; not only because the translation itself (invariably the King James) contained anti-Catholic bias, but also because of the absence of the deuterocanon. This refusal was misinterpreted by Protestant missionaries as hostility to the Bible itself. As the American historian Ray Allen Billington records,

> A clash developed as soon as the American Bible Society attempted to spread the Protestant version of the Bible among Catholics. The indignation of the Catholic hierarchy and papal letters denouncing the society all were interpreted by Protestants as an attack on the Bible rather than on one version of the Bible. Thus the illusion was created that papists were hostile to the scriptures and that their Church rested not on divine but on man-made authority. These beliefs bore particular weight with a populace under the fundamentalistic influence of the New Measure. This supposed Catholic attack on the Bible interested the church in the No-Popery crusade and led them to take their first exploratory steps against Catholicism.[638]

The expulsion of the deuterocanon from Protestant bibles came at great cost. For the British and Foreign Bible Society it meant the loss of many auxiliaries, including the Scottish societies; the damage took years to repair. The establishment of the American Bible Society and the propagation of bibles without the deuterocanon fanned the flames of persecution for Catholics in America by providing fodder for the fledgling No-Popery movement and later the Nativist movements in the United States.[639] American anti-Catholicism can be traced in part to the historical ripple effects of the deuterocanon debate.

Books In Exile

On Bible Sunday, December 6, 1915, Episcopal minister Rev. Milo H. Gates rose to his pulpit in Manhattan to preach a sermon about the exodus of the "Apocrypha" from Protestant bibles and Protestantism in general. Gates urged,

> The time has come when all real Protestants should demand from the Bible societies the whole Bible. The day was, and it was not long ago, when every true Protestant had as the motto on his banner, "The Bible and the Bible only; our rule of faith and practice." Therefore the true Protestants should now make a fight for the restoration of the Bible. One of the greatest libraries of sacred writings is contained in what is known as the Apocrypha . . . [I]t is the fault of Bible societies that this wonderful part of holy writ has been stolen from the Bible. If these Bible societies were truly Protestant they would not commit such a grievous theft. They would not keep the Bible from the common people. What we need today is either a reform or the retirement of the so-called Bible societies. If they are permitted to go on, I fear that they will continue more seriously to hinder the use of the holy scriptures. What we need is a new Luther to arouse us and to lead a

> new Reformation for the freedom of the Bible. He will find its most powerful enemy not at Rome, but in the "Bible Houses" of the United States and England.[640]

Even at the beginning of the twentieth century such voices persisted, but their cry was in vain. Much of Protestantism preferred to forget the Apocrypha controversy. Anti-Catholicism in both America and England sapped the will of non-Catholics who wished to preserve the Bible as the Reformers had left it. The Apocrypha had disappeared from the Protestant landscape. The deuterocanon's expulsion was so thorough that it was even removed from a Protestant reproduction of the *Codex Vaticanus*.[641] The few Protestant bibles that still included the deuterocanon relied on old and antiquated translations. For example, a considerable part of the deuterocanon in the 1895 English Revised Version was translated from the Latin Coverdale Bible of 1535. Likewise, the two-volume work *The Apocrypha and Pseudepigrapha* (1913), edited by R.H. Charles, provided more than half of the books with new translations. A minority of the books were copied from the English Revised Version.[642]

The discovery of the Dead Sea Scrolls in the 1940s renewed interest in intertestamental studies, and it spawned several new Protestant translations with the deuterocanon. Despite this renewed interest, however, the anti-Catholic winds of the last century and a half have eradicated the place these books formerly held in Protestant devotion. Today, practically no one (Protestant or Catholic) is aware that an Apocrypha controversy existed in Protestantism, much less that these books were once part of the Protestant Bible.

12

Answering the Ultimate Question

We have come to the point in our survey where can give an answer to the question: did the Council of Trent add seven books to the Old Testament in reaction to Protestantism, or did Protestantism remove these books? Since the history of the deuterocanon is complex, it's easy to become lost in all the nuances and details. Therefore, let's strip them away and look at the core issues.

Did Trent add seven books to the Old Testament canon? We must define first what is meant by *canon*. As we've seen, the word is a theological term that wasn't applied to the contents of Scripture until the fourth Christian century. Obviously, Scripture existed before anyone referred to it as "canon." *Scripture* is a more fundamental term; but is there an even more fundamental way to describe what Scripture is?

St. Paul says, "All Scripture is inspired by God" (2 Tim. 3:16). Here we reach the most fundamental term: *inspiration* is what sets Scripture apart from any other religious writing. It alone has God as its primary author. It alone is, as Paul says, "God-breathed." If a book is inspired, it is Scripture, and if it is inspired Scripture it is canonical. We can also add that inspiration also makes a writing, as Paul says, "profitable for teaching, for reproof, for correction, and for training in righteousness." It can be used to teach revealed truth (teaching), it can be used as a proof (reproof and correction), and it can be used to train one in virtue ("training in righteousness").

Therefore, if a writing is *inspired* it is capable of confirming doctrine, and it is Scripture. If a writing isn't inspired, it is not capable of confirming doctrine, and it is not Scripture. Inspiration is the bottom line, not whether or not someone calls it "canonical."

Given these two indicators, we can now ask whether the Catholic Council of Trent declared the deuterocanon to be inspired when it had not been previously thought to be? Our survey of the deuterocanon's history shows that this is not the case. Early Christians believed that the deuterocanonical books were inspired. These books were explicitly quoted as inspired Scripture and used to confirm doctrine, even by some Fathers who didn't call them "canonical."[643] True, there were detractors. Outside of Julius Africanus's dispute with Origen, though, it wasn't until the end of the fourth century and the beginning of the fifth century, with St. Jerome, that anyone denied the inspiration of the deuterocanon and placed it among the Apocrypha. After Jerome, the most ardent denials of the deuterocanon came from people who were the most ardent followers of Jerome.

Furthermore, the deliberations of the Council of Trent show that its canon was the product of previous councils. The council fathers who wished to add other material in addition to what was affirmed and defined by Hippo, Carthage, Florence, and numerous papal decrees never won favor. The decrees of Trent were little more than a rubber-stamp reaffirmation of previous councils. If there was an innovation at Trent, it was the addition of an *anathema*, which supplied a much needed corrective to the abuses and exaggerations of a few Jeromist Catholic theologians.

If Trent didn't *add* books to Scripture (by calling uninspired books inspired), did Protestantism remove books from Scripture by denying the inspiration of the deuterocanon? The answer must be in the affirmative.

Although Martin Luther had several influences that would have pushed him to the "Jeromist" position, he didn't follow them, at least not at first. Luther was Augustinian on this point. Luther's *protestatio* declarations, his usage, and quotations show that he initially believed that the deuterocanon could be admitted into debate to prove doctrine. The Second Leipzig Disputation (1519) signaled a change. When Johann Eck entered 2 Maccabees into the debate, Luther rejected its canonicity, its admissibility in debate, and its ability to confirm doctrine, something that he had not done in previous controversies.

Why Luther made this about-face on the deuterocanon can only be guessed at. Bruce Metzger suggests that it may have been doctrinally motivated:

> It appears that Luther was first led to disparage the books of the Apocrypha when his opponents appealed to passages in them as proof for the doctrines of purgatory and the efficacy of prayers and Masses for the dead (2 Macc. 12:43–45). Likewise the emphasis that certain apocryphal books lay upon merit acquired through good works (Neh. 8:33; 13:46, Tob. 12:9, Sir. 3:30; etc.) was naturally distasteful to him.[644]

This may explain why, at Leipzig, Luther disputed Johann Eck's interpretation of several classic prooftexts for purgatory but he did not dispute Eck's interpretation of 2 Maccabees. Instead, Luther disputed its admissibility, canonicity, and authority. Second Maccabees 12:43–46 was a particularly difficult passage for Luther since it not only speaks to a fuller Catholic understanding of purgatory than what he accepted at the time, but it has applications to the doctrine of indulgences as well.[645]

A second motivation may have been Luther's development of the "canon-within-a-canon" idea, according to which a book is only canonical to the extent that one hears "Christ preached." Luther's comments during the debate also support this position.[646] Furthermore, the *Resolutions to the Leipzig Disputation*, published in August of the same year, includes Luther's earliest disparaging remarks about the epistle of James, which was a temporary victim of Luther's "canon-within-a-canon" approach.

Whatever the motive, the deuterocanon's inspiration was denied along with its ability to confirm doctrine. From that moment on, Protestants could not allow the deuterocanon to enjoy its former status. However, there is a problem. Whether Luther rejected the deuterocanon because of doctrine or because of his "canon-within-a-canon" approach, neither motive could legitimately justify that rejection. Both would be seen as self-serving. Almost by default, the burden of justifying the Protestant Old Testament canon was almost entirely historical, and the one person who perfectly reflected the Protestant position was St. Jerome. Luther appealed to Jerome at Leipzig. Later, Joseias Osiander did as well. The Anglican *Thirty-Nine Articles* explicitly cites Jerome, as did John Calvin. In fact, according to Wilhelm Neuser,

> The Reformed theologians and confessions of the sixteenth and seventeenth centuries basically follow the Church Father Jerome, who "is the only person in the early Church who took up a position against the [Old Testament] Apocrypha."[647]

Protestants appealed to Jerome's *Helmeted Prologue* because, as Neuser observes, "It serves on the one hand as evidence for the exclusion of the apocryphal writings from the canon, and their inappropriateness as scriptural proof, and on the other hand as encouragement for their profitable use."[648] For Protestants, Jerome became an exemplar of the common view of the deuterocanon in antiquity.[649] The evidence presented in this book debunks this idea.

Jerome fails not only as a witness to the common view of antiquity, but also in his reasons for rejecting the deuterocanon in the first place. Put simply, Jerome reasoned that since there was only one Hebrew text (and several Greek translations that appeared to him to be a translation of that same text), then the Hebrew text must be identical to the inspired original. Hence, whatever is not in the Hebrew text is apocrypha, and whatever is included is inspired Scripture. But as the Dead Sea Scroll expert Emmanuel Tov points out,

> Since the discovery of the Qumran Scrolls, it has become clear that a unified text tradition before the turn of the eras never existed. In the last centuries B.C.E., a large number of copies of the biblical text, attesting to a large number of different texts, circulated in ancient Israel. . . . [B]iblical research postulates that the text preserved in the various manuscripts and editions of the MT [Jerome's Hebrew text] does not reflect the "original text" of the biblical books.[650]

But why didn't Jerome know about these other texts? Tov answers,

> The notion of textual uniformity was later perpetuated in the Judaism of the first century C.E. onward, together with the understanding that only the MT represents the Hebrew Bible.[651]

Without the benefit of the discoveries at Qumran, Jerome bought into this rabbinic belief. All the available data seemed to support it. There weren't any competing Hebrew texts; even Origen's *Hexapla* only gave one Hebrew text. Only one Hebrew text in existence was the one that the rabbis prized as *the* normative copy of the original. The discoveries at Qumran proved Jerome's idea of Hebrew Verity to be wrong.

The Church, interestingly enough, knew that Jerome was wrong. Its proof was that it had always accepted the deuterocanonical books as inspired texts, being read, as Origen said, "in every church of Christ." Based on this knowledge, the Councils of Hippo and Carthage, as well as Pope St. Innocent I, reaffirmed the historic Christian canon. Although the Church knew Jerome was wrong, they couldn't demonstrate it. In fact, he couldn't be demonstrated to be wrong until the 1940s with the discovery of the Dead Sea Scrolls. Now there is no doubt.

If Jerome falls, so does the historic case for the Protestant rejection of the deuterocanon. As the Lutheran scholar A.C. Sundberg observes,

> But now, it has been shown, Jerome's case falls hopelessly to the ground since it was based on the misconception that that Jewish canon was the canon of Jesus and the apostles. Any continuing appeal through the Reformers to Jerome and the Hebrew canon comes to this same end. . . . If Protestant Christianity is to continue its custom of restricting its [Old Testament] canon to the Jewish canon, then an entirely new rationale and doctrine of canon will have to be described. And any Protestant doctrine of canonization that takes seriously the question of Christian usage and historical and spiritual heritage will lead ultimately to

> the Christian [Old Testament] as defined in the Western Church at the end of the fourth and the beginning of the fifth centuries.[652]

These councils from the end of the fourth and the beginning of the fifth centuries were the very councils on which the Council of Trent placed its stamp of approval.

Why Retain the Books?

Another piece of evidence showing that Protestantism changed the status quo when it rejected the deuterocanon as apocrypha is the fact that the deuterocanon remained in early Protestant bibles. It doesn't make sense. If these books were *never* considered inspired, why put them in the Bible at all—even in an appendix with a cautioning preface? The only answer is that these books *were* considered authentic parts of Sacred Scripture, and so removing them outright would have been too radical a change. The preface in the Zurich Bible (1531) stated that the "Apocrypha" were included "so that no one may complain of lacking anything, and each may find what is to his taste."[653] Even in the early years of Protestantism there was a strong feeling that these books needed to be included in the Bible.[654] As the Anglican scholar John Hey observes, "At the Reformation, when men had been brought up to revere them [the deuterocanonical books], it would have been both imprudent and cruel to set them aside."[655] As we saw even the Edinburgh Bible Society acknowledged "circumstances [that] discouraged" the removal of the deuterocanon from bibles.

Why would it have been "imprudent and cruel?" What possible circumstances could have discouraged these men from even attempting to remove the deuterocanon from

Protestant bibles? Long before Trent was alleged to have "added" the deuterocanon, Protestants (who were all former Catholics) grew up reading bibles with these books in them, just as their parents and grandparents and the generations who lived before them had done. To the rank and file, the dispute over the canonicity of these Old Testament books must have seemed like scholarly quibbling, but making these books vanish from the Bible could not be dismissed as trivial. Less drastic measures needed to be taken first.[656]

We've chronicled the path of the deuterocanon out of Protestant bibles:

- Luther gathered together the deuterocanonical books and placed them in an appendix between the Old and New Testaments.
- The Synod of Dort moved Luther's appendix to the back of the Bible.
- Nineteenth-century Protestant Bible societies first suppressed them, then removed them altogether.
- Anti-Catholicism, especially in the United States, added fuel to the anti-deutero fire. Supporting the printing of a Bible with the "Apocrypha" was nothing short of "aiding and abetting Rome."
- By the twentieth century, the deuterocanon's removal was so complete and the memory of its former place so faded that in 1915 Rev. Gates opined that part of the Bible had been "stolen" and a "new Reformation" was needed to get it back. Will this new Reformation ever happen?

Today, Protestantism has largely traded in its anti-Catholic sentiments for indifference. I imagine the Protestant associate pastor who spoke at my neighbor's funeral would have said, "What difference does it make which books are in your Bible as long as you know Jesus?" Maybe one day, as anti-Catholic prejudices continue to fade and the news of the collapse of the historical case for the Protestant canon spreads, perhaps there will come a newfound courage in all of us to embrace the word of God in its entirety and to follow it where it may lead—even if that road eventually leads us (as all roads do) back to Rome.

APPENDIX 1

Sola Scriptura and the Problem of the Canon

Luther taught that Scripture alone is the ultimate authority for the individual Christian. When confronted with Scripture that contradicted his theology (as he was with 2 Maccabees 12:43–46, used as a defense of purgatory), Luther took advantage of the doubts raised by Jerome to deny that ancient book's full canonical weight. Therefore, it was not Scripture alone that gave birth to Luther's novel theology, but a refusal to permit Scripture to fully speak.

Many since Luther's time have attempted to provide a justification for the Protestant canon in a manner logically consistent with *sola scriptura*. Coming up with such an after-the-fact justification, however, has proved to be easier said than done, since *sola scriptura* effectively destroys any logically consistent and cogent explanation of how we come to the knowledge of which books make up Scripture to begin with.

Dozens of *sola-scriptura*-friendly explanations for the canon have been offered over the years, but only three have gained any sizable number of adherents: 1) the historical-investigative approach; 2) the "canon-within-a-canon" approach; and 3) the self-attestation/inner witness approach.

Historical-Investigative Approach

Evangelicals and mainline Protestants typically favor this

argument, supposedly based on the results of historical investigation. According to this method, the investigator uses various historical-critical methods to examine the beliefs of the early Church Fathers and councils. Trends of thought are outlined, and the results, they claim, point to a consistent (or nearly consistent) affirmation of the legitimacy of the shorter Old Testament canon. The canon, therefore, is determined by *historical research*.

The historical-investigative approach has substantial merit in that it provides an objective and verifiable means of determining a closed fixed canon. Critics are quick to point out, however, that it has more than a few equally substantial failings. For example, practitioners of this method often presume the legitimacy of a shorter Protestant canon, and then proceed to select those Fathers who appear to agree with their *a priori* assumption. Evidence to the contrary (such as a Father who affirms the deuterocanon) is either ignored or dismissed as the product of ignorant men. In other words, this method is prone to special pleading.[657]

Critics of this method note that the results of this historical approach never reach the level of certitude necessary to establish the limits of something as fundamental as the word of God. A river, as they say, cannot rise higher than its source. In other words, because the historical investigation approach relies on the inductive reasoning of fallible men, moving from particulars to the general, it can never produce an *infallible* conclusion, but only a highly probable one. But high probability, these critics point out, is not enough to bind the consciences of all believers. There must be *no* possibility of error when it comes to the contents of God's word since the certainty of faith rests on those contents. If Scripture is uncertain, one's faith is uncertain.

Finally and most decisively, critics have argued that the historical-investigative approach contradicts *sola scriptura* because it sets the results of external historical investigation as the norm *above the norm of Scripture*. Historical research becomes the ultimate judge and arbitrator of what should and should not be permitted to pass muster as the word of God. Although this approach is often lauded for being of secondary usefulness, it most certainly does contradict *sola scriptura*.

Canon-Within–a-Canon Approach

Martin Luther developed this second approach. He believed that the canonical scriptures demonstrated their own canonicity by their contents. Luther reasoned that the first duty of an apostle was to *preach Christ*. Therefore, if a book preached Christ it was to that extent apostolic and canonical Scripture. Conversely, if a book did not preach Christ it was to that extent not apostolic and canonical Scripture.[658]

Luther's approach attempts to avoid appealing to any criterion outside of Scripture so as not to violate *sola scriptura*. Instead, the contents of Scripture itself are used to determine the canon. But critics are quick to point out that this method also fails its objectives in two ways.

First, the approach suffers from circular reasoning. How did Luther learn that an apostle's first duty is to preach Christ, if he did not learn it from a book of Scripture? And how did he know, before reading it, that said book was canonical? By rejecting an authoritative and authentic tradition of the canon, *sola scriptura* cuts itself off from the only avenue of escape from this circle. The "canon-within–a-canon" approach assumes at the outset the canonicity of a certain group of books and then, based on those books, formulates what constitutes "preaching Christ." It then uses this formulation to confirm those very same books as canonical—thus begging the question.

Second, this approach, it is sometime argued, also cannot provide the level of certitude necessary to establish the limits of the word of God. Even Luther admitted that not all books "preach Christ" equally. Some "preach" him more forcefully and clearly than others (something which hardly anyone has ever doubted). And thus this method produces not a set number of books but a continuum of canonicity, each book more or less canonical than another. Indeed, some New Testament books (e.g., 2 and 3 John, James, Hebrews, Jude, and Revelation) were said to be of questionable canonical status. Who or what determines if a given book possesses sufficient canonicity to overturn a conviction or to bind the conscience of the believer? The answer is Martin Luther. Not surprisingly, non-Lutherans are less than satisfied with this answer.

This approach, though aiming to preserve *sola scriptura,* also violates it by setting up an extrabiblical standard for determining what is and what is not the word of God (Luther's own understanding of what constitutes having "Christ preached"). Anyone who adopts this method erases Luther's name and fills in his own, but the process does not become more reliable by the change.

The Self-Attesting/Inner Witness Approach

John Calvin offered a two-fold witness approach to this problem, and Reformed Protestants generally follow his approach today. According to this method, the canonicity of a given writing can be known—not by the contents of a given book, as in Luther's approach—but by the quality or nature of the writing itself. The canonical scriptures are said to be so holy, true, powerful, harmonious, elevated, and beautiful that their inspired character unmistakably imposes itself upon the reader. This impression made by inspired Scripture is so strong and unmistakable that the Protestant theologian Charles Briggs argues,

> If men are not won by the holy character of the biblical books, it must be because for some reason their eyes have been withheld from seeing it.[659]

Therefore, this approach concludes, the inspired canonical Scripture is *autopisteuo* (self-attesting). In addition to the self-evident nature of Scripture, the Holy Spirit is said to also provide an inner witness within the believer's heart that assures and confirms to him that what is being read is the inspired word of God.

This approach masterfully avoids two of the most serious flaws of the "canon-within-a-canon" approach. By moving the criterion from a believer's theology (Christ preached) to qualities perceivable to every human (truth, harmony, beauty, etc.), the self-attesting approach avoids, at least at first glance, the placing of one's theology above Scripture. It also avoids Luther's canonical continuum, by insisting that the impression made by an inspired work is such that degrees of canonicity are neither needed nor discernible. In theory, this approach seems formidable. When put into practice, however, the self-attesting approach discloses several serious deficiencies.

If the nature of Sacred Scripture is so plain and unmistakable, how is it that so many people were wrong on the canon? Martin Luther is perhaps the best example. How could he have missed the unmistakable canonicity of the book of Revelation, the epistle of James, or Esther? Reformed Protestants generally argue that it was Luther's zeal for the gospel that blinded his eyes from seeing the obvious. If this logic is true, however, then how do the Reformed Protestants (also zealous for the gospel) know that *their* perception is correct, and that Luther's was incorrect?

Moreover, how do they know that it was Luther's *zeal* that caused him to err? Proponents noticed that Luther's views on the canon differed from theirs. They investigated Luther's life, noted his zeal for his beliefs, and concluded that it is probable that Luther's zeal blinded him on the canonicity of these books. In other words, they knew that they were right and Luther was wrong based on the results of historical investigation. But the determining factor isn't Luther's views on the canon, but our interpretation based on historical research that determines whether his zeal blinded him or not. But relying on historical research shares the same weaknesses as the historical investigative approach, namely that it cannot produce certain results and it violates *sola scriptura*.

There are other problems as well. The self-attestation approach could never provide a closed or fixed canon. Even if a person could infallibly discern whether certain books were part of inspired Scripture, this perception could never tell anyone that these books *alone* made up the canon. There would always be the possibility that there are books yet to be read—or even *yet to be written*—that will also give a self-attestation. Many good Protestants, in fact, have been led into Mormonism by just this rationale—feeling the "burning in the bosom" that supposedly attests to the inspiration of the Book of Mormon.

The Protestant divine John Bunyan, author of the famed allegory *Pilgrim's Progress*, writes in his autobiography,

> One day, after I had been so many weeks oppressed and cast down, as I was now quite giving up the ghost of all my hopes of ever attaining life, that sentence fell with weight

> upon my spirit, "Look at the generations of old, and see: did ever any trust in the Lord and was confounded?" At which I was greatly lightened, and encouraged in my soul.[660]

Drawing spiritual strength from this passage, Bunyan searched his Protestant Bible for it, but to no avail. Eventually he did discover its location—in Sirach 2:11! Shocked that he had felt such divine consolation from a book in the Apocrypha, he dissembled, only to admit later that this passage continued to bring him spiritual comfort. Is this not an instance of Sirach's attesting its own divine character to John Bunyan? And if so venerable a figure as Bunyan can be wrong about such a thing, perhaps the same could happen to you and me?

Conclusion

Ironically, the principle of *sola scriptura* is the chief impediment to defining the exact limits of the Scripture within Protestantism. It places the scriptures as the final court of appeal, but it is unable to identify which judges are to sit on its bench. A *sola scripturist* may say, "Thus says the Lord," provided he qualifies his statement with the words ". . . I think." *Sola scriptura* is a self-refuting proposition. No one can know, with sufficient certainty, what the Scripture is unless he adopts a norm outside of Scripture that sets the limits of Scripture. But then *scriptura* has ceased to be *sola*.

No solution is possible in this matter because all of these methods are *a posteriori* in nature. They are attempts to justify a position that has, for other reasons, already been determined.

The only alternative to these *a posteriori* solutions is to treat the canon as something handed down or received, as did some of the early Protestant confessions. However, the question must be asked: received from *whom*? St. Francis de

Sales, an ardent leader of the Catholic Counter-Reformation, argued that no ancient canon squares perfectly with that accepted by Protestants:

> I pray you, Reformers, tell me whence you have taken the canon of the Scripture which you follow? You have not taken it from the Jews, for the books of the Gospels would not be there; nor from the Council of Laodicea, for the Apocalypse would not be in it; nor from the Councils of Carthage or of Florence, for Ecclesiasticus and the Maccabees would be there. Whence, then, have you taken it? In good sooth, like canon was never spoken of before your time. The Church never saw canon of the Scripture in which there was not either more or less than yours. What likelihood is there that the Holy Spirit has hidden himself from all antiquity, and that after 1,500 years he has disclosed to certain private persons the list of the true scriptures?[661]

Ironically, the exaltation of Scripture, as envisioned by *sola scriptura*, can only be experienced and practiced within the Catholic Church. The Church accepts the Scripture as something received from our Lord and his apostles. It does not determine what Scripture is, but it manifests its inspired status by reading it in its liturgy as the word of God. When the canon is contested, the Church reaffirms the gift it has received from the apostles. It is only within the confines of the historic Catholic and apostolic Church that Scripture stands predetermined, untampered with by mere traditions of men. Outside of it, the Bible can never achieve the highest aspirations of Protestant Reformation.

APPENDIX 2

The Deuterocanon and Biblical Inerrancy

Protestants sometimes allege that the deuterocanon contains historical, logical, theological, and moral errors. Since Scripture is immune from errors, they argue that the deuterocanon must not be part of Scripture.

The historical response to these accusations has been either to attempt to reconcile these supposed errors or to show similar difficulties in the protocanon. These tactics often fall on deaf ears. John Henry Newman once said of believers, "Ten thousand difficulties do not make one doubt." But for those who are not inclined to see the deuterocanon as Scripture, one doubt sufficiently establishes ten thousand difficulties. Even if one were to harmonize with ninety-nine percent certainty that a given error does not exist, the non-Catholic would deem the remaining one percent sufficient to reject the work. Appealing to similar problems in the protocanon likewise falls on deaf ears because such arguments appear to be denigrating Scripture. The "real errors" of the deuterocanon cannot compare to the mere "difficulties" of the protocanon.

Herein lies the problem. What constitutes a real error, as opposed to a "Bible difficulty"? Can either of these two be established beyond all doubt? Let us answer the second question first. All Scripture is inspired or God-breathed, but inspiration applies only to the original text. Subsequent copies are not immune from error or corruption. Over centuries of manually re-copying the sacred text, copyists undoubtedly made errors. Fortunately, we possess a large number of copies of the New Testament, some of which were created not long after the original inspired text (called the autograph) was made. Through the science of textual criticism, we possess a theoretic text of the New Testament that is nearly identical to the original inspired text. The Old Testament text does not share these benefits. Even after the discoveries of the Dead Sea Scrolls, the earliest manuscripts we own are still centuries removed from the originals. Despite the remarkable fidelity of Jewish scribes over the centuries, difficulties and corruptions exist in the Old Testament; and the ability to solve these difficulties conclusively is quite beyond our reach. It is, therefore, impossible to *demonstrate* the existence of errors in a given text without looking at the autograph. All that can be produced is a high degree of the probability for a given error.

Even if it were possible to show that an "error" did exist in the autograph, it remains to be proved that the author made the "error." An inspired writing is without error only if it is interpreted in line with the *author's original intent.* It is, obviously, possible for the reader to *understand* a text incorrectly, so as to make it appear to constitute or contain an error. For example, our Lord said, "If anyone comes to me, and does not hate his own father and mother and wife and children and brothers and sisters, yes, and even his own life, he cannot be my disciple" (Luke 14:26). Interpreted one way, our Lord could be made to teach a moral error.[662] Those interpreting this passage in the spirit of the Church, however, understand Christ to be using the literary form of *hyperbole*, which is a deliberate exaggeration or overstatement to make a point. In this case, the error existed in our interpretation and not in the document itself.

If then, we can never know with certainty of the presence or absence of an error, how do we know if *any* book of the Bible is inerrant? Inerrancy is the *product* of inspiration. The Holy Spirit, who is the primary author of inspired Scripture, can never deceive nor be deceived. The inspired books, therefore, can neither be mistaken nor deliberately deceive others. It is the inspired status of a given book that guarantees for us its inerrancy, not our own critical historical investigations. And the determination of inspiration *must necessarily* come *before* any other question is asked. If a text is inspired, then all difficulties are understood to be errors only in appearance. If, on the other hand, one believes that a text is not inspired (i.e., it does not have the Holy Spirit as its primary author), then there is a possibility that the difficulty may be in fact a real error. The reason why the supposed moral "error" committed in Luke 14:26 above was so easy to solve comes from our pre-determination that the Gospel of Luke is, in fact, an inspired text and it cannot err. Based on this presupposition, we endeavor to harmonize the difficulty.

The appeal to "errors" in the deuterocanon ultimately ends up committing the formal fallacy of *begging the question* because the Protestant begins all his inquiries with the presupposition that the deuterocanon is *not* inspired. When difficulties are found in the deuterocanon, the reader assumes that these difficulties are true errors and concludes that the deuterocanon must not be inspired.[663] The deuterocanon cannot be inspired because it has errors, and it has errors because it is not inspired. For this reason, neither Catholics nor non-Catholics are persuaded to change their position by arguments based on supposed errors. The same is true with pointing out similar difficulties in the protocanon or the New Testament. For Protestants who reject the inspiration of the deuterocanon and accept the inspiration of the New Testament, comparing difficulties between the two texts would be like comparing apples to oranges. The *a priori* conviction of inspiration and inerrancy renders the appeal moot.

The best way out of this dilemma is not to enter it at all. Biblical inerrancy is not based upon our feeble abilities to solve every problem. Our faith rests upon the God who inspired the text, not in our own abilities. First determine if a text is inspired and only then determine if errors exist. Doing otherwise is not only anti-Protestant (placing ourselves as judges over Scripture), but it has also served to destroy belief in biblical inerrancy within mainline Protestantism.

Appeals to supposed errors in the deuterocanon have long peppered Protestant/Catholic debates and rendered them far uglier than they need be. And because Catholicism was this method's target, few had the foresight to realize that this method could be used against the rest of the Bible, too. As the Reformed scholar Edward Reuss noted,

> Not one of the ardent champions of the purity of the canon foresees that criticism so puerile, so unworthy of the subject, and so pointless, will end in showing to superficial and scoffing minds the ways and means of sapping the authority of the whole Bible; and that the scoffs thrown at the head of the little fish of Tobit will sooner or later destroy Jonah's whale.[664]

Reuss's prophetic words have been fulfilled by the extravagances of higher criticism. After the Apocrypha controversy had subsided, critics turned the same weapons against not only the Prophet Jonah but the rest of the Bible. So-called errors and absurdities were quickly expunged from the protocanon of the Old and New Testaments. Whole books were labeled (or libeled) as myths and fables. The end result is a Bible where only a few passages are worthy of belief. Anti-Catholic polemicists unwittingly opened a Pandora's Box. They assumed no one would ever dare charge the rest of Scripture with errors and absurdities, yet the advent of liberal Protestantism brought with it individuals who did not fear to apply these arguments consistently throughout the entire Bible.

The problem at the heart of this line of argumentation is one of pride. It places the intellect in the role of judge, allowing it to sit in judgment upon the word of God. Yet we must know in advance what the word of God *is* before offering it this kind of allegiance. That is why the canon of Scripture *must* be received as Sacred Tradition.

It takes humility to accept the canon of Scripture as given to the Church. But once we have made such an act all the glories of the Bible open up to us. We may humbly submit our intellect to the text, sitting at the Master's feet like little children, knowing that even if the power to solve all difficulties is beyond us, there is nevertheless a solution. To do otherwise would be not only anti-Protestant (since it violates *sola scriptura*), but anti-Catholic and anti-Christian as well.

APPENDIX 3

Esdras, Carthage, and Trent

Non-Catholics have asserted for some time that the Council of Trent rejected a book that the Councils of Carthage and Hippo listed as canonical, namely the book of Esdras. Is this true? Did Trent really reject a book that Carthage accepted?

The Problem of Esdras

Where the Council of Carthage addresses the books of Ezra and Nehemiah it simply says, "Esdras, two books."[665] One would assume that this means the books of Ezra and Nehemiah, but some have called this into question. The "books of Esdras" are numbered differently in different translations and in various recensions of those translations. For example, the book of Esdras is listed as 1 Esdras (or Esdras A) in the Syrian versions and in several important Greek manuscripts. 2 Esdras (or Esdras B) is the combination of Ezra and Nehemiah. However, in the Lucian recension of the Septuagint the two are reversed. 1 Esdras (Esdras A) is Ezra-Nehemiah and 2 Esdras (Esdras B) is the book of Esdras. The Latin Vulgate separates Ezra and Nehemiah so that 1 Esdras is the book of Ezra, 2 Esdras is Nehemiah, and 3 Esdras is the book of Esdras.[666] The question that is posed is what did the Council of Carthage mean when it said "Esdras, two books"? Did it mean Ezra and Nehemiah, or did it mean the book of Esdras and Ezra-Nehemiah?

The Case for Hippo/Carthage Accepting Esdras

Critics offer the following reasons why they think the Council of Carthage accepted the book of Esdras as one of the two books:

First, the early Church Fathers who lived before the time of the council sometimes quoted the book of Esdras as Scripture. Therefore, this opens the possibility that Carthage likewise may have accepted this book.

Second, Augustine, who was a major influence in these councils, accepted the book of Esdras as inspired Scripture since he quotes it as such in his work *City of God* 18, 36. Moreover, Augustine believed that the Septuagint was inspired, and since the book of Esdras was in the Septuagint he must have accepted it as inspired. Carthage's canon, therefore, must have reflected his opinion.

Third, the Council of Carthage affirmed the Septuagintal canon, and most copies of the Septuagint have two books of Esdras (1-2 Esdras or Esdras A-B) that is the book of Esdras and Ezra-Nehemiah combined.

From these points, it is asserted that the African councils and all subsequent decrees (Innocent I, Gelasius, etc.) must have affirmed the book of Esdras as a canonical book. Since, it is argued, Trent rejected Esdras as apocrypha; Trent's decree contradicts these previous councils.

The problem with this argument is that it is too simplistic and it is in some areas factually incorrect. Let's look at why.

Ezra and Nehemiah

It is commonly claimed that Jerome was the first Christian to separate 2 Esdras into the two books of Ezra and Nehemiah. There is a sense that this is correct. The Vulgate separates the two books where the Septuagint most often does not. However, there is evidence that Christians prior to Jerome understood Esdras B (Ezra and Nehemiah combined) to be two books. Jerome himself speaks about this Christian custom when he says, "The eighth is Ezra, which itself is likewise divided *amongst Greeks and Latins* into two books."[667] Even though Ezra and Nehemiah were combined in one book, Jerome says, all Christians (both East and West) divide this one book into two. Origen of Alexandria (185–254), when speaking of the books of the rabbinic Bible, seems to speak of the same Christian understanding: "Esdras, first and second in one, *Ezra*, that is, 'an assistant.'"[668] We can add to this list comments by Cyril of Jerusalem and Rufinus as well.[669] It certainly is plausible, if not likely, that Carthage's "Esdras, two books" does indeed refer to Ezra and Nehemiah and not the book of Esdras and Ezra-Nehemiah.[670]

But even if Carthage did refer to the book of Esdras and Ezra-Nehemiah, there is still a deeper problem concerning the book of Esdras. Is it really a book?

Is the Book of Esdras a *Book*?

But doesn't the fact that several early Church Fathers and Augustine quoting the book of Esdras as Scripture prove that it is a standalone book? Normally, yes. But the book of Esdras is not a typical book. According to Vriezen and Van Der Woude's *Ancient Israelite and Early Jewish Literature*,

> No single apocryphal book of the Old Testament exhibits such a high degree of kinship with the canonical literature of the Hebrew Bible. The document consists for the most part of a translation of 2 Chronicles 35-36 (although differing from time to time in terms of content from the

> Masoretic Text and not in harmony with the LXX), the entire book of Ezra (with the exception of Ezra 4:6) and Nehemiah 7:72–8:14a.[671]

In other words, the book of Esdras (with the exception of some original material in Esdras 3–5:6) is composed entirely of canonical material.[672] The canonical material makes up so much of the book of Esdras that it is questionable whether it should be considered a standalone work or perhaps something akin to the category of writings found at Qumran known as "Rewritten Scripture." As Bruce Metzger notes,

> What the relation is between 1 Esdras and the canonical narratives has perplexed scholars of many generations. There are three possible solutions: Ezra-Nehemiah may have been derived from 1 Esdras; or 1 Esdras may be a modification of Ezra-Nehemiah; or both forms may derive from a common original.[673]

Regardless of what option, the end result is the same. The book of Esdras is another Greek version of the canonical texts of 2 Chronicles, Ezra, and Nehemiah. Like the "Rewritten Scripture," material is added and omitted and the order of events is arranged differently.

This point is made by none other than Roger Beckwith in his book *The Old Testament Canon in the New Testament Church,* who writes,

> 1 Esdras diverges widely from the Masoretic Text of Ezra-Nehemiah, but it is regarded by many as the old LXX version of *that* book, which would make it another example of the unusual freedom displayed in the LXX Hagiographa.[674]

It's an "old LXX [Septuagint] version of" . . . what book? The book of Ezra-Nehemiah! Since the book of Esdras (1 Esdras or Esdras A) appears to have been, according to Beckwith, an older version of the Greek Ezra-Nehemiah, the early Christian may have used the book of Esdras, not as a single standalone work, but as a different version of the canonical books of Ezra and Nehemiah. Beckwith later observes,

> [The book of Esdras] . . . is a second, possibly older and certainly freer, Greek translation of Ezra, with additional material but with very little Nehemiah. The early Church seems to have used both translations as equally authoritative, but to have preferred Esdras A (1 Esdras) for the earlier part of the history and Esdras B (Ezra-Nehemiah) for the later part.[675]

If Beckwith is correct, this would account for why the early Church Fathers and Augustine quoted the book of Esdras as one would the canonical Scripture. It wasn't because the book of Esdras was seen as a standalone separate work, but because it was another Greek version of Ezra-Nehemiah. Beckwith's conclusion is important:

> Although 1 Esdras occurs in the Septuagint manuscripts as Esdras A, and appears to have been used by Josephus and the Fathers of the first four centuries in preference to the corresponding, part of Esdras B (Ezra-Nehemiah), the simplest explanation of this phenomenon is not that they regarded it as a different book, but that they regarded it as an alternative (and fuller) Greek translation of the same book. The question of the canon, therefore, is probably not involved.[676]

If the early Church Fathers quoted the book of Esdras as an alternative (and fuller) Greek translation of Ezra-Nehemiah, then obviously whatever they say about it should be attributed to the canonical books Ezra and Nehemiah, not to the book of Esdras itself. This also means, if Beckwith is correct, that whatever Carthage meant by "Esdras, two books" the council was affirming Ezra and Nehemiah either directly (by dividing 2 Esdras or Esdras B into two books, like Jerome says) or indirectly by affirming the book of Esdras, which would be nothing more than an "alternative (and fuller) Greek translation of the same book." Therefore, if the book of Esdras is simply a manuscript (and not a standalone work) it imposes no difficulty in regard to Carthage's canon since the only *books* it affirmed are Ezra and Nehemiah.

Trent's "Rejection" of Esdras

The argument also makes a factual error. It is assumed that since the Council of Trent didn't include the book of Esdras in its canon, it rejected it. If all we had to look at was the canon itself that might be a possible interpretation. It could be argued that Trent intended its canon to be exhaustive so that whatever is not included is to be considered rejected. But there is no reason to guess. We possess the Acts of Trent and the various diaries and letters of its participants, so we can know how the fathers of the council wished the decree to be interpreted. Once these primary sources are consulted, rather than commentators on those sources, it becomes clear that Trent did not implicitly or explicitly "reject" Esdras. Instead, they wished that the decree be silent on the issue. How do we know this?

On March 29, 1546, fourteen questions (called *capita dubitationum*) were proposed to the council fathers to provide direction for the framers of the document. Question four asked whether the books that were not included in the official list of the canon, but were included in the Latin Vulgate (the book of Esdras, 3 Ezra, and 3 Maccabees), should be rejected by the decree by name or passed over in silence.[677] Only three fathers voted for an explicit rejection. Forty-two voted that these books should be passed over in silence (Latin, *libri apocryphi sub silentio*). Eight were undecided.[678]

Therefore, not only did Trent *not* explicitly reject the book of Esdras, but the fathers did *express a wish* that the decree not name these books as being rejected. This is a subtle but important point. It's not altogether accurate to say that Trent "rejected" the book of Esdras.

Does this mean that Catholics can accept the book of Esdras as canonical Scripture or that the contents of the canon of Scripture is an open question? Not at all. The canon of Scripture is what is given at the Council of Trent, the Council of Florence, and the African councils. I suppose it could be *theoretically* possible at some future date to admit Esdras to the canon since it was never explicitly rejected, but this would be *practically* impossible since the book has fallen into disuse. Moreover, if Beckwith and others are correct, there really is no need for the book of Esdras to be affirmed since it was virtually affirmed by the adoption of Ezra and Nehemiah.

Conclusion

The claim that Trent contradicted Carthage is plainly false, and this may be the reason why most Protestant scholars ignore it. There is good reason to believe that Carthage's "Esdras, two books" refer to Ezra and Nehemiah. Moreover, it would have to be proven that the book of Esdras is a standalone work and not "Rewritten Scripture," or what Beckwith calls an ancient "fuller" Greek version of Ezra-

Nehemiah. Even more problematic is the fact that Trent's decree was framed to be silent in regard to Esdras and the other books. It's true that the book wasn't affirmed, but that's not to say that it was therefore rejected. There is a third possibility that the council fathers didn't wish to address the question and that is what the *capita dubitationum* suggest.

All this is nothing more than a tempest in a teapot if the book of Esdras is another version of the canonical books of Ezra and Nehemiah, which most scholars believe it to be.

ENDNOTES

1 Since it would be too tedious to refer to these books and sections of books as the "disputed books," we are going to refer to them as the deuterocanon or deuterocanonical books.

2 *Tanakh* is a Hebrew acronym for the three-fold division of the *Torah, Nebi'im, and Ketuvim* (Law, Prophets, and Writings).

3 The earliest certain references from the Babylonian *Baba Bathra* 14b generally dated around this time.

4 *Prologue to the book of Sirach*. Emphasis added.

5 *CD* 7:15–17; *1QS* 1:1, 8:15–17. The closest parallel to Luke 24:44 is an incomplete fragment known as *Miqsat Maʿase Ha-Torah* (designated *4QMMT*). Its reconstructed reading of C, lines 10–11, is "[W]e have [written] to you so that you may study (carefully) the book of Moses and the books of the prophets and (the writings of) David [and the] [events of] ages past," as quoted in Eugene Ulrich's *The Dead Sea Scrolls and the Developmental Composition of the Bible* (Boston: Brill, 2015), 300. Lee McDonald asks, "[I]s there a fourth category, namely 'annals of each generation?' that refers to Chronicles, Ezra-Nehemiah, and possible Esther or something else? (Lee McDonald, *The Origin of the Bible: A Guide for the Perplexed* (London: T & T Clark International, 2011), 62.

6 Philo wrote of the Jews in Therapeutae, "And in every house there is a sacred shrine which is called the holy place, and the monastery in which they retire by themselves and perform all the mysteries of a holy life . . . studying in that place *the law and the sacred oracles of God enunciated by the holy prophets and the hymns, and psalms and all kinds of other things* by reason of which knowledge and piety are increased and brought to perfection." *Contemplative Life*, 25–26. Yonge, Charles Duke. *The Works of Philo: Complete and Unabridged* (Peabody: Hendrickson, 1995), 700. Emphasis added. Anywhere from a three-fold to a five-fold division of writings can be discerned in this passage.

7 Matthew 5:17; 7:12; 11:13; 22:40; Luke 16:16; John 1:45; Acts 13:15; 24:14; 28:23; and Romans 3:21.

8 The *Psalms* is a very strange descriptor for the books found in the Writings. Could anyone ever consider Ezra, Esther, and Chronicles to be a member of "the Psalms"? Moreover, the book of Psalms is somewhat unique in the Writings. No other book in the Writings is psalmic, and no other books

was written or attributed to David. The appeal to the Dead Sea Scrolls fragment called *Miqsat Ma'asch Torah* (4QMMT) fails to connect the Psalms to the Writings. Indeed, it is fraught with problems. Besides the fact that several important words are missing in this fragment, making its correct reading little more than an educated guess, it still doesn't say "Psalms" but "David." The argument, therefore, assumes that "David" is a synecdoche for the Psalms, and the Psalms is a synecdoche for the Writings, not exactly the meaning that jumps off the page. As noted in Endnote 6, the addition of the "book of days" may be problematic to this argument since it appears to be a reference to books of Chronicles, which are also found in the Writings. In the end, *Miqsat Ma'asch Torah* (4QMMT) doesn't link the Psalms with the Writings. Moreover, the fragment may very well have been written after Luke composed his Gospel, making it less valuable for showing that the *Tanakh* existed before the time of Christ.

9 Edward W. Reuss, *History of the Canon of the Holy Scriptures in the Christian Church*, trans. David Hunter (Edinburgh: R.W. Hunter, 1891), 10.

10 See *The Case for the Deuterocanon: Argument and Evidence*, 86–94.

11 Those candidates are Zechariah, the son of Jeberechiah (Isa. 8:2); Zechariah, the son of Baruch (Josephus, *Wars of the Jews*, 4, 5, 4); Zechariah, the son of Jehoiada (2 Chron. 24:22); the prophet Zechariah; the son of Barachiah (Zech. 1:1); Zechariah, the father of John the Baptist (see *Protoevangelium of James,* 23, et al.); and an otherwise unknown contemporary of Jesus who was killed in the temple area.

12 Emphasis added. Here the patronym (X, the son of so-and-so) is not used, but rather a different construction altogether. The Greek Septuagint (*Iõdae ho patêr autou*) and the Hebrew (*yᵉhô·yã·dã''ã·bîw'*) explicitly state that Jehoiada is his father.

13 See *Encyclopedia of Bible Difficulties* (Grand Rapids: Zondervan Publishing House, 1982), 337–38.

14 There also appears to be textual evidence that suggests that Ezra originally may have followed 2 Chronicles. If you look at the concluding verses of 2 Chronicles (2 Chron. 36:21–23), you find that they are virtually repeated at the beginning of Ezra (Ezra 1:1–3). It's possible—although not certain—that Ezra-Nehemiah followed Chronicles rather than preceded it at some time in the distant past.

15 See Edmon L. Gallagher, "The Blood from Abel to Zechariah in the History of Interpretation," in vol. 60, no. 1 of *New Testament Studies,* (2014), 121–138.

16 See Roger Beckwith, *The Old Testament Canon of the New Testament Church and its Background in Early Judaism* (Eugene, OR: Wipf and Stock, 1985), 369–370.

17 Genesis 4:10: "The Lord then said: 'What have you done! Listen: your

brother's blood cries out to me from the soil!'" and 2 Chronicles 24:22: "And as he [Zechariah] was dying, he said, 'May the Lord see and avenge.'" This interpretation is proposed by H.G.L. Peels in his article, "'The Blood of Abel to Zechariah' (Matthew 23, 35; Luke 11,50f.) and the Canon of the Old Testament," *ZAW* 113 (2001), 584–85.

18 Zechariah's martyrdom in the temple (see the Protoevangelium of James, Origen, *Commentary on Matthew* 10:18, et al.) Jesus' reference to otherwise unknown contemporary events (e.g., Luke 13:4).

19 Norman Geisler is perhaps the strongest proponent of the "Jewish province" argument. See Norman Geisler and Ralph MacKensie, *Roman Catholics and Evangelicals: Agreements and Difference* (Baker Academic, 1995), 162. Also, Geisler's "Apocrypha" article in the *Encyclopedia of Christian Apologetics* (Baker Academic, 1998).

20 Josephus (*Antiquities*, 18, 16), Hippolytus (*Refutation* 9, 29), Origen (*Against Celsus* 1, 49; *Commentary on Matthew* 17, 35), and Jerome (*Commentary on Matthew*, 22:31–32). Some scholars dispute this claiming that the early Fathers were dependent upon the misunderstanding of Josephus. However, two key Fathers (Origen and Jerome) show no indication of dependence upon Josephus. Rather Origen and Jerome had independent access to two different Jewish communities, and both indicated the belief that the Sadducees only accepted the Torah. For an excellent discussion on this see, Lee McDonald's, *The Formation of the Biblical Canon: Volume 1: The Old Testament: Its Authority and Canonicity* (London: Bloomsbury T & T Clark, 2017), 256.

21 The Qumran community didn't publish a canon, and there is no discussion about which books were Sacred Scripture and which were not. The "canon" of Qumran is little more than educated guesses. However, it is generally understood that the Qumran community accepted a larger group of sacred texts. See *Scribes and Schools: The Canonization of the Hebrew Scriptures*, ed. Philip Davies (Kentucky: Westminster John Knox Press), 164–165.

22 Mishnah, *Yadayim* 3:5, et al. See William Osterley's *The Books of the Apocrypha: Their Origin, Teaching, and Contents* (New York: Fleming Revell Company, 1914), 170–171.

23 The New American Standard Bible (NASB), which is known for its precision in rendering Greek verb tenses, translated this clause as "the Jews *were entrusted* with the oracles of God" (Greek, *episteuthêsan ta logia tou theou*). Emphasis added.

24 God also revealed his will through other means. For example, his will was made known through casting lots (1 Sam. 14:41–42; Prov. 16:33; Jon. 1:7; Acts 1:24–26) and by the high priest's breastplate, which contained a device known as the Urim and Thummin (Exod. 28:30; Num. 27:21; 1 Sam. 28:6). These authorized forms of divination, which also informed Israel of

God's will, also gave the Israelites an advantage over the Gentiles.

25 Josephus, *Against Apion*, 1, 38–41. Josephus, Flavius, and William Whiston, *The Works of Josephus: Complete and Unabridged.* (Peabody: Hendrickson, 1987), 776.

26 *b. Baba Bathra* 12b, as quoted in Jacob Neusner, vol. 15 of *The Babylonian Talmud: A Translation and Commentary* (Peabody: Hendrickson Publishers, 2011), 551.

27 *Tosefta Sotah* 13:2, as quoted in *The Contents of the Soncino Babylonian Talmud*, trans. I. Epstein (London: The Soncino Press, 1948), folio 11a.

28 Seder Olam Rabbah, as quoted in Seder Olam: *The Rabbinic View of Biblical Chronology*, trans. Heinrich W. Guggenheimer (Oxford: Rowman & Littlefield Publishers, Inc., 2005), 260.

29 *J. Ta'anith* 2, 1 as quoted in Beckwith, *Old Testament*, 370.

30 *Prophets, Prophecy, and Prophetic Texts in Second Temple Judaism*, ed. M.H. Floyd and R.D. Haak (New York: T & T Clark International, 2006), 242. Per Bilde likewise sees the same implication: "This sentence . . . seems to indicate that Josephus also regarded these authors as 'prophets'" (Per Bilde, "Contra Apionem 1.25–56: An Essay on Josephus's View of His Own Work In the Context of the Jewish Canon," in *Contra Apionem: Studies in its Character & Context with a Latin Concordance to the Portion Missing in Greek*, ed. L.H. Feldman and J.R. Levison (New York: Brill, 1993), 103). Bilde, Gray, and others even go so far as to suggest that Josephus may have been himself a prophet/priest and his records as being akin to that of a sacred history.

31 *Antiquities* 1, 240–241; 3, 218; 13, 311–313; 20, 97–99; 20, 167–168; 20, 169–172; 20, 188; 20, 167–168; 6, 283–287; 14, 22–24, et al.). Alexander Polyhistor even identifies a Jew named Cleodemus as "the prophet" who wrote "a history of the Jews, in agreement with the History of Moses" (*Antiquities*, 1.240). This took place during the period of time when, supposedly, prophets ceased to exist.

32 *Against Apion*, 1, 1.

33 *Against Apion*, 1, 2.

34 *Against Apion*, 1, 8: "For we have not an innumerable multitude of books among us, disagreeing from, and contradicting one another: [as the Greeks have] but only twenty-two books."

35 Since Josephus never explains exactly what the "succession of prophets" is or how he knows that it existed during this time period, I believe Rebecca Gray offers the most plausible explanation. She argues that since the histories presented in these books are continuous and even at times overlapping, as opposed to the later histories, which make up a more sporadic and discontinuous historical narrative, Josephus reasoned that an exact succession of prophets must have existed for the earliest histories, but not for the later ones. See Rebecca Gray, *Prophetic Figures in Late*

Second Temple Jewish Palestine: The Evidence from Josephus. (Oxford: Oxford University Press, 1997), 12–13.

36 Jacob Neusner. *The Jerusalem Talmud: A Translation and Commentary.* (Peabody: Hendrickson Publishers, 2008). y. Taan. 2:1, III.3.G–K.

37 Neusner, y. Mak. 2:6, III.3.A.

38 Neusner, y. Hor. 3:2, II.1.DD.

39 Neusner, b. Yoma 1:8, II.3.E–F (emphasis in original).

40 John R. Levison, "Did the Spirit Withdrawal from Israel? An Evaluation of the Earliest Jewish Data" *NTS* 43 (1997), 35–57.

41 "When R. Eliezer died, the glory of the Torah ceased" (14:3); "When R. Joshua died, men of counsel ceased, and flection ended in Israel" (14.8); and "When R. Akiba died, the arms of Torah were taken away, and the springs of wisdom ceased" (15.3).

42 Does the overshadowing of the Holy Spirit give the ability to compose inspired writings? The *Canticle of Canticle Rabbah 1.8* says that "Rabbi Judan said: 'It is to teach you that whoever preaches on the Torah in public merits that the Holy Spirit should rest on him. From whom do you learn this? From Solomon; for, because he discoursed on the Torah in public, he earned the privilege that the Holy Spirit rested on him and he composed three books, Proverbs, Ecclesiastes and the Songs of Solomon.'" Although Hillel and Samuel the Little didn't compose inspired Scripture, this passage seems to suggest that the overshadowing of the *Shekinah* could, like when it happened to Solomon, produce such texts. At this point in rabbinic history (i.e., c. 200), the rabbinic Bible had already closed the canon, and so this is question was moot.

43 *Sedar Olam Rabban* was written ca. A.D. 165–200; *Tosefta Sotah* 13:2 was written sometime around 200; *b. Baba Bathra* was written around the third or fourth century.

44 The fact that Sirach's grandson felt it necessary to translate Sirach into Greek (as was done with the other books of Scripture in his day) indicates that it was well received by the Jews in Egypt. This acceptance could only happen if it were first accepted in Palestine. See John E. Steinmuller, *The Companion to Scripture Studies: General Introduction* (London: B. Herder, 1950), 63. Also see Pfeiffer, *IBD*, 1:499.

45 Preface to Sirach. Emphasis added. Sirach's study of the Law and subsequent composition of the book of Sirach sounds similar to what we read earlier from the *Canticle of Canticles Rabbah* 1.8 that taught, "The *Canticle of Canticle Rabbah 1.8* says that 'Rabbi Judan said: It is to teach you that whoever preaches on the Torah in public merits that the Holy Spirit should rest on him' just as Solomon discoursed in public and earned the Holy Spirit to rest upon him and write three books."

46 Emphasis added.

47 When the Edinburgh Bible Society argued against Protestant bibles being printed with the "Apocrypha" (deuterocanon), it claimed, "so plainly does it [the deuterocanon] affect to have the sanction of heaven, that it actually apes the phraseology of inspiration. It contains messages to mankind *which are sometimes represented as proceeding immediately from God himself*" (second statement, 16–17, paragraph 1). Our passage from Sirach clearly fits this description.

48 See Emmanuel Tov, *Hebrew Bible, Greek Bible and Qumran: Collected Essays* (Mohr Siebeck, 2008), 126–127.

49 For further detail see *The Case for the Deuterocanon*, 102–106.

50 Matthew 11:9–10; 21:26–27, 46; Mark 11:32; and Luke 7:26; 20:6.

51 Jesus is identified both as "a prophet" like the others (Matt. 16:14; 21:11; Mark 6:15–16; 8:28; Luke 7:16; 24:19; John 4:19; 9:17) and also as the prophet that was prophesied by Moses (Luke 1:76; John 6:14; 7:4).

52 For example, Jude 14–15 quotes formally quotes the apocryphal book 1 Enoch 1:9. Likewise, James 4:5 formally quotes as Scripture an otherwise unknown work.

53 Several early Protestant bibles included New Testament cross-references (e.g., Coverdale Bible (1535), Matthew's Bible (1537), Great Bible (1541), Taverner's Bible (1551), Geneva (1557, 1560, 1583), Bishops' Bible (1568), as well as the French Olivetan NT (1535), Stephanus's Greek NT (1550), the Spanish "Bear" Bible (1569) and others). Because the Authorized Version or King James Bible (1611) was put together by Protestants, there can be no hint of pro-Catholic bias; its cross-references cannot be rejected for "reading into" the New Testament deuterocanonical references that aren't there.

54 Matthew 27:43, Wisdom 2:17–18, and Psalm 22:8 (LXX) all use the same Greek word for *rescue*.

55 Wisdom 2:17–18 cf. Romans 1:4.

56 W.H. Daubney, *The Use of the Apocrypha in the Christian Church* (London: C.J. Clay and Sons, 1900), 21 quoting *The Cambridge Paragraph Bible of the Authorized English Version, with the Text Revised by a Collation of Its Early and Other Principal Editions, the Use of the Italic Type Made Uniform, the Marginal References Remodeled, and a Critical Introduction Prefixed*, ed., F.H.A. Scrivener, (Cambridge: Cambridge University Press, 1873), *lvi*.

57 Cf. Matthew 7:12.

58 See *JB.C.* 63:119, 445.

59 John 1:9.

60 Paul demonstrates this by noting that Abraham had two children, Ishmael and Isaac, but "Through Isaac shall your descendants be named" (Gen. 21:12; Rom. 9:7). Likewise, Isaac's wife Rebecca "had conceived children *by one man* . . . she was told, 'the elder will serve the younger'" (Rom. 9:10–12). Therefore, God, like a potter, was free to form from one man—

Abraham and Isaac—as a lump a clay good and bad, the line of promise and the line to be rejected.

61 See Metzger, *Introduction*, 161.

62 See Wisdom 7:22 and Proverbs 8:30.

63 W.J. Deane, in his commentary on the book of Wisdom, states that "The similarity here is too close to be accidental" (W.J. Deane, *The Book of Wisdom*, (Oxford: Clarendon Press, 1881), 36). For a fuller explanation of implications of this important passage, *see The Case for the Deuterocanon*, 15–19.

64 2 Maccabees 7:9 states, "[H]e said, 'You accursed wretch, you dismiss us from this present life, but the King Of The Universe will raise us up to an everlasting renewal of life, because we have died for his laws.'" Likewise, the fourth son in 2 Maccabees 7:14 says, "[H]e said, 'One cannot but choose to die at the hands of men and to cherish the hope that God gives of being raised again by him. But for you there will be no resurrection to life.'"

65 William Heaford Daubney, *The Use of the Apocrypha in the Christian Church* (London: C.J. Clay and Sons, 1900), 22. Also Metzger, *Introduction,* 163–164.

66 The reference to the non-canonical book *The Ascension of Isaiah* in Hebrews 11:37 does not negate my point. It is *not* my contention that Hebrews 11 used only information supplied by Scripture, but that it uses only *biblical figures* to illustrate supernatural faith. This is clear from the preceding context. The reference to those who were "sawn in two" is an expansion on *the biblical figure of* the prophet Isaiah. One can find numerous expansions of biblical figures in the New Testament (e.g., 2 Tim. 3:8; Jude 14) from apocryphal sources, but none *introduces new biblical characters.*

67 J.B. Lightfoot, *Notes on the Epistles of St. Paul* (Peabody, MA: Hendrickson Publishers, 1995), 252. Emphasis added.

68 Metzger, *Introduction*, 163.

69 From Bishop Ellicott's *Commentary for English Readers*, as quoted in Daubney, *Use of the Apocrypha*, 19.

70 *The Commentary for Schools: Corinthians, the First Epistle,* ed. C.J. Ellicott, commentary by E.H. Plumptre (London: Cassell, Petter, Galpin & Co., 1883), 45.

71 *The Speaker's Commentary, Apocrypha* (Murray, 1888), vol. 2, 22-23 as quoted in *The General Epistles of St. James and St. Jude,* Alfred Plummer (London: Hodder and Stoughton, 1891), 70.

72 Both accuse God of bringing about sin, whether it be temptation to evil in James or God doing something to set a person astray in Sirach.

73 The Greek word translated "have rusted" is *katioō*. It occurs only twice in the entire Greek Bible (Sirach 12:11 and James 5:3). Moreover, the noun translated "rust" [Greek: *ho ios*] in James 5:3 is not found anywhere else in the New Testament. Yet, the same word in its verbal form is used in Sirach 29:9–10.

74 *Speaker's Commentary*, 22 as quoted in Daubney, *Use of the Apocrypha*, 24 FN 1.

75 The New Testament authors quote several works that are not part of anyone's Bible, formally citing (with introductory remarks) works non-canonical and even totally unknown (e.g., John 7:38; James 4:5). Perhaps the most famous of these is the formal citation of the apocryphal book of Enoch found in Jude 14:

> It was of these also that Enoch in the seventh generation from Adam prophesied, saying, "Behold, the Lord came with myriads of his holy ones, to execute judgment on all, and to convict all the ungodly of all their deeds of ungodliness which they have committed in such an ungodly way, and of all the harsh things which ungodly sinners have spoken against him."

Notice that Jude even goes so far as to say that the writer of Enoch "prophesied" when he composed this passage! Yet would anyone argue today, based on this formal citation alone, that the book of Enoch must be considered Scripture? Quotation does not equal canonicity, nor does the absence of citation argue *against* canonicity since several Old Testament protocanonical books are never directly or formally quoted (e.g., Judges, Ruth, Ezra, Nehemiah).

76 Our focus is to answer whether the deuterocanon was added or removed from the Bible. The texts presented here are sufficient to show a continuity between the New Testament and Catholicism and the current state of discontinuity within Protestantism. For a fuller explanation of how the New Testament usage affirms the inspiration of the deuterocanon, see *The Case for the Deuterocanon*, 1–37, 38–53.

77 See endnotes 20 and 21.

78 *Yadaim* 3:5, *Eduyoth*, 5:3.

79 As Eusebius puts it, "The leader of the Jews at this time was a man by the name of Barcocheba, who possessed the character of a robber and a murderer, but nevertheless, relying upon his name, boasted to them, as if they were slaves, that he possessed wonderful powers; and he pretended that he was a star that had come down to them out of heaven to bring them light in the midst of their misfortunes" *(Church History*, 4, 6, 2). Also see Finkelstein, *Akiba: Scholar, Saint, and Martyr*, (New York: Covici Friede Publishers, 1936), 269.

80 Moore, *Jewish Canon*, 140.

81 Justin Martyr, in his *First Apology*, 31 writes, "For in the Jewish war which lately raged, Barchochebas, the leader of the revolt of the Jews, gave orders that Christians alone should be led to cruel punishments, unless they would deny Jesus Christ and utter blasphemy." This blasphemy uttered was that

Bar Kokhba was the promised messiah.

82 Cf. Revelation 13:5.

83 *Avot of Rabbi Natan*, ch. 18.

84 Finkelstein, *Akiba*, 155–156.

85 Although Akiva was not the first to use "inclusion and exclusion" (he learned it from Nachum Ish Gamzu or Gimzo), it was a decisive change from his predecessor Eleazar ben Azariah who rebuked Akiva's methodology saying, "Even if you persist the whole day in extending and limiting, I shall not harken to you" (*Menahot* 89a). See Finkelstein, *Akiba*, 171–174.

86 John Bowman, "The Fourth Gospel and the Jews: A Study in R. Akiba, Esther, and the Gospel of John," Pittsburgh Theological Monograph Series, No. 8, (Eugene, OR: Pickwick Publications, 1975), 6.

87 *IDB* 4:585. Also see, *Qumran and the History of the Biblical Text*, ed. F.M. Cross and S. Talmon (Harvard University Press, 1975), 228–229.

88 "Owing to the influence of Akiba . . . there became predominant a school of rabbinic interpretation which laid emphasis upon every letter of the sacred text, and which drew the most farfetched and often the most singular conclusion from the most unimportant of details . . . It is quite evident that this type of interpretation, adhering firmly, as it does, to every single letter, could not rest satisfied which such a manifestly free translation as the Septuagint. As a result, the Judaism of this period [first thirty or so years of the second century A.D.] fashioned an entirely new Greek translation of the Old Testament. Aquila, a Greek proselyte and a disciple of Akiba, rendered every detail of the sacred text as precisely as possible into Greek, and he did not shrink from perpetrating the most appalling outrages to the whole essence of the Greek language." Alfred Rahlis, "History of the Septuagint Text" (in *Septuaginta: Id est Vetus Testamentum Graece Iuxta LXX Interpretes Editit Alfred Rahlfs, Deutsche Bibelgesellschaft*, lviii. Also, Gigot, *Introduction*, 284–285. Also Julio T. Barrera, *The Jewish Bible and the Christian Bible: An Introduction to the History of the Bible*, trans. W.G.E. Watson (Grand Rapids: Eerdmans, 1998), 314.

89 See Mishnah, *Yadayim* 3:5. Also see, John Bowman's *The Fourth Gospel and the Jews: A Study in R. Akiba, Esther, and the Gospel of John* (Pittsburgh: Pickwick Press, 1975). Also see *The Case for the Deuterocanon*, 95–99.

90 Akiva also made several other declarations that imposed the new norm, such as the reading of non-canonical books at service would lead to the loss of the future life. See Finkelstein, *Akiba,* 187.

91 *Tosefta Yadayim* 2:13 as it is quoted in Leiman, *Canonization,* 109. Also see Moore, *Jewish Canon*, 117–21.

92 Holy works required careful handling since they "defiled" the reader when touching it, which required ritual washing. Secular (that is non-inspired,

purely human works) could be read without any special care.

93 Louis Ginzberg, "Akiba Ben Joseph" in vol. 1 of *The Jewish Encyclopedia*, ed. Isidore Singer (New York: Funk and Wagnalls), 306.

94 The New Testament reflects this use. Last chapter, we saw how the New Testament employs Sirach, Wisdom, 2 Maccabees, and Tobit in debate and to establish certain Christological points. We will also see a continuing use of the deuterocanon to confirm doctrine within Christian theology and in debates against Jews. For a comprehensive analysis of the Christian use of the deuterocanon to confirm doctrine for the first four centuries of the Church, see *The Case for the Deuterocanon*, 105–249.

95 Ginzberg, "Akiba Ben Joseph," 306.

96 Finkelstein, *Akiba*, 270–271.

97 Ibid., 272.

98 "The reason for the Sanhedrin's frequent change of seat is to be sought in the turbulence of the period, but mainly, perhaps, in the Hadrianic persecutions; this, therefore, approximately establishes the *terminus a quo* of the Synod of Usha, while the *terminus ad quem* is indicated by the fact that Shefar'am, the later residence of Judah I., is mentioned as the next seat of the synod after Usha. The Galilean synod was convened, then, between these two dates—more exactly during the reign of Antoninus Pius, and after that emperor had, about 140, annulled the anti-Jewish laws instituted by Hadrian. For while Judah b. Baba had to suffer a martyr's death for his ordinations and these, therefore, must have taken place under Hadrian, this synod, though it was attended by large numbers of people and marked by special festivities, met unhindered; it must, therefore, have been convened after the annulment of the laws mentioned. The rabbinic sources give various and inconsistent accounts of the synod. Wilhelm Bacher and Samuel Krauss," "Synod of Usha," *JE*, vol. 11, 645.

99 Louise Ginzberg, "ANTONINUS PIUS (Titus Aurelius Fulvus Boionius Arrius Antoninus)," *JE*, vol. 1, 657. Emphasis added.

100 See J.N.D. Kelly, *The Oxford Dictionary of the Popes* (Oxford/New York: Oxford University Press, 1988), 7.

101 1 Clement 3:4 and 1 Clement 7:5 quote Wisdom 12:10, referencing a "place of repentance" [Greek, *metanoias topon*], the same words as Wisdom 12:10 [Greek, *topon metanoias*].

102 This allusion is confirmed by W.H. Daubney, F.X. Glimm, E.J. Goodspeed, R.M. Grant, A. Harnack, J.A. Kleist, D.R. Knopf, K. Lake, J.B. Lightfoot, J.P. Migne, C.C. Richardson, and J. Sparks. Westcott, however, calls this connection into doubt (Brooke F. Westcott, *The Bible in the Church: a Popular Account of the Collection and Reception of the Holy Scriptures in the Christian Churches* (New York: Macmillian and Co., 1887),

84–85), but elsewhere acknowledges that Clement did not restrict himself to only the protocanonical books (Westcott, *Bible*, 123).

103 Oesterley, *Introduction*, 125.

104 Emphasis added.

105 Greek, *dia charitos tou theou.*

106 1 Clement 42:1 and 47:1 respectively.

107 The Hebrew Esther never mentions God and refrains from explicitly religious actions, where Septuagint Esther—which includes the deuterocanonical sections—is replete with fasting, prayer, etc. Clement's description clearly comes from the Septuagint, not the Hebrew version. See Ralph J. Brabban II, *The Use of the Apocrypha and Pseudepigrapha in the Writings of the Apostolic Fathers* (Ph.D. diss., Baylor University, 1984), 350–351. Also, Martin Hengel, *The Septuagint As Christian Scripture: Its Prehistory and The Problem of the Canon* (Baker Academic, 2004), 115.

108 Wisdom 2:12 and Isaiah 3:9–10 indicate that both were of equal authority (Oesterley, *Introduction*, 125). Similarly, the *The Ante Nicene Fathers*, eds. Roberts and Donaldson (Grand Rapids: Eerdmans Publishers) acknowledges both passages. See *ANF* 1.140, FN. 19. Likewise, Migne, Muilenburg, Kraft, Goodspeed, Lake, and Sparks confirm this connection, as does Brabban, who calls it a "loose paraphrase" (Brabban, *Use of the Apocrypha*, 358–359). Westcott (Westcott, *Bible*, 84), Beckwith (Rodger Beckwith, *The Old Testament Canon of the New Testament Church and Its Background in Early Judaism* (Grand Rapids: Eerdmans, 1985), 427, FN. 208), Norman L. Geisler and Ralph E. MacKenzie's *Roman Catholics and Evangelicals: Agreements and Differences* (Grand Rapids: Baker Book House, 1995), 161, and others dispute this connection.

109 Irenaeus of Lyons, *Against All Heresies*, 3, 3, 4.

110 Polycarp, *Letter to the Philippians* 10:1–3. Emphasis added. The biblical references are cited. See *ANF* 1.35 FN 12–15. Also see Kirsopp Lake, *Apostolic Fathers* (Harvard University Press, 1960) 24, 294–297.

111 For example, Breen sees a link between *Similitude* 9:23 and Sirach 28:3 (Breen, *Introduction*, 64–65). Others see links between *Visions* 3.7.3 and Sirach 18:30; *Visions* 4, 3, 4 and Sirach 2:5; *Mandates* 5, 2, 3 and Tobit 4:19; also *Mandates* 10, 1, 6 and Sirach 2:3.

112 *The Shepherd of Hermas*, First Commandment, 1.

113 Did God create everything out of nothing, or did he create everything from pre-existing matter? Christians believe the former. Some protocanonical passages imply creation *ex nihilo* (e.g., Gen. 1:1; Ps. 124:8; 146:6; and Rom. 4:17), but only 2 Maccabees 7:28 teaches this doctrine explicitly.

114 Emphasis added.

115 *The Apostolic Fathers*, 2 eds. J.B. Lightfoot, et al., (Grand Rapids: Baker

Book House, 1990), 150, FN 12.

116 *Didache* 4:3–5.

117 Cf. *Second Clement* 16:4 and Polycarp's *Letter to the Philippians* 10:1–3.

118 Brabban, *Use of the Apocrypha*, 367–68.

119 See Thomas B. Falls and Justin Martyr, *The First Apology, The Second Apology, Dialogue with Trypho, Exhortation to the Greeks, Discourse to the Greeks, The Monarchy or the Rule of God.* Vol. 6. The Fathers of the Church. (Washington, DC: The Catholic University of America Press, 1948), 139.

120 Justin Martyr, *Dialogue with Trypho*, 71.

121 Ibid. Emphasis added.

122 Ibid., 72.

123 Ibid., 120. Emphasis added.

124 Justin may have inferred that it was Scripture since Hebrews 11:37 seems to allude to Isaiah's martyrdom. But the New Testament sometimes uses extra-biblical pseudepigraphic sources to expand on biblical characters (e.g., 2 Timothy 3:8 produces the names of the otherwise unnamed Egyptian magicians who opposed Moses apparently from the *Apocryphon of Jannes and Jambres* (Origen, *Commentary on Matthew* 27:8); Jude 14–15 expands on Enoch's condemnation of the world through a passage in the book of Enoch (1 Enoch)). This is substantially different from Hebrews 11:35, where the author introduces characters only mentioned in the deuterocanon (i.e., the Maccabean martyrs). For more arguments as to how the deuterocanon can be differentiated from true apocrypha, see *The Case for the Deuterocanon*, 259–274.

125 Eusebius's *Church History*, books 4, 26, 12–14.

126 Melito's list omits the books of Lamentations, Nehemiah, and Esther—and it possibly even includes the book of Wisdom. Even if Lamentations and Nehemiah are present (being included in other books), as some have argued, the omission of Esther remains unaccountable. Later Christian lists of the rabbinic canon will also point to doubts concerning Esther.

127 Some argue that Melito could not have had contact with the synagogue because dialogue between Jews and Christians had all but ceased due to tensions between the two groups. Antagonism indeed existed, but dialogue did nevertheless continue, as we saw in Justin's *Dialogue with Trypho the Jew* written only a few years earlier. Moreover, Melito's inquiry would be for information, not debate, and there is no reason to expect the rabbis to be antagonistic. When the two prospects of either inquiring at the synagogue in Sardis or making the arduous trek to Palestine to receive essentially the same answer are considered, Melito certainly would have chosen the former. If the Jews in Sardis were so antagonistic as not to answer Melito's inquiry, what hope would there be of an answer being secured among the rabbis in

Palestine? We do know that Jewish/Christian dialogues, as evidenced in the writings of the early Fathers, continued unabated throughout the first several centuries of the Church. They were pointed, but they continued.

128 Philip Schaff, *The Nicene and Post-Nicene Fathers Second Series Vol. I* (Eusebius *Church History, Life of Constantine the Great,* and *Oration in Praise of Constantine*) (Oak Harbor: Logos Research Systems, 1997), 3. Emphasis added.

129 Athenagoras, *Plea for Christians*, 9.

130 Irenaeus of Lyon, *Against Heresies*, 3, 3, 4.

131 Gigot, *Introduction*, 45 FN 4. For example, Irenaeus unambiguously attributed the deuterocanonical chapter in Daniel known as "Bel and the Dragon" to "Daniel the Prophet" (*Against Heresies*, 4, 5, 2 [Latin, *Quem (Deum) et Daniel Propheta, cum dixisset ei Cyrus rex Persarum*]) and does the same for the other deuterocanonical chapter "Susanna." Irenaeus twice quotes Baruch as the words of the prophet Jeremiah (*Against Heresies*, 4, 38, 1 [Latin, *Hoc significavit Jeremias Propheta;* and *Against Heresies*, 5, 35, 1]). He did this because Baruch was Jeremiah's secretary (Jer. 32:12–16; 36:1–32; esp. 45:1ff). The books of Jeremiah and Baruch became so closely associated in the early Church that Baruch was sometimes combined with Jeremiah, a practice goes back to the Jewish LXX scrolls (see Hengel, *Septuagint*, 113–14, esp. 114 FN 31). Irenaeus therefore contradicts the notion that only prophets can write prophetic writings since Baruch was Jeremiah's secretary.

132 *Against Heresies*, 2, 30, 11. Some Fathers (e.g., Ambrose and perhaps Bede) also understood Tobit to be prophetic.

133 Some scholars have challenged this early dating. For our purposes here, we will use its traditional dating.

134 The fragment reads, in part, "[T]he epistle of Jude, indeed, and two belonging to the above-named John—or bearing the name of John—are reckoned among the Catholic epistles. And the book of Wisdom, written by the friends of Solomon in his honor." Somehow—no one knows quite how—the Old Testament book of Wisdom made its way into this fragment as a part of somebody's New Testament. It may be that the relatively recent date of its composition (as late as 40 B.C., according to some scholars) led to the error. Alternately, the well-known prophecies of the "Son of God" in chapter two (combined with an awareness that the Jews had already rejected the book) led it to be identified so closely with Christianity. Later, Epiphanius also put Wisdom with the New Testament—along with Sirach as well (see Daubney, *Use of the Apocrypha*, 51).

135 Clark D. Lamberton, "Early Christian Painting and the Canon Of Scripture" in vol. 17, no.8:8 *Western Reserve University Bulletin.*

136 Since Tertullian's view of the canon remained unchanged through all three

periods, we will not differentiate these periods in our quotes. Tertullian's consistency in usage throughout these periods suggests that both Catholics and Montanists accepted the deuterocanon.

137 Like Clement of Rome, who offered Judith and Esther as examples of grace at work in godly women, Tertullian offers Rebecca and Susanna (*The Crown*, 4). The book of Baruch and the deuterocanonical portions of Daniel are undoubtedly treated as authentic continuations of Jeremiah and the protocanonical Daniel (Scorpion's *Antidote*, 8; *Against Hermogenes*, 44; *Against Idolatry*, 18; *Against the Gnostics*, 8). Tertullian attributes the book of Wisdom to Solomon (*Against the Valentinians*, 2; also, *Prescription Against the Heretics*, 7). In *Against Hermogenes*, Tertullian explicitly identifies 2 Maccabees 7:28 as "Scripture"; in another book (*Against Hermogenes*, 21) he does the same for Sirach: "Then, if God had been unable to make all things of nothing, the Scripture could not possibly have added that he had made all things of nothing [2 Macc. 7:28]." He refers to the book of Wisdom as one of "our Christian authorities" and affirms that its precepts were "taught by God" (*Concerning the Soul*, 1, 6). Beckwith believes Psalms 139:23 is quoted here instead of Wisdom 1:6. Roberts and Donaldson, on the other hand, reference only Wisdom 1:6 (see *ANF* 3.194). He makes no distinction between his quotations from the book of Wisdom and those from the protocanonical books (*Concerning the Soul*, 15). In fact, Tertullian references every book in the deuterocanon at least once—except for Tobit, but it is likely that he accepted it as well .

138 Tertullian, *In Answer to the Jews*, 4.

139 In his *Commentary on the book of Daniel,* Susanna he presents as a model for Christian imitation (*Commentary on Daniel*, 6:1 and 6:61). Hippolytus makes no distinction between protocanonical and deuterocanonical books, often quoting from both groups without qualification or distinction (*Commentary on Daniel*, 6:1, 55). In his treatise *Against Noetus* (2), he explicitly refers to the book of Baruch as "Scripture." Hippolytus is using Baruch as a prooftext for the Incarnation: "But they make use also of other testimonies, and say, Thus it is written: 'This is our God.'" Hippolytus cites 1 Maccabees 2:33 as the fulfillment of a prophesy given by Daniel (*The Anti-Christ,* 49 and *Commentary on Daniel*, 2:23 respectively). In his book, *Against the Jews,* he states twice that the book of Wisdom contains a prophecy about Christ. *Against the Jews*, 8–9, 10: "I produce now the prophecy of Solomon, which speaketh of Christ, and announces clearly and perspicuously things concerning the Jews; and those which not only are befalling them at the present time, but those, too, which shall befall them in the future age, on account of the contumacy and audacity which they exhibited toward the Prince of Life; for the prophet says [quotes Wisdom 2:12–20]." Hippolytus

makes no distinction or qualification between the Wisdom quote and the protocanonical quotations that surrounded this passage. In fact, he lists Wisdom among those books in which the knowledge of the mysteries of the Incarnation resides (*Commentary on the Song of Songs*, 1–2).

140 *Commentary on Daniel,* 6:1.

141 Clement of Alexandria, *Stromata* 1, 11.

142 Baruch he understood as the words of the prophet Jeremiah (*The Instructor*, 1, 10) and refers to it explicitly as "divine Scripture" (*The Instructor*, 2, 3). Clement also quotes the book of Sirach and calls it Scripture five times. The book of Wisdom Clement lauds as "the divine Wisdom" (*Stromata* 4, 16: "The divine Wisdom says of the martyrs [quotes Wisdom 3:1–4]"). Tobit is also quoted as Scripture in *Stromata* 2.23 (*Stromata* 2, 23: "This Scripture has briefly showed, when it says . . . [quotes Tob. 4:15]"). Also *Stromata* 4, 12.

143 See Westcott, *Bible*, 126–127. A simple quotation without distinction or qualification from Judith occurs in *Stromata* 2, 7. Cornely believes that the book of Maccabees is mentioned in *Stromata* 1, 21 and 5, 14. See E.P. Cornley, *Manuel D'Introduction Historique et Critique* à *Toutes les Saintes Ecritures*, Tome Premier (Paris: P. Lethielleux, Libraire-Editeur, 1907), 437. Like Tertullian, Clement appears to have accepted the book of Esdras as inspired Scripture as well.

144 Cyprian held Sirach to be inspired Scripture, actually stating that its author was "established in the Holy Spirit." Elsewhere, he refers to it as "[the] divine Scripture" (*On Morality*, 9: "Holy Scripture teaches and forewarns, saying . . . [quotes Sirach 2:1–5]"). Many of his quotes from Sirach are prefaced with the solemn formula "It is written" (see *Letter* 5, 2; also *On the Gift of Patience*, 17; *Glory of Martyrdom*, 16). Wisdom is likewise introduced as "divine Scripture" (*Letter* 80, 6; *On the Dress of Virgins*, 10). In chapter twelve of his *Exhortation to Martyrdom*, Cyprian introduces Wisdom 3:4 with these words: "The Holy Spirit shows and predicts." Wisdom is frequently quoted without apology or proviso of any kind (*Letter* 61, 1 quotes Wisdom 3:11 between Jeremiah 3:15 and Psalms 2:12 (LXX); *On the Dress of Virgins,* 1 quotes Wisdom 3:11 between Psalm 2:12, 49:16–17 and Proverbs 3:11–12; *Against the Jews* 3, 16 quotes Wisdom and Proverbs, et al.). He considers Bel and the Dragon and Susanna as authentic parts of Daniel. These deuterocanonical sections are said to have come from the prophet filled with the Holy Spirit (see *Exhortation to Martyrdom*, 9). They are also said to record the actions of God (*On the Lord's Prayer*, 21). Baruch is an authentic part of Jeremiah, according to Cyprian, and contains the true words of the inspired prophet (*On the Lord's Prayer*, 5). Baruch precedes quotes from 1 Kings 1:13 and Psalms 4:5. The book of Tobit, which is quoted without qualification or stipulation, is offered as an example

for Christian living (*On Morality*, 10 and *On the Gift of Patience*, 18). It is used to explain the power of prayer before God (*On the Lord's Prayer*, 33). Cyprian also cites, as did Polycarp before him, the book of Tobit for scriptural proof of the spiritual efficacy of almsgiving (*On Works and Alms*, 5.20). Cyprian found solace within the books of the Maccabees also and recommends the Maccabean martyrs to his Christian readers facing similar persecution (*Against the Jews*, 3, 17, especially *Exhortation to Martyrdom*, 9). The books are also used as Scripture in argument (*Against the Jews*, 3, 15). First Maccabees 2:62–63 is quoted as "holy Scripture" (*Letter* 54.3). And again: "And fear not the words of a sinful man, for his glory shall be dung and worms. Today he is lifted up, and tomorrow he shall not be found, because he is turned into his earth, and his thought shall perish," quoting Hebrews 2:5 and 1 Maccabees 2:62–63. Both 1 and 2 Maccabees are quoted right along with protocanonical sources, with no hesitation or expectation of contradiction. Cyprian clearly considers both deuterocanon and protocanon to be equally authoritative portions of the same inspired corpus (see *Against the Jews*, 3, 4 and *Against the Jews*, 3.52).

145 *History of Susanna*, 1: "Your letter, from which I learn what you think of the Susanna in the book of Daniel, which is used in the churches." *History of Susanna*, 2: "In answer to this, I have to tell you what it behooves us to do in the cases not only of the History of Susanna, *which is found in every Church of Christ*" (emphasis added). For a further discussion on the implications of Origen's assertions for the canon, see *The Case for the Deuterocanon*, 253–254.

146 He makes this known both in the *History of Susanna* (e.g., *History of Susanna*, 13), as well as his other works (e.g., *Homily 1 On Leviticus*, I. *History of Susanna*).

147 See Edward W. Reuss, *History of the Canon of the Old Testament* (Edinburgh: James Gemmell George IV, 1890), 130–31.

148 Latin, *sacris libris*; Greek, *hierais biblous*.

149 Origen, *Letter to Africanus*, 4.

150 Hengel, *Septuagint*, 10.

151 This is seen in Origen's employment of Proverbs 22:28 and Deuteronomy 19:14.

152 The same accusation is made elsewhere in Origen's works. For example, in his *Homilies on the Book of Leviticus*, Origen addressed the "impious" Jewish presbyters who read the book of Leviticus literally. He writes, "But it behooves us to use against the impious presbyters the words of the blessed Susanna, which they indeed repudiating, *have cut off from the catalogue of divine Scripture the history of Susanna. But we receive it, and appositely adduce it against them, saying,* 'I am straitened on every side: for if I do this thing (follow the letter of the Law) it is death to me; and if I do it not. I shall not

escape your hands.'" *Homily 1, Commentary on Leviticus* 1. Emphasis added.

153 *History of Susanna*, 5.

154 *First Principles*, 2, 2. Emphasis added. Also *Commentary on John 28, 122*, where after quoting Psalms 51:13 [11], he wrote, "And if someone accepts in addition the saying [quotes Wisdom 1:5]. It will appear clearly to be proven that the Holy Spirit flees from the soul that has dealt treacherously, even if he was there previously before deceit and sin." These two texts are the only qualifications Origen makes in regard to the deuterocanon. See *The Case for the Deuterocanon: Evidence and Arguments*, 234–235.

155 *Commentary on the Psalms*, 1 quoted in Eusebius's *Church History*, 6, 25.

156 "By this drowning, however, it is not to be supposed that God's providence as regards Pharaoh was terminated; for we must not imagine, because he was drowned, that therefore he had forthwith completely perished: 'for in the hand of God are both we and our words; all wisdom, also, and knowledge of workmanship' [Wis. 7:16], *as Scripture declares*" (*First Principles*, 3, 1, 14) and "For, naturally, whatever is infinite will also be incomprehensible. Moreover, *as Scripture says*, "God has arranged all things in number and measure [Wis. 11:20] . . . " (*First Principles*, 2, 9, 1). Emphasis added.

157 *Commentary on the Psalms*, 1 quoted in Eusebius's *Church History*, 6, 25.

158 See Westcott, *Canon*, 180; Reuss, *History*, 185–186; Gigot, *Introduction*, 54; H.H. Howorth, "The Influence of Jerome on the Canon of the Western Church," *JTS* 11 (1909/1910), 323; et al. Given Hilary's dependence on Origen, we may, with caution, use Hilary's work to point us in the right direction in understanding Origen's list.

159 *Prologue to Psalm*, 15. Emphasis added.

160 This fascination with the mystical correspondences behind numbers and letters is also found in Epiphanius. It should also be noted that Hilary's list differs from Origen only in that he includes the twelve and omits Maccabees (Hengel, *Septuagint*, 63).

161 Hengel, *Septuagint*, 11.

162 Origen understood the deuterocanon to be "divine Scripture" containing "divine things" (see *Homily* 1, *Commentary on Leviticus*, 1 and *History of Susanna*, 15).

163 See *Homily* 5 *in Psalms* 36, 5.

164 *Contra Celsum*, 3, 72: "In reply to which we say that, since wisdom is the knowledge of divine and human things and of their causes, or, as *it is defined by the word of God*, the breath of the power of God, and a pure influence flowing from the glory of the almighty; and the brightness of the everlasting light, and the unspotted mirror of the power of God, and the image of his goodness."

165 *Contra Celsum*, 3, 60.

166 See *Selecta in Psalms* 34:2; *Homily* 5 *in Psalms* 36:5; *Selecta in Psalms* 88:32;

Prologue to Song of Songs; and *Homily* 6 *in Isaiah* 5.

167 Reuss, 85. Reuss's statement is directed toward Theophilius of Antioch's description of Saint Paul's letter to Timothy. Theophilius calls Paul's letter *ho theios Logos* (the divine Word). Since the exact same phrase is used here in Origen to describe a passage in Sirach, Reuss's words are equally applicable.

168 Origen, *Contra Celsum*, 7, 12: "But he ought to know that those who wish to live according to the teaching of Sacred Scripture [Greek, *kata tas theias zoen graphas*] understand the saying, "The knowledge of the unwise is as talk without sense" [Sir. 21:18], and have learned "to be ready always to give an answer to every one that asks us a reason for the hope that is in us" [1 Pet. 3:15].

169 See *Homily 18 in the book of Numbers*, 3; *Homily 24 in Joshua*, 2; and *Selecta in Psalms 120:6*.

170 *First Principles*, 2, 1, 5. He also quotes *The Shepherd of Hermas, Commandment* 1, 1 and Psalms 33:6.

171 *Homily on Numbers*, 27, 1.

172 Dionysius quotes Tobit in *Against Germanus*, 10. He also uses Wisdom 7:25 to show how fitting is John 4:24's definition that "God is Spirit" (see *Letter to Dionsyius of Rome*, 4). Most strikingly, Dionysius introduces Sirach as "*divine oracles*" [Latin, "*oraculorum vocem*"] in *On Nature*, 3. In the same work, Dionysius quotes Sirach after a string of quotations from Psalms, as if Sirach 16:29–30 came from the same inspired corpus (*On Nature*, 5).

173 Archelaus, *The Acts of the Disputation with the Heresiarch Manes*, 29.

174 Methodius quotes Sirach, Wisdom, and Proverbs in the same passage without any qualification or distinction (see *The Banquet of the Ten Virgins, Discourse* 1, 3). Similarly Wisdom 4:2 is included among the quotations from the Protocanon without distinction or qualification. (Also see *Banquet of the Ten Virgins, Discourse*, 11.1; *Concerning Simeon and Anna*, 6; et al.) He explicitly introduces a passage from Wisdom as Scripture (*The Banquet of the Ten Virgins, Discourse* 2, 3: "bringing forward the Scripture which says [quotes Wis. 3:16]"). The deuterocanon he uses often to confirm doctrine. In the *Banquet of the Ten Virgins,* Sirach and Wisdom are both employed as scriptural proof against the idea that polygamy ended during the time of the prophets (*The Banquet of the Ten Virgins, Discourse* [Marcella ed.], 1, 3). Wisdom is also used to show how "the Word" accuses idolaters (see *The Banquet of the Ten Virgins, Discourse* 2, 7. The book of Wisdom is also said to be a book "full of virtue." Methodius also follows this quote from Wisdom 15:10–11 with a quote from 1 Timothy 2:4 without any distinction or qualification). Quotations from the same book are employed to confirm the good of Creation, as well as certain matters of eschatology (see *Concerning the Resurrection*, 8 and 14). He uses Sirach against certain teachings of Origen

(*Extracts from Created Things*, 9). The same book is elsewhere quoted with the solemn formula "It is written" (see *Concerning Simeon and Anna*, 12: "as it is written [quotes Ps. 13:8] and in another place . . . [quotes Sir. 22:7] which plainly, in the revered Gospels, our Lord signified, when he said to the Jews . . . [quotes Matt. 23:38]"). Methodius quotes Baruch without qualification or distinction (*Concerning Simeon and Anna*, 10) and praises Judith and Susanna as models of Christian virtue (*The Banquet of the Ten Virgins, Discourse* 11, 14). For these reasons and others, there is no controversy that Methodius accepted the deuterocanon as Scripture in the fullest sense (see Westcott, *Bible*, 138).

175 Lactantius, *Institutes*, 4, 8 quoting Sirach 24:3–5.

176 The Arians denied that Christ was fully divine, consubstantial with the Father. They believed that there was a time where the Son was not. Nicaea defined that the Son is consubstantial (*homoousios*) with the Father.

177 Breen, *Introduction,* 361 FN.

178 Ibid.

179 *Church History* lists the book of Wisdom as being among the New Testament books used by Irenaeus of Lyon (5, 8, 8); Baruch was referred to as a prophet of God in *Demonstratio Evangelica*, 6, 19; Wisdom is quoted as a divine oracle (*Praeparatio Evangelica*, 1, 9); Susanna is quoted as Scripture (ibid., 6, 11); and Wisdom is likewise quoted as Scripture (ibid., 11, 14).

180 Eusebius includes the deuterocanon under the category "controverted and yet familiarly used by many." See Westcott, *Bible*, 153.

181 Modalism is the belief that the three persons of the Trinity are not three distinct eternal persons, but three manifestations or modes of the one God.

182 Alexander of Alexandria, *Letter to Alexander*, preserved in Theodoret's *Church History*, 1, 3. Emphasis added.

183 Earlier, we quoted from Ginzberg who recognized this point when he wrote, "The religious persecutions of Hadrian had devastated the country, depopulated the cities, *and made the intellectual development of the Jews impossible.* Had these conditions lasted much longer there would have been an end to the Jewish people in the Roman empire" (Louis Ginzberg, "ANTONINUS PIUS," *JE*, vol. 1, 657).

184 Origen wrote to Julius Africanus, "In all these cases consider whether it would not be well to remember the words, 'You shall not remove the ancient landmarks which your fathers have set.' Nor do I say this because I shun the labor of investigating the Jewish scriptures, and comparing them with ours, and noticing their various readings. This, if it be not arrogant to say it, I have already to a great extent done to the best of my ability, laboring hard to get at the meaning in all the editions and various readings; while I paid particular attention to the interpretation of the Seventy, lest I might to be found to accredit any forgery to the Churches which are

under heaven, and give an occasion to those who seek such a starting point for gratifying their desire to slander the common brethren, and to bring some accusation against those who shine forth in our community. And I make it my endeavor not to be ignorant of their various readings, lest in my controversies with the Jews I should quote to them what is not found in their copies, and that I may make some use of what is found there, even although it should not be in our scriptures. For if we are so prepared for them in our discussions, they will not, as is their manner, scornfully laugh at Gentile believers for their ignorance of the true reading as they have them" (*History of Susanna*, 5). As a side note, Epiphanius of Salamis claims that Origen's work eventually included two more columns that sported two unknown Greek texts as well (*Weights and Measures*, 18).

185 Origen wrote, "For so Aquila, following the Hebrew reading, gives it, who has obtained the credit among the Jews of having interpreted the Scriptures with no ordinary care, and whose version is most commonly used by those who do not know Hebrew, as the one which has been most successful" (*History of Susanna*, 2).

186 Athanasius uses the Greek word for "canonized" (*kanonzomena*), and it appears that he is one of the first known authors to apply this term to Scripture (see Bruce, *Canon*, 77). Beckwith places its first usage sometime in the fourth century (Beckwith, *Canon*, 1). Oesterley holds that Amphilochius, bishop of Iconium is the first (Oesterley, *Introduction*, 3). Robert and Tricot identify both Origen and Athanasius among the first (Robert and Tricot, *Guide to the Bible* (New York: Tournai, 1960), 69; also *ABD*, 1.838). Regardless of which is correct, Athanasius is one of the earliest Fathers to use the term *canon* to refer to a collection of books in Scripture.

187 Mishnah *Yadayim* 3:5 says that "All holy scriptures defile the hands."

188 The Old Testament background of the formal reading of Scripture can be traced back to Ezra and Nehemiah. Nehemiah 8:2–4 speaks about Ezra reading the Law of Moses to the people while standing on a wooden pulpit which was specially constructed for this purpose. The synagogue adopted the use of an elevated platform (sometimes called a *bema*) for this station in the liturgy. An elevated place for the reading of Scripture was incorporated into Christian architecture as well. The fact that Christian liturgical practice inherited the reading of Scripture is so well accepted that it hardly needs proof. Justin Martyr, for example, provides one of the earliest accounts of the Christian liturgy and he speaks of the special place for the reading of Scripture (see Justin Martyr, *First Apology*, 67).

189 The strict identification of canon and inspiration may not be shared by all Protestant groups (e.g., Lutherans).

190 Translated by R. Payne-Smith. From *Nicene and Post-Nicene Fathers, Second*

Series, Vol. 4., eds. Philip Schaff and Henry Wace. (Buffalo: Christian Literature Publishing Co., 1892), 550–555.

191 Ibid.

192 Melito (*Extracts*) omits Esther, Baruch, and the Letter; Origen (*Commentary on Psalms*) includes Esther and the Letter; Hilary (*Prologue to the Psalms*) includes Esther, Baruch, and the Letter; Cyril of Jerusalem (*Catechetical Lectures*) includes Esther, Baruch, and the Letter; Amphilochius (*Iambis of Seleucus*) accepts Esther with qualification and omits Baruch and the Letter; Gregory of Nazianzus (*Carmen Dogmatica*) omits Esther, Baruch and the Letter; Epiphanius (*Against Judaism*) includes Esther and Baruch; (*Against the Anomoeans*) includes Esther; (*On Weights and Measures*) includes Esther, Baruch, and the Letter; Jerome (*prefaces*) includes Esther and omits Baruch and the Letter.

193 Athanasius's exclusion of Esther and inclusion of Baruch in the canonical category may reflect Jewish practice. For example, Melito of Sardis omitted Esther from the books accepted by the Jews in Palestine, and Epiphanius of Salamis states that Baruch was still read in the synagogues of his day.

194 Those who have difficulty believing that Athanasius did not believe that the first category alone was entirely accurate should pay attention to his own words. He himself says that for "greater accuracy" (*All' heneka ge pleionos akribeias*) he added the second category. Its addition to Athanasius's Festal Letter, as he himself says, was a matter of necessity (*anankaiōs*). The Greek text used for the *Thirty-Ninth Festal Letter* comes from Johannes Kirchhofer, *Quellensammlung zur Geschichte des Neutestamentlichen Kanons bis auf Hieronymus* (Zürich: Meyer and Zeller, 1844), 7–9. Emphasis added.

195 Unfortunately, some translators (like the one cited above) add "merely" so that it reads, "the latter being [merely] read." The word "merely" is rightly bracketed because it is not part of the original text [*Kai homōs agapêtoi, kakeinōn kanonizomenōn kai toutōn anaginōskomenōn oudamou tōn apokryphōn mnêmê*]. The insertion, however, does give a false impression to the reader that Athanasius didn't think much about the books in the second category. Even when the reading of these books certainly refers to being read from the special station in the liturgy for the reading of Sacred Scripture.

196 The two books of Maccabees are omitted. However, most scholars believe that they too were included in the second category.

197 Athanasius, *Homily on the Book of Numbers 27:1.*

198 For example, Athanasius in his work *Against the Heathen*, 1, 17, 3, cites Wisdom 14:21 as "Scripture" and later in the same work (*Against the Heathen*, 2, 44), he places the words of Wisdom 13:5 on the lips of the Son in *On the Opinion of Dionysius*, 9, Wisdom 7:25 as coming "from the Scripture." He also quotes the deuterocanon explicitly as "Scripture" in the anti-Arian work *Four Discourses Against the Arians*, 2, 32, which seems

to quote Wisdom 13:5 as Scripture in *Four Discourses Against the Arians*, 2, 35, he quotes Judith 8:16 as "Scripture." And in *Four Discourses Against the Arians*, 2, 45, he cites Wisdom 9:2 within a series of citations from "divine scriptures." Even more telling is his use of the deuterocanon in the *Letter of the Council of Egypt*, 3, that quoted Wisdom 1:11 as "holy Scripture" and later in the same chapter quotes Psalms 49:16 and Sirach 15:9 as the words of the Holy Spirit. Also, in his letter to Alexander of Thessalonica (284–305) Athanasius cites Sirach 30:4 as "holy Scripture."

199 Athanasius, *On the Incarnation of the Word*, 4.

200 Athanasius writes, "And Dionysius accordingly acted as he learned from the apostles. For as the heresy of Sabellius was creeping on, he was compelled, as I said before, to write the aforesaid letter, and to hurl at them what is said of the Savior in reference to his manhood and his humiliation, so as to bar them by reason of his human attributes from saying that the Father was a son, and so render easier for them the teaching concerning the Godhead of the Son, when in his other letters he calls him from the scriptures the word [John 1:1], wisdom [1 Cor. 1:24, 30], power [1 Cor. 1:24], breath [Wis. 7:25], and brightness of the Father [Wis. 7:26; Heb. 1:3]."

201 Athanasius wrote, "Again, when the bishops said that the Word must be described as the true power and image of the Father, in all things exact and like the Father, and as unalterable, and as always, and as in him without division (for never was the Word not, but he was always, existing everlastingly with the Father, as the radiance of light." Compare this with Wisdom 7:26: "For she [God's wisdom] is a reflection of eternal light, a spotless mirror of the working of God, and an image of his goodness."

202 "Thus they have called the Father the Fount of Wisdom (Bar. 3:12) and Life (Ps. 36:9; Prov. 13:14), and the Son the Radiance of the Eternal Light (Wis. 7:26), and the Offspring from the Fountain, as he says, 'I am the life,' and, 'I wisdom dwell with prudence' (Prov. 8:12; John 14:6). But the Radiance from the Light, and Offspring from Fountain, and Son from Father, how can these be so fitly expressed as by 'coessential' [*homoioousios*]? And is there any cause of fear, lest, because the offspring from men are coessential, the Son, by being called coessential, be himself considered as a human offspring too? Perish the thought! Not so; but the explanation is easy. For the Son is the Father's word and wisdom; whence we learn the impassibility and indivisibility of such a generation from the Father . . . [Athanasius concludes later in the next paragraph] . . . though we know God to be a Father, we entertain no material ideas concerning him, but while we listen to these illustrations and terms, we think suitably of God, for he is not as man, so in like manner, when we hear of 'coessential,' we ought to transcend all sense, and, according to the proverb, 'understand by

the understanding what is set before us' (Prov. 23:1); so as to know, that not by will, but in truth, is he genuine from the Father, as Life from Fountain, and Radiance from Light."

203 This quote is persevered in Theodoret's *History of the Church*, II. 8, 18–43, 45–8.

204 This evidence flatly contradicts Churton's claim that the Council of Sardica formally excluded the book of Wisdom from the canon. See W.R. Churton, *Uncanonical and Apocryphal Scriptures* (London, 1884), 14.

205 Cyril and Athanasius's *Thirty-Ninth Festal Letter* lists 22 books that include Baruch and the epistle of Jeremiah. Cyril differs from Athanasius in that he includes Esther among the "canonical" books where Athanasius places it among those that are read.

206 Cyril of Jerusalem, *Catechetical Lectures,* 4, 33, 35–36.

207 Ibid., 11, 15.

208 Cyril uses Sirach 3:21–22 to confirm the incomprehensibility of God (*Lectures* 6, 4). Wisdom 13:5 is used to demonstrate that God can only be known through our observations by analogy. And he uses Baruch 3:14–15 to demonstrate Christ's deity.

209 Cyril of Jerusalem, *Catechetical Lectures,* 14, 25 and 16, 31 respectively.

210 Ibid., 9, 16.

211 Cyril and Athanasius made similar prohibitions.

212 See Bruce, *Canon*, 80.

213 Origen: "found in all the Church" and "[Tobit and Judith are] . . . used in all the churches" (*History of Susanna*, 2, 13, etc.); Athanasius: "the Fathers decreed [that these books] should be read to those who have lately come into the fold, and seek to be catechized, and who study to learn the Christian doctrine" (*Thirty-Ninth Festal Letter*); Cyril of Jerusalem: "But let all the rest [not listed as canonical, but is read in the Church] be put aside in a secondary rank. And whatever books are not read in churches, these read not even by yourself" (*Catechetical Lectures*, 4, 36).

214 This appears to be the consensus among Protestant scholars. Westcott believes this canon to be a later addition (Westcott, *Bible*, 170). Ryle and Reuss call it spurious (Ryle, *Canon*, 228 and Reuss, *History*, 180). Ellis, following Theodore Kahn, calls it a later appendage (Earle E. Ellis, *The Old Testament in Early Christianity: Canon and Interpretation in Light of Modern Research* (Wipf and Stock Publishers, 2003), 21). F.F. Bruce, likewise, calls its genuineness into question (*Canon*, 80). The Protestant historian Philip Schaff (*History of the Christian Church*, vol. 2, 420) likewise states, "This catalogue is omitted in several manuscripts and versions, and probably is a later insertion from the writings of Cyril of Jerusalem."

215 For example, there are instances in Church history where copies of the

Bible were prohibited due to the pervasive circulation of adulterated translations and/or heretical footnotes. These measures were disciplinary in that they only affected the practice in limited localities and they lasted only until the problem was resolved. These prohibitions were not doctrinal (i.e., they did not constitute a repudiation of Scripture per se nor the publication and distribution of Scripture), but disciplinary. Had they been doctrinal the prohibition would have been applied universally throughout the Church and would have lasted in perpetuity.

216 Hilary of Poitiers, *Prologue to the Psalms,* 15.

217 See Howorth, *Jerome*, 324.

218 Hilary of Poitiers, *On the Trinity*, 4, 42: "As you have listened already to Moses and Isaiah, so listen now to Jeremiah inculcating the same truth as they [quotes Baruch 3:36–38]."

219 Hilary of Poitiers, *On the Trinity*, 1, 7: "from the prophet's voice." Also, *Tract*. In Ps. 118:8 [Latin, "*et rursum propheta*"]; Ps 118. *Lettera* 19, 8; Ps. 118. *Lettera* 19, 8 [Latin, "*Et Spiritus Dei, secundum prophetam, replevit orbem terrarum*"]; Wisdom 1:7 [quoted between Acts 17:28 and Jeremiah 23:24 without qualification]; *Tract*. In Ps. 135, 11 [Latin, "*docet propheta dicens*"]; *Letter*, 9, [Latin, "*Clamat propheta dicens*"].

220 Hilary of Poitiers, *Letter 8;* Psalms 118 (Littera V.9); *Tract. Psalms* 128, 9; and *Tract. De Psalms* 41, 12.

221 Hilary of Poitiers, *Prologue to Psalms,* 20, *Tract*. In *Psalms* 140:5; and *Ex Operibus Historicis Frag*. 3, 24.

221 Hilary of Poitiers, *Tract in Psalms* 125, 6 (Jth. 16:3). Hilary continues by quoting Isaiah, John, and Colossians without any distinction or qualification.

223 Hilary of Poitiers, *Tract in Psalms* 129, 7.

224 Hilary of Poitiers, *On the Trinity*, Book 4, 8 quotes Isaiah, John, Mark, 1 Timothy, Malachi, Psalms, and Matthew before Susanna and follows with quotes from Isaiah, Acts, Psalms, John, 1 Timothy, and Exodus all without distinction or qualification. Also see *Tract in* 52; Ps. 19.

225 Hilary of Poitiers, *Tract in Psalms* 134.25; *Lib. Contra Const. Imp*. 6.

226 Hilary of Poitiers, *On the Trinity*, Book 4, 16. Emphasis added.

227 Latin, "*Sed haec divinae Scripturae ratio non recipit. Omnia enim secundum Prophetam facta ex nihilo sunt.*"

228 Basil the Great, *On the Holy Spirit,* 19.

229 Basil the Great, *Letter 6, Ad Nectarii Uxorem*, 2.

230 Basil the Great, *Letter* 8, 10.

231 Ibid., 12.

232 Basil the Great, *Letter* 38, 8.

233 Basil the Great, *Hexaemon Homilies,* 6, 10.

234 See Westcott, *Bible*, 168.

235 Gregory of Nazianzus, *Oration,* 30, 13.
236 Gregory of Nazianzus, *Oration,* 43, 23.
237 *Oration* 7, 14, 19 quotes Job, Wisdom, Psalms, and Jeremiah; *Oration* 21, 17 quotes John, Psalms, 1 Corinthians, Hebrews, Wisdom, John, Genesis, Psalms, and Revelation; *Oration* 40, 6 quotes 2 Kings, Luke, Matthew, Acts, and Wisdom; in *Oration* 41, 14 Wisdom is used to confirm that the Holy Spirit is the author of spiritual regeneration. It is quoted between quotes from John and 1 Samuel; *Oration* 42, 6 quotes Romans, Ezekiel, Psalms, Wisdom, Zechariah, and Hebrews.
238 Gregory of Nazianzus, *Oration* 2, 64.
239 See *Oration* 37, 18.
240 Gregory of Nazianzus, *Oration* 45, 15: "which are also called in the Scripture *the Seed of the Chaldeans*." Emphasis added.
241 *Oration*, 43, 70. The examples run from chapter 70 to 75.
242 Gregory of Nazianzus, *Orations* 37, 18 quotes Sirach 3:10 with the qualification, "and if you will accept this saying." Despite this single qualification, Gregory still uses Sirach to confirm doctrine.
243 Gregory of Nazianzus, *Carmen*, 1, 1, 12, as quoted in W.A. Jurgens's *The Faith of the Early Fathers* (Collegeville, Minnesota: The Liturgical Press, 1979), 2, 42.
244 Amphilochius writes, "Here then most certainly you have the canon of the divinely inspired scriptures" (*Carmen*, 2, 2, 8 as quoted in Jurgens, *FEF*, 2, 66).
245 Breen, *Introduction*, 397. Also see *Iambics to Seleucus*, 2.
246 Amphilochius, *Oration I*, 2: "Hence, do we confirm that? Out of the other prophet's voice, saying, 'After this he is seen on earth and conversed with men.'"
247 See *The Oxford Dictionary of the Christian Church*, 2 ed., eds. F.L. Cross and E.A. Livington, (New York/Oxford: Oxford University Press, 1983), 232.
248 *DS-H* 84. Baruch is omitted, but it can be reasonably assumed that it was included in Jeremiah.
249 This assumes, of course, that canon 60 of the Council of Laodicae is spurious. As a side note, Howorth believes Jerome, who was Pope Damasus's secretary at this time and was in sympathy with its pronouncement on the canon (that accepted the deuterocanon), but later abandoned it for his new idea of Hebrew Verity (which adopted the shorter rabbinic canon). See Howorth, *Jerome*, 322.
250 Ibid.
251 Epiphanius of Salamis, *Panarion*, Section 1, Heresy 8 (Judaism continued), 6, 1–4.
252 For a discussion of retention of the deuterocanon within Judaism and its implications, see *The Case for the Deuterocanon*, 85–94.
253 Epiphanius of Salamis, *Panarion*, Heresy 76 ("Against Anomoeans"),

Refutation of Proposition 5, 22.5.

254 Epiphanius, On Weights and Measures, ed. James Dean (Chicago Ill: Chicago University Press), 1934, 19-20.

255 Epiphanius quotes Wisdom 3:13–14 as "another passage the Holy Spirit says prophetically, both for the ancient and for [the] future generations" (*Panarion*, Section 2, Heresy 6, 15, 7); Sirach 13:16 as "Scripture" (*Panarion*, Section 2, Heresy 13, 8, 1); Sirach 14:5 as "Scripture" (*Panarion*, Section 3, *Scholion* 70a); Baruch 3:36 as "Scripture" (*Panarion*, Section 4, Heresy 37, 2, 1); Wisdom 7:2 and Sirach 10:11 as "Scripture" (*Panarion*, Section 4, Heresy 44, 18, 1); Wisdom 3:1–4 is quoted as "[The Lord] . . . taught it through Solomon in a book entitled Wisdom" (*Panarion*, Section 4, Heresy 43, 44, 2); and Wisdom 3:4–7 is said to be corroborated by the "other scriptures" (*Panarion*, Section 4, Heresy 43, 48, 2).

256 Epiphanius appeals to Baruch 3:20 to refute Patripassianism (*Panarion*, Section 4, Heresy 37, 2.1 "Against Noetus"); Sirach 17:24 to show that post-baptismal forgiveness of sins is still possible (*Panarion*, Section 4, Heresy 38 "Against the Valesians" 6, 1); quotes Wisdom 7:2 and Sirach 10:11 to explain Origen's theory of the Resurrection (*Panarion*, Section 4, Heresy 43 "Against the Origenists" 18, 1); quotes Wisdom 2:23; 1:13; 2:35 to demonstrate that Adam, though created immortal, was changed in the fall and that God is not the origin of death (*Panarion*, Section 4, Heresy 43 "Against the Origenists" 28, 2); he uses Wisdom 1:14 to demonstrate that God ordered Creation so that it would endure (*Panarion*, Section 4, Heresy 43, "Against the Origenists" 39, 4); Photinus had cited Baruch 3:38, and Epiphanius uses it to prove that the Son pre-existed before he became incarnate (*Panarion*, Section 6, Heresy 51 "Against the Photinians" 3, 6); uses Wisdom 1:7 as an "authoritative proof" that the Holy Spirit is Lord (*Panarion*, Section 6, Heresy 54 "Against the Pneumatomachi" 1, 4).

257 Nestorianism believed that there are two separate persons (divine and human) in the incarnate Christ.

258 See Westcott, *Bible*, 174; Bruce, *Canon*, 81.

259 John Chrysostom, *Concerning Statues*, 7.

250 John Chrysostom, *Against Marcionists and Manicheans.*

261 See *Homilies on First Corinthians*, 15.

262 John Chrysostom, *Homilies on John*, 48

263 Ambrose holds up Tobit as a model of virtue (*On the Duty of the Clergy*, 3, 16, 96); he also uses Tobit as explicitly as a prophetic book (Hengel, *Septuagint*, 68 FN 33); Judith, Jephthah, Isaac, Moses, and Elisha are all held up as Christian models (*On the Duty of the Clergy*, 3, 13, 82–85); Ambrose draws parallels between Judith and Rahab as if they both came from the same sacred text (*Concerning Virgins*, 2, 4, 24); Wisdom is quoted

as "Scripture" (*On the Duty of the Clergy*, 2, 13, 64–65, "[quotes Wisdom 7:29] . . . We have spoken of its beauty, and proved it by the witness of Scripture [continues with other quotes from Wisdom]." It is also quoted as containing the words of the Lord (*On the Holy Spirit*, 3, 6, 36), and he also quotes Wisdom explicitly as Scripture with the formal introduction "it is written" (*On the Holy Spirit*, 3, 18, 135: "Let them learn that we teach by *authority of the Scriptures*; for it is written: [quotes Wisdom 7:22]." Emphasis added). Sirach is called "Scripture" (*On the Duty of the Clergy*, 1, 2, 5). The Maccabees are used as examples of godly courage (*On the Duty of the Clergy*, 1, 40, 205–208 and *On the Duty of the Clergy*, 2, 24). The book of 2 Maccabees is formally quoted with "It is written" (*On the Duty of the Clergy*, 3, 18, 107): "The sacrifice which was consumed in the time of Moses was a sacrifice for sin, wherefore Moses said, as is written in the book of the Maccabees" and the words of 1 Maccabees are said to come from the lips of a saint (*Letter* 40, 33: "And now, O Emperor, I beg you not to disdain to hear me who am in fear both for yourself and for myself, for it is the voice of a Saint which says [quotes 1 Maccabees 2:7]"). The deuterocanonical portions of Daniel are also quoted as authentic parts of that prophetic book (see *On the Duty of the Clergy*, 1, 3, 9; 2, 4, 11; and 2, 11, 57–58; *On the Holy Spirit*, 3, 6, 39; and *Concerning Virgins*, 2, 4, 27–28).

264 The Septuagint groups modern day 1 and 2 Samuel with 1 and 2 Kings into four books of Kings (1 Samuel=1 Kings (or Kingdoms) and 2 Kings=4 Kings (or Kingdoms)).

265 See Ellis, *Old Testament*, 25.

266 Rufinus of Aquileia, *Commentary on the Symbol of the Apostles*, 36–38.

267 Origen, *First Principles*, Preface, 8. Emphasis mine.

268 Rufinus of Aquileia, *Commentary on the Twelve Patriarchs, Blessing of Joseph*, 5. Latin, "*Quod et propheta praedixerat, ubi ait* [quotes Baruch 3:36–38].

269 Rufinus of Aquileia, *Commentary on the Twelve Patriarchs, Blessing of Gad*, 3, and in his *Commentary on the Twelve Patriarchs, Blessing of Joseph*, 3.

270 Rufinus of Aquileia, *Commentary on the Twelve Patriarchs, Blessing of Joseph*, 46.

271 Rufinus of Aquileia, *Apology Against Jerome*, 2.33. Emphasis added.

272 Wisdom 7:26 (which Hebrews 1:3 uses to describe the Son's relation to the Father) was also used by several Church Fathers to describe the consubstantial relationship of the Son and Father. Rufinus uses this same text, without explicitly citing it, to do the very same thing. Rufinus says that Christ is the brightness of the eternal light (Latin, *aeternae lucis*). Wisdom 7:26 says that God's wisdom is the brightness (candor) of God's "eternal light" (*lucis aeternae*). Wisdom also describes God's wisdom as "unique" or "only-begotten" (Greek, "*monogenes*," and Latin, *unicus*) in Wisdom 7:22: the same Latin term that Rufinus uses to describe the Son ("*Et ideo recte unicus dicitur*

Filius. Unicus enim et solus est") (Migne, *PL* 21, 348).

273 "They were added in our Church, as is well known, on account of the Sabellian heresy, called by us 'the Patripassian,' that, namely, which says that the Father himself was born of the Virgin and became visible, or affirms that he suffered in the flesh. To exclude such impiety, therefore, concerning the Father, our forefathers seem to have added these words, calling the Father 'invisible and impassible.' For it is evident that the Son, not the Father, became incarnate and was born in the flesh, and that from that nativity in the flesh the Son became 'visible and passible.' Yet so far as regards that immortal substance of the Godhead, which he possesses, and which is one and the same with that of the Father, we must believe that neither the Father, nor the Son, nor the Holy Ghost is 'visible or passible.' But the Son, in that he condescended to assume flesh, was both seen and also suffered in the flesh. Which also the prophet foretold when he said, 'This is our God: no other shall be accounted of in comparison of him. He has found out all the way of knowledge, and has given it unto Jacob his servant and to Israel his beloved. Afterward he showed himself upon the earth, and conversed with men' (Bar. 3:36–38) (Rufinus, *Commentary on the Symbol of the Apostles*, 5). Note that Rufinus did not list Baruch among the canonical books.

274 Although this is jumping the gun a bit, we should note that the Fathers up to this point who expressed the most doubt about the deuterocanon (Amphilochius, Gregory of Nazianzus, Rufinus) all had personal contact with or were admirers of St. Jerome.

275 More than eighty percent of the Old Testament quotations that appear in the Greek New Testament are direct quotes from the Septuagint.

276 Kelly, *Jerome*, 160. Also see *The Cambridge History of the Bible: The West from the Father to the Reformation*, vol. 2, ed. G.W.H. Lampe (Cambridge: Cambridge University Press, 1969), 92.

277 Fuller, *Old Testament Canon, NCC*, 26.

278 Gigot, *Introduction*, 58. Emphasis added.

279 Jerome's manuscripts circulated extensively throughout the Western Church, much to the chagrin of Rufinus, who complained, "But how are we to regard those translations of yours which you are now sending about everywhere, through our churches and monasteries, through all our cities and walled towns?" (*Apology Against Jerome*, 2, 32). Indeed, the rapidity and expansiveness of Jerome's writings is impressive. For details, see H.H. Howard's "The Influence of St. Jerome on the Canon of the Western Church," *JTS* (1911), 13, 1–17.

280 Jerome, *Preface to Samuel and Kings, Helmeted Prologue*. Emphasis added.

281 Jerome, *Preface to the Books of Solomon*.

282 Jerome, *Preface to the Book of Ezra*. Emphasis added.

283 Jerome, *Letter*, 107, 12, *To Laeta*.

284 Metzger, *Introduction*, 178.

285 Howorth, *Jerome*, 319. Also see *Dictionary of Christian Antiquities*, eds. William Smith and Samuel Cheetham (London: John Murray, 1876), 1,278; Bruce, *Bible*, 90–93; and Hengel, *Septuagint*, 50 FN 80.

286 See Howorth, *Jerome*, 339.

287 Rufinus, *Apology*, Book 2, 33.

288 *Apology Against Jerome*, 2, 33–34. Emphasis added. Rufinus's argument concerns the primacy of the Septuagint as well as other issues. However, Jerome's rejection of the deuterocanon is a logical consequence of his Hebrew Verity. Therefore, Rufinus's comments are *ad rem* to our discussion.

289 See Appendix 1, "*Sola Scriptura* and the Problem of the Canon," for a more in-depth discussion of the problem of individuals determining the canon.

290 Reuss, *History*, 194.

291 See Gigot, *Introduction*, 58–59, 81; Steinmueller, *Companion*, 78.

292 Breen, *Introduction*, 443.

293 Jerome, *Prologue to John* [Latin, "*Liber quoque Tobiae, licet non habeatur in Canone, tamen quia usurpatur ab Ecclesiasticis viris*"].

294 Jerome, *Commentary in Eccles.*, 8.

295 Jerome, *Prologue to Jeremiah*.

296 Jerome, *Letter* 77, 4, *to Oceanus*.

297 Jerome, *Commentary on Isaiah*, Book 2, 3:12; *Letter* 77, 6; 108, 22; 118, 1; 148:2,16, 18.

298 Jerome, *Commentary on Jeremiah*, Book 4, 21:14; *Commentary on Ezekiel*, Book 6, 18:6; and *Letter* 64, 5.

299 Jerome, *Commentary on Isaiah*, Book 8, 24:4; *Commentary on Ezekiel*, Book 6, 18:6; *Letter* 57, 1 *To Pammachius;* and *Letter* 125, 19, *To Rusticus*.

300 Jerome, *Commentary on Isaiah*, Book 1, 1:24; *Commentary on Zechariah*, Book 3, 14:9; and *Commentary on Malachi*, 3:7ff.

301 Jerome, *Commentary on Galatians*, Book 1, 3:2, [Latin, "*de quo (Spiritu Sancto) alibi scribitur*"] and *Breviarium in Psalmos*, Ps 9, [Latin, "*Et alibi (ipse Deus ait)*"].

302 Jerome, *Against Pelagians*, Book 2, 30; *Letter* 7, *To Chromatius, Jovinus, and Eusebius,* and again in *Against the Pelagians,* 2, 30.

303 Jerome, *Letter* 3, 1 (374) *to Rufinus the Monk*; *Letter* 22, 9–10 *to Eustochium; Letter* 1, 9 *To Innocent*.

304 Jerome, *Letter* 48 *To Pammachius*, 14.

305 Jerome, *Letter* 54, 16, *To Furia*, 16.

306 Jerome, *Letter* 65, 1 [Latin, "*Ruth et Esther et Judith tantae gloriae sunt, ut sacris voluminbus nomina indiderint.*"].

307 Examples in history abound. The Gnostic Marcion, who believed the Old

Testament chronicled the work of an evil materialistic god, disparaged the Old Testament and the Gospels, accepting only the writings of Paul and an adulterated version of Luke. The Ebionite sect did away with the letters of Paul, preferring to accept only the Gospels since Paul's statements about the Jewish ceremonial law contradicted their beliefs. Others can be listed as well. In all cases, the heretics placed their own personal theological views over the word of God.

308 Augustine, *On Christian Doctrine*, book 2, 12.

309 "The authority of these books has come down to us from the apostles through the successions of bishops and the extension of the Church, and, from a position of lofty supremacy, claims the submission of every faithful and pious mind" (*Against Faustus,* 11, 5). Also see *Against Faustus*, 28, 2 and 33, 6.

310 Augustine, *On Christian Doctrine*, book 2, 13.

311 Augustine, *Against Faustus*, book 33, 9.

312 Charles J. Costello, *St. Augustine's Doctrine on the Inspiration and Canonicity of Scripture* (Ph. D. diss., The Catholic University of America, 1930), 78.

313 Augustine discusses the inspiration of the Septuagint later in chapter 15 of the same book. His concern at this point is not the canon, but how to correctly interpret the text when comparing the Old Latin, the Septuagint, and the Hebrew.

314 Augustine, *On the Soul and Its Origins*, 1, 1, (Migne, *PL* 44, 980–981).

315 Augustine, *City of God,* 17, 19–20. Emphasis added.

316 Augustine, *City of God*, 18, 36.

317 Augustine, *City of God*, 11, 30 [Latin, "*multis sanctarum Scripturum locis*"]; *City of God*, 13, 16 and 2, 21: "Holy Scripture" [Latin, "*sacra Scriptura*"]; *On the Trinity* Book 13, 16, 21: "Holy Scripture" [Latin, "*sacra Scriptura*"]; *On the Trinity* Book 14, 1, 1: "Holy Scripture" [Latin, "*sacra Scriptura*"]; *On Lying*, 30–31: "Scripture"; *Of the Morals of the Catholic Church*, 27: "could anything agree better with these passages than what is said in the Old Testament of wisdom [quotes Wisdom]". In *Reply to Faustus the Manichaean* Book 11, 9, he appeals to Wisdom in a controversy as a "divine authority." *Concerning the Nature of Good, Against the Manicheans*, 24; in *A Treatise on Grace and Free Will*, 8, Wisdom is said to contain "divine commandments"; *Sermons on the Gospel*, Sermon 12, 12: "holy Scripture."

318 Augustine, *Of the Morals of the Catholic Church*, 29. Also, *Of the Morals of the Catholic Church*, 31–32.

319 Augustine, *Sermons on the Gospel, Sermon* 8, 7.

320 Augustine, *City of God*, 14, 7.

321 Costello, *St. Augustine's Doctrine on the Inspiration and Canonicity of Scripture*, 78.

322 Augustine, *City of God,* 14, 11 also refers to it a part of the "ancient

Scriptures"; *City of God,* 21, 9 [Latin, "*Legitur quippe et in veteribus Scripturis*"]; *On the Trinity,* 15, 11, 20; *The Enchiridion* 66: "saying of Scripture"; *On the Spirit and the Letter,* 26: "Scripture," and later in the same passage it is described as being from the "holy Scriptures"; *On Nature and Grace,* 33: "Scripture"; *On Marriage and Concupiscence,* book 1, 29–32; *Sermons on the Gospel,* Sermon 56, 4.

323 Augustine, *On the Sermon on the Mount,* 48: "From this carelessness and ruinous security the Holy Spirit recalls us, when he says by the prophet [quotes Sirach 5:5–6]."

324 Augustine, *City of God,* 15, 23; *Of Holy Virginity,* 44; *On Patience,* 11; *On Care to Be Had for the Dead,* 21: "holy Scriptures."

325 Augustine, *Of Holy Virginity,* 19–20.

326 Augustine, *Reply to Faustus the Manichaean,* 20, 35.

327 Augustine, *Concerning Man's Perfection in Righteousness,* Book 1, 8 [31].

328 Augustine wrote, "But since we are speaking here of bearing pain and bodily sufferings, I pass from this man, great as he was, indomitable as he was: this is the case of a man. But these Scriptures present to me a woman of amazing fortitude, and I must at once go on to her case. This woman, along with seven children, allowed the tyrant and executioner to extract her vitals from her body rather than a profane word from her mouth, encouraging her sons by her exhortations, though she suffered in the tortures of their bodies, and was herself to undergo what she called on them to bear [2 Macc. 7]. What patience could be greater than this? And yet why should we be astonished that the love of God, implanted in her inmost heart, bore up against tyrant, and executioner, and pain, and sex, and natural affection? Had she not heard, 'Precious in the sight of the Lord is the death of his saints'? [Ps. 116:15]. Had she not heard, 'A patient man is better than the mightiest'? [Prov. 16:32]. Had she not heard, 'All that is appointed you receive; and in pain bear it; and in abasement keep your patience: for in fire are gold and silver tried'? [Sir. 2:4–5]. Had she not heard, 'The fire tries the vessels of the potter, and for just men is the trial of tribulation'? [Sir. 27:6]. These she knew, and many other precepts of fortitude written in these books, which alone existed at that time, by the same divine Spirit who writes those in the New Testament" (*Of the Morals of the Catholic Church,* 43).

329 Augustine, *On the Soul and Its Origin,* book 1, 13 and book 3, 18.

330 See Augustine, *On Grace and Rebukes,* 41.

331 Bruce, *Canon,* 97.

332 *DS-H* 186.

333 Bruce, *Canon,* 97.

334 Pope Innocent I approved these canonical lists as did subsequent North

African councils (e.g., the Sixth Council of Carthage (419) and the later Council of Trullo (Quinisext) in the East in 692).

335 The title is "*Commentariorum Zachariam Prophetam ad Exsuperium Tolosanum Episcopum, Libri Duo*" Migne, *PL* 25, 1450. See William Barry, *The Tradition of Scripture: Its Origin, Authority and Interpretation*, (London/New York/Bombay: Longmont, Green and Company, 1906), 138.

336 See Gigot, *Introduction*, 61.

337 Pope St. Innocent I, Letter *Consulenti tibi* to Bishop Exsuperius of Toulouse, 7. *DS-H* 213.

338 From Kevin Knight, *Nicene and Post-Nicene Fathers*, Second Series, vol. 14, eds. Philip Schaff and Henry Wace. Trans. Henry Percival (Buffalo, NY: Christian Literature Publishing Co., 1900.) *NPNF*, 14, 438, revised and edited for New Advent. http://www.newadvent.org/fathers/3816.htm.

339 Ibid., 453–454, canon 24 (Greek, canon 27).

340 Ibid., 438. Emphasis added.

341 The canon of the church in Ethiopia appears to be one of the most unique collections of the ancient Church. In addition to the deuterocanon, the Ethiopian canon included books, such as Enoch, Jubilees, 3 and 4 Ezra, and Psalms 151, which were not part of anyone's canon. (See Hans Peter Rüger's "The Extent of the Old Testament Canon" in *The Bible Translator* 40 (1989): 301–303; also Bruce Metzger's article "Bible" in the *Oxford Companion to the Bible*, (New York: Oxford University Press, 1993), 79. Metzger adds one more book to the list above: Joseph ben Gurion's (Josippon's) *Medieval History of the Jews and Other Nations*).

342 It is generally agreed that the Christian churches in Armenia accepted the larger canon for its canonical scriptures. See Breen, "*Introduction*," 468; Westcott, "*Bible*," 239–240.

343 A native of France, Cassian traveled east and entered a monastery in Bethlehem and for some time visited the desert Fathers in Egypt. John Chrysostom ordained him a deacon in Constantinople. He traveled to Rome and was ordained a priest, and then finally to Marseilles, France where he founded two monasteries.

John Cassian quotes Sirach as Scripture: "Wherefore, as Scripture says, 'when you go forth to serve the Lord stand in the fear of the Lord, and prepare your mind'" (*Institutes*, 4:37). And he references Wisdom as Scripture: "[A]s Scripture itself testifies: 'For God made not death, neither does he rejoiceth in the destruction of the living'" (*Third Conference of Abbot Chaermon*, 7, quoting Wisdom 1:13).

344 Theodoret was born in Antioch near the end of the fourth century. At an early age, he became bishop of Cyrus. He is known for his role in combating Monophysitism and Nestorianism. Theodoret accepted the

deuterocanon as inspired Scripture. See Theodoret, *Church History*, 3, 11 and *Letter* 136, *To Cyrus Magistrianus*.

345 Vincent was a semi-Pelagian monk at Lerins's island monastery who opposed Augustine's and Prosper's definitions of grace. Vincent's most famous work is his *Commonitorium,* in which he gives his famous "canon of Vincent of Lerins," which gives the marks of authentic teaching. Vincent's only use of deuterocanonical books appears in these words: *"[T]he divine Oracles cry aloud,* 'Remove not the landmarks, which your fathers have set,' [Prov. 22:28] and 'Go not to law with a Judge,' [Sir. 8:14] and 'Whoso breaketh through a fence a serpent shall bite him,' [Eccles. 10:8]" (*Commonitory*, 21, 51). Vincent makes no distinction among the quotes from Proverbs, Ecclesiastes, and Sirach. All three are included among the divine oracles.

346 Although attributed to Denis the Areopagite (mentioned by the apostle Paul in Acts 17:34) the author of the works bearing this name was almost certainly a sixth-century Christian. Pseudo-Dionysius's *The Divine Names,* which became quite popular in the early Church, especially in the Middle Ages, was a major influence on the theology of St. Thomas Aquinas. Pseudo-Dionysius unquestionably accepted the deuterocanon. The books are used so extensively in *The Divine Names* that to enumerate the references would go quite beyond the scope of our survey.

347 Pope Anastasius II, Letter to the Bishops of Gaul "*Bonum Atque Iucundum*" (August 23, 498). Pope Anastasius II quotes Sirach with the formal appellation "It is written." It is followed by a quote from the Gospel of John with no qualification or distinction between the two.

348 *Synopsis of Sacred Scripture,* 1–3. It reads, "All divinely inspired Scripture belongs to us Christians. The books are not undefined but defined, and have canonical status. The books of the Old Testament are [lists the protocanon omitting Esther]. The canonical books of the Old Testament are therefore twenty-two in number, equal in number to the letters of the Hebrew alphabet. Beside these there are also other books of the same Old Testament, which are not canonical and which are read only to the catechumens. These are [lists the deuterocanon with Esther] . . . these are not canonical. So much then for the books of the Old Testament, to the canonical and the non-canonical."

349 Judith is missing in some manuscripts.

350 There is much dispute over the exact nature of this papal decree. According to Breen, "This decree is not found the same in the different codices. It is by some scribed to Damasus (366–384); by others to Gelasius (492–496); and by others to Hormisdas (514–523). Cornely believes that it was originally a decree of Damasus that was afterwards enlarged by Gelasius. All agree that it was an authentic promulgation from the Roman see in that

period" (Breen, *Introduction*, 366).

351 Reuss, *History*, 158–159.

352 Ellis, following Swete, dates this work around the second or early third century (Ellis, "*Old Testament*," 24 FN. 74).

353 These lists are based on Henry B. Swete's *Introduction to the Greek Old Testament* (KTAV, 1978).

354 The Codex Ephraemi Rescriptus was once a complete copy of the Septuagint composed around the fifth century. However, it was taken apart, partially erased, and used over again. Today, it survives only in parts. The original order of its boo*ks cannot be determined.*

354 The Codex Basilano-Vaticanus (N) and Codex Venetus (V) appear to be two halves of an *original codex. They were compiled in the eighth century* (Swete, *Introduction*, 130).

356 The Septuagint includes 1 and 2 Samuel and 1 and 2 Kings under the heading 1–4 Kings.

357 The Codex Alexandrinus contains some late Christian *additions. For example, the Psalms of Solomon (which Hengel argues was never part of the LXX) and the Odes (which contain prayers from the New Testament) were added in the fifth century.* See Hengel, *Septuagint*, 58 FN 3, 59.

358 Hengel believes the omission of 2 and 3 Maccabees, 1 Ezra, Baruch, and Letter of Jeremiah may be lacunae in the text (Hengel, *Septuagint*, 57).

359 Breen, *Introduction*, 468.

360 Leontius of Byzantium quotes Sirach, Wisdom, and Baruch as Scripture, *Contra Nestor. Et Eutych.* [Latin, *ait Scriptura* (quoting Sirach 21:21)/Greek, *kata ten Graphen*] and [Latin, quem Scriptura dicit (Wisdom 2:10)/Greek, *kata ton hen Graphe*] and [Latin, *Verum et illud ostendemus e Scriptura veteri. Nam manifesto Jeremias id alicubi dicit his verbis: Hic deus noster est* (Baruch 3:36–38)/Greek, . . . *touto Jeremias anaphandon, Outos ho Theos* . . .].

361 Leontius, *Adversus Nestorianos*, Book 3.

362 Gregory the Great, *Moral Treatises*, 19, 21.

363 See Gigot, *Introduction*, 66; also Breen, *Introduction*, 469.

364 Gregory the Great, *Pastoral Care*, Part 3, 20; *Commentary on Job* 10:8 and 6:24.

365 Art Sippo, "Dr. Sippo utterly refutes Webster on the Canon."

366 See *Pastoral Care,* Book 3, 30 and *Commentary on Job* Book 2, 2, 20 respectively.

367 Breen, *Introduction*, 474. It appears likely that Gregory accepted Baruch and Judith, but didn't have an occasion to quote them.

368 Art Sippo, "Dr. Sippo utterly refutes Webster on the Canon."

369 Primasius, *Commentary on the Book of Revelation*, 1 (Migne *PL* 77, 119).

370 Primasius, *The Incarnation of Christ*, 4, 13.

371 Breen, *Introduction*, 467.

372 As quoted in Westcott, *Bible*, 193.

373 Reuss, *History*, 239.

374 2 Timothy 3:15. The Greek literally reads, "Every Scripture"—that is, every individual Scripture contains these qualities.

375 John B. O'Connor, "Isidore," *CE*, 8:187.

376 Isidore of Seville, *Etymologies*, Book 1, 3–9.

377 Ibid. Emphasis added. Baruch is likely included with Jeremiah.

378 Isidore of Seville, *De Ecclesiasticis Officiis*, 1, 9, 4–5, and 7. Emphasis added.

379 Isidore of Seville, *Prologue to the Books of the Old Testament*, Book 1, 7–8. Emphasis added.

380 See Breen, *Introduction*, 467–468.

381 See D. S. Margoliouth, "The Use of the Apocrypha by Moslem Writers," *IJA* 12.44 (1916), 10–12.

382 See Breen, *Introduction*, 477.

383 Ildefonsus, *Treatise on Baptism*, 79.

384 This may be Anastasius Sinaita's work, but this identification is doubtful. See Westcott, *Bible*, 224–25.

385 It also commends the Wisdom of Sirach to those who have recently joined the Church. See Barry, *Tradition*, 136.

386 "Dr. Sippo utterly refutes Webster on the Canon," on Art Sippo's website, accessed August 24, 2017, http://art-of-attack.blogspot.com/2008/01/dr-sippo-utterly-refutes-webster-on.html.

387 Oesterley, *Introduction*, 128.

388 Bede, *Ecclesiastical History*, Book 5, 24.

389 Bede, *De Temporum Ratione*, (Migne, *PL* 90, 539). Emphasis added.

390 Breen, *Introduction*, 486–87.

391 Daubney also finds Bede, in his *Church History*, 1, 27, giving an answer from Pope Gregory to Augustine where the pope's remarks appear to be echoing 2 Maccabees 5:19. See Daubney, *Use of the Apocrypha*, 57.

392 Bede, *Commentary on the Revelation*, 4.

393 The Iconoclasts forbade Christians from using religious art (particularly icons and statues) because they wrongly believed the use of these objects to be idolatrous.

394 John Damascene, *The Orthodox Faith*, 4, 17.

395 Ibid.

396 See Epiphanius, *On Weights and Measures*, 4. This dependence is noted in Westcott, *Bible*, 220; Reuss, *History*, 249; Gigot, *Introduction*, 65; and Breen, *Introduction*, 477.

397 John Damascene, *Orthodox Faith*, 4, 15: "The divine Scripture likewise says that 'the souls of the just are in God's hand' [Wis. 3:1] and death cannot lay hold of them."

398 John Damascene, *Orthodox Faith*, 4, 6: "And although the holy Scripture says, 'Therefore God, your God, has anointed you with the oil of gladness,' it is to be observed that the holy Scripture often uses the past tense instead of the future, as for example here: '*Thereafter he was seen upon the earth and dwelt among men*' [Bar. 3:38]. For as yet God was not seen nor did he dwell among men when this was said. And here again: 'By the rivers of Babylon, there we sat down; yea wept.' For as yet these things had not come to pass." As you can see, Baruch 3:38 is quoted as Scripture between Psalms 14:7 and 137:1 without distinction or qualification.

399 John Damascene, *Orthodox Faith*, 4, 16 [quoting Bar. 3:38] and *Orthodox Faith*, 4, 18.

400 John Damascene, *Orthodox Faith*, 1, 9: "For God is a fire consuming all evils: or from [the Greek] *theasthai*, because he is all-seeing [2 Macc. 10:5]: for nothing can escape him, and over all he keepeth watch."

401 Alcuin, *Carmina*, 6. Migne, *PL* 101, 731–734.

402 Alcuin, *Against Elipandus*, book 1, 18.

403 Alciun, *De Virtutibus et Vitiis*, 15, 18.

404 Second Council of Nicaea, *Action VII Under Proof II* and *Canon,* 16.

405 Breen believes this manuscript is evidence of Pope Gregory the Great's acceptance of the deuterocanon as Scripture (Breen, *Introduction,* 481).

406 The name of Nicephorus's work is *Stichomentry.*

407 Nicephorus, *Letter to Pope Leo III*, (Migne, *PG* 100, 189–190); *Antirrheticus I Adv. Constantinus Corp.*, (*PG* 100, 249–250); *Antirrheticus I Adv. Constantinus Corp.*, (Migne, *PG* 100, 443–444).

408 See *Apologeticus pro Sacris Imaginibus*, (Migne, *PG* 100, 727–728).

409 Nicephorus, *Antirrheticus III Adv. Constantinus Corp.*, (Migne, *PG* 100, 473–474).

410 Nicephorus, *Apologeticus pro Sacris Imaginibus*, (Migne, *PG* 100, 751–752).

411 Rhabanus Mauras, *De Institutione Clericorum*, II, ch. 53. Rhabanus, like Isidore, notes the correspondence of seventy-two books of Scripture with the number of prophets elected by Moses and the number of disciples Jesus sent to preach.

412 On the other hand, Walafrid introduces the book of Baruch with the following: "The book which is called Baruch is not found in the Hebrew canon, but only in the Vulgate edition, as also the epistle of Jeremiah. For the knowledge of the readers, they are written here, for they contain many things relating to Christ and the last times" (*Preface to Baruch* as quoted in Breen, *Introduction,* 489).

413 Migne, *PL* 113, 732.

414 Migne, *PL* 113, 740.

415 Compare Strabo's words in Migne, *PL* 113, 1167, with Jerome's words in his preface to the books of Solomon in Migne, *PL* 27, 1308.

416 See Migne, *PL* 113, 1183–1232A.
417 Pope Nicholas I, *Ad Universos Episcopos Gallae* (Migne, *PL* 119, 902). Also see Gigot, *Introduction,* 67 and A. F. Loisy's *Histoire du Canon de l'Ancien Testament*, (Paris: Letouzey et Ane, 1890), 158–159.
418 Despite the contradictions within these decrees, the East may have understood them as affirming the deuterocanon as Scripture along with 3 and 4 Maccabees.
419 Westcott, *Bible*, 223; Breen, *Introduction,* 478; Oesterley *Introduction*, 128; and Steinmueller, *Companion*, 79.
420 This number is debatable. Only a few bishops attended at the beginning, but the number grew to about 102 as the council proceeded.
421 Constantinople IV, Canon 10 (Latin, *divina manifesto clamente scripture* / Greek, *tes theias . . . graphes*).
422 Reproduction of Codex Toletanus can be found at http://bdh-rd.bne.es/viewer.vm?pid=d-1723042.
423 Notker Balbulus, *De Interpretibus Divinae Scripturae*, 3 (Migne, *PL* 131.996) as quoted in Breen, *Introduction,* 490–91. Emphasis added.
424 See *The Case for the Deuterocanon*, 222–231 for a partial survey of these unqualified intermixed quotations.
425 Daubney, *Use of the Apocrypha*, 57.
426 Gigot, *Introduction*, 68–69. Emphasis added.
427 Westcott, *Bible*, 209.
428 Burchard of Worms, *Decr.* III. 217.
429 Ivo of Chartres, *Decr.* IV. 16.
430 Gratian, *Decr. I. dist.* 15. C. 3.
431 See *Dispute of a Jew with a Christian.*
432 Honorius of Autun, *Gemma Animae*, IV. 118.
433 Hugh of St. Victor, *De Scripturis et Scriptoribus Sacris.*
434 Ibid.
435 "There are, besides, in the Old Testament certain other books, which are read, indeed, but are not within the *Corpus Scripturarum*, or in the authentic canon. These are Tobias, Judith, Maccabees, and that which is inscribed the Wisdom of Solomon, and Ecclesiasticus [Sirach] (*De Sacramentis*, Preface).
436 Bruce, *Canon*, 99–100.
437 Breen, *Canon,* 497.
438 Rupert of Deutz, *Commentary on Genesis*, 31.
439 Compare with Jerome's *Preface to the Book of Judith.*
440 Peter of Cluny, *Letter Against Peter of Bruys*, Letter 2, Book 1 (Migne, *PL* 188, 751) as quoted in Breen, *Introduction*, 499. Also see Reuss, *History*, 257. Emphasis added.
441 For example, Peter of Cluny calls 1 Maccabees "the truthful Scriptures"

(*Letter Against Petrobrusiani*); he introduces Sirach as "the divine philosopher" (*Letter*, 34); in this treatise against the Jews, Peter quotes Baruch as coming from "the prophet or the prophetic man" (*Against the Jews*, 2), and Sirach is quoted as coming from God (*Against the Jews*, 4).

442 Rudolf of Flavigny, *In Leviticus*, 14, Preface.

443 Peter Comestor, *Preface to the Book of Joshua.*

444 Peter Comestor, *Historia Scholastic*, 13.

445 Peter Comestor, see *Commentary on Daniel*, 2 and *Against Rufinus*, 11:33.

446 *Epistola ad Hugonem. De modo et ordine legendi Script* (Migne, *PL* 139, 1129–39).

447 John of Salisbury, *Letter* 143. Emphasis added.

448 Peter of Blois, *Rationale div. Off.* 59.

449 See "The Fourth Lateran Council" (1215), *CE* 9, 18.

450 Latin, *Cum Autem Scriptum Sit* (section 70).

451 Bonaventure, *Preface to Commentary on the Book of Wisdom*, as quoted in Breen, *Introduction*, 503–504.

452 Breen, *Introduction*, 503.

453 Hugh of St. Cher, *Preface to the Books of Judith and Sirach* as quoted in Breen, *Introduction*, 506.

454 Thomas appeals to the deuterocanon throughout his *Summa Theologiae* not only in his objections, but also in the replies and his *sed contra*. He calls the book of Wisdom "divine Wisdom" (*Summa Theologiae*, I. Q. 109, Art. 2, *sed contra* et al.) and quotes it explicitly as holy Scripture (*Summa Theologiae*, I. Q. 1, Art. 3, *sed contra*; also, I. Q. 19, Art. 12, Obj. 2). Thomas uses Wisdom 11:20 to answer whether the particular punishments of Adam and Eve were suitably appointed in Scripture; also *Summa Theologiae*, II. Q.164, Art. 2, *sed contra*. He quotes it as an authentic part of the Old Testament (*Summa Theologiae*, I-II, Q. 106, Art. 1, Obj. 1). He even put the words of the book of Wisdom on the lips of Christ, who *is* the Divine Wisdom (*Summa Theologiae*, III. Q. 55, Art. 6. *sed contra*). Tobit is seen as Scripture (*Summa Theologiae*, III. Q. 5. Art. 6. Reply 1.). First Maccabees is included among other citations from the Old Testament without qualification (*Summa Theologiae*, II-II, Q. 64. Art. 4. Obj. 1). Based on 2 Maccabees, St. Thomas responds to difficulties as to whether suffrages can be made for the damned (*Summa Theologiae*, III. Q. 71. Art. 5. Obj. 1 and Reply). He interprets Baruch 3:38 as a prophecy concerning Christ (*Summa Theologiae*, III. Q. 40. Art. 1. Obj. *sed contra*). All of these examples come from a single one book of Thomas Aquinas. The examples could be multiplied.

455 *Summa Theologiae*, II-II, Q. 110, Art. 3, Reply 3. Emphasis added.

456 Robert Holet, *Postilla super Lib. Sapientiae*, 1, lect. 2 as quoted in Breen, *Introduction*, 503. Emphasis his.

457 Thomas Netter, *Doctrinale Fidei*, II, 20.

458 In section 14, the council fathers quote Sirach 24:23. Wisdom 5:6 is quoted in section 24. Sirach 24:28–29 and 1:5 are quoted as the words of God. Susanna (Dan. 13:42) is also used in section 38 (see *Decrees of the Ecumenical Councils*, ed. Norman P. Tanner (Georgetown University Press, 1990).

459 Emphasis added.

460 As quoted in Westcott, *History*, 211. Emphasis his.

461 See Breen, *Introduction*, 507.

462 *DS-H* 1025.

463 Westcott, *Bible*, 211.

464 As quoted in Westcott, *Bible*, 212–213. Emphasis added.

465 Daubney, *Use of the Apocrypha*, 62.

466 *Sacrorum Concilium Nova et Amplissima Collectio* (Mansi), 21, 885 as quoted in Breen, *Introduction*, 504. Emphasis added.

467 Including Alfrick, Burchard of Worms, Ivo of Chartres, Gratianus, Peter of Cluny, Stephen Harding, Gilbert Crispin, Honorius of Autun, Aegidius, Peter of Riga, John Beleth, Peter of Blois, the Fourth Lateran Council, Albert the Great, Bonaventure, Alexander Neckam, Robert Grosseteste, Thomas Aquinas, Robert Helot, Thomas Netter, the Council of Vienne, Andrew Horne, Clement VI, and John of Ragusa.

468 See Norman Geisler and Ralph MacKenzie, *Roman Catholic and Evangelicals: Agreements and Differences* (Grand Rapids: Baker Books, 1997), 164.

469 *DS-H* 1333–1335.

470 Previous ecumenical councils may have only sanctioned the canons of Hippo and Carthage as part of the African Code.

471 As done in the most ancient Christian bibles, including the Great Codices *Aleph, A,* and *B*.

472 Council of Florence, session 6 quotes Tobit 12:20; session 7 quotes Susanna (Dan. 13:9), and session 9 quotes Wisdom 5:21.

473 Geisler, *Roman Catholicism*, 164 FN 20.

474 *DS-H* 1304.

475 According to the *Acts of Florence*, 2 Maccabees was mentioned by the Catholic Doctors, but it was largely irrelevant to the discussion. As James Jorgenson notes, "The tradition of the Catholic Church, whether Latin or Greek, witnesses that it prays and has always prayed for the dead. Unless there is a purification after death, this prayer would be in vain; for this prayer is neither for those who are already in glory nor for those who are banished to hell . . . The point of dispute will center upon whether the scriptures, the Fathers, and the universal liturgical custom of prayer for the dead justify the doctrine of purgatory. In other words, does purification for sins take place after death, and if so, how is it accomplished?" (James Jorgenson, volume 30, no. 4 of "The Debate Over the Patristic Texts

on Purgatory at the Council of Ferrara-Florence, 1438," (St. Vladimir's Theological Quarterly, 1986), 311–312). In fact, the whole debate centered not on prayers for the dead, but "purgatorial fire" and the Greek's fear that such a "fire" smacks of Origenism and his doctrine of *apocatastasis* (ibid., 326) (see *Acta Sacri Oecumenici Concilii Florentini ab Horatio Instiniano* (*Romae: Typis Sac. Congr. de Fide Propaganda*, 1638)).

476 Although Nicaea was a watershed moment, Arianism still persisted. Many Eastern bishops still disputed Nicaea's use of the word *homoousios*, and even when uniformity was achieved in the late fourth century, Arianism continued among medieval Germanic tribes until the seventh century.

477 Breen, *Introduction*, 510.

478 The *Decree on the Reunification of the Jacobites* was accepted.

479 Jerome's *Prologue to the Book of Kings*. Emphasis added.

480 As quoted in Breen, *Introduction*, 512.

481 See Breen, *Introduction*, 512.

482 *Prologue to the Gospels* as quoted in Breen, *Introduction*, 267–268. Emphasis added.

483 Quoted in Breen, *Introduction*, 268.

484 Breen, *Introduction*, ibid. Breen points out that in Chronicle III, 11, 2 Antoninus was unable to recall the issues addressed in the reunion of the Jacobites and Armenians.

485 See Breen, *Introduction*, 513, and Westcott, *Bible*, 199, and Gigot, *Introduction*, 71.

486 See Breen, *Introduction*, 514.

487 James Lyell, *Cardinal Ximenes, with an Account of the Complutensis Polyglot Bible*, (London: Grafton, 1917), 27.

488 As quoted in Gigot, *Introduction*, 72.

489 Lyell, *Cardinal Ximenes, with an Account of the Complutensis Polyglot Bible*. 29.

490 As quoted in Westcott, *Bible*, 252.

491 *Exposition on the Creed*, 10 as quoted in Westcott, *Bible*, 253.

492 Erasmus, Malou, II, 108 as quoted in Breen, *Introduction*, 514.

493 Warren H. Carroll, *The Cleaving of Christendom* (Christendom Press, 2001), 4, 10.

494 *Commentary on Esther*, as quoted in Breen, *Introduction*, 514–515.

495 Like Tostatus and Erasmus, Cajetan confuses the usefulness of Scripture with its inspired authority.

496 *Conc. Senonse*, Decr., 4, ap. Hard., ix, 1939. See Reuss, *History*, 273.

497 The Council of Trent is the first council in history to raise the belief in Scripture to the level of an article of faith. As Daubney comments, "But to those who regard the Church of Rome as an enemy to the full use of the scriptures, the fact that Pope Pius's creed should be the first to contain an express declaration of belief in holy Scripture must seem strange."

Daubney, *Use of the Apocrypha*, 49.

498 *DS-H* 1502–1505.

499 That is, the Creed, or "Symbol of the Faith."

500 Peter G. Duncker, "The Canon of the Old Testament at the Council of Trent," *CBQ* 15 (1953), 281.

501 Asked by Cardinal Cervini. See Duncker, "Canon," *CBQ 15* (1953): 283.

502 Breen, *Introduction*, 517.

503 Duncker, *Trent*, 284.

504 See Duncker, *Trent*, 285; Breen, *Introduction*, 517; R.E. Murphy, "Old Testament Canon," *CBQ* 28 (1966), 192.

505 Breen, *Introduction*, 518.

506 It appears that Cardinal Madruzzo, the bishop of Trent, was willing to accept Florence's canon. He wished that the council would also refute the arguments of the heretics. See Duncker, *Trent*, 284.

507 Non-Catholics often misunderstand the meaning of the *anathema*, believing that it damns those under it to hell and that Protestants, by rejecting Catholic doctrine, are under an anathema. But, since anathema means the application of the canonical penalty of excommunication, it applies only to those who are under canon law. Non-Catholics are not members of the Catholic Church and therefore do not fall under canon law. Moreover, they cannot be excommunicated since they are not in communion with the Church. Finally, it should be noted that the anathema as a technical theological term does not mean damning someone to hell. As Jimmy Akin puts it, "An anathema was a formal way of signaling him that he had done something gravely wrong, that he had endangered his own soul, and that he needed to repent. Anathemas, like other excommunications, were thus *medicinal* penalties, designed to promote healing and reconciliation." Jimmy Akin, "Are YOU 'Anathema'? How about Your Protestant Friend?" National Catholic Register, http://www.ncregister.com/blog/jimmy-akin/are-you-anathema-how-about-your-protestant-friend.

508 Duncker, *Trent*, 288; Jedin, *Council of Trent*, 2:55-57.

509 See Duncker *Trent*, 290.

510 G. Reid, "Canon of the Old Testament" in the *Catholic Encyclopedia* (New York: Robert Appleton Company, 1908) accessed May 12, 2017 from New Advent. http://www.newadvent.org/cathen/03267a.htm. Emphasis added.

511 Unfortunately, when this thought was condensed into a brief summary for the *New Catholic Encyclopedia* (1968), the author rephrased the point inaccurately: "According to Catholic doctrine, the proximate criterion of the biblical canon is the infallible decision of the Church. This decision was not given until rather late in the history of the Church (at the Council of Trent). Before that time there was some doubt about the canonicity

of certain biblical books, i.e., about their belonging to the canon" (L.F. Hartman, "Canon, Biblical" in vol. 3 of the *New Catholic Encyclopedia* (New York: McGraw Hill, 1968), 29). By phrasing it this way, Hartman makes it sound as if Trent was the first infallible pronouncement on the canon since others didn't bring about uniformity on the issue. This, of course, is not a proper text for whether a pronouncement is dogmatic. Trent was the first pronouncement that was infallible *and* effectual.

512 See *Pope Nicholas I.*

513 Duncker, *Trent*, 291; *Letter* 303, CT, X, 382–383.

514 See Breen, *Introduction*, 430; Reuss, *History*, 285.

515 See Westcott, *Bible*, 227–228.

516 In later centuries, Philaretes incorporated these views in the *Russian Catechism* of 1868. See Breen, *Introduction*, 430.

517 Breen, *Introduction*, 430. The Synod of Jerusalem (Jassy) understood that the omission of books from lists (e.g., the Council of Laodicea) and those of some of the early Fathers (e.g., Gregory of Nazeanzus) was not a rejection of the book's inspired status. They were not treated as apocrypha ("pagan or profane"), but Scripture (accepted as "good and excellent"). See Westcott, *Bible*, 229.

518 *DS* 1787 and *DS* 1808. Vatican I attached an anathema to any who deny Trent's decree on the canon. Emphasis added.

519 Owen Chadwick, no. 6 of the UBS Monograph Series in *The Apocrypha in Ecumenical Perspective*, United Bible Societies, ed. Siegfried Meurer (trans. Paul Ellingworth), (Read, New York), 120. Moreover, every Bible produced by the Protestant *Society for the Promotion of Christian Knowledge* (SPCK) before 1743 contained the deuterocanon.

520 These influences include Johann Reuchlin (1455–1522), who in 1506 published a Hebrew grammar and dictionary called *Rudimenta Hebraica*, which later became a standard manual for learning Hebrew for all students north of the Alps. He certainly influenced Johann Staupitz, Martin Luther (who became the friend of Staupitz in Erfurt), Andrew Bodenstein (also known as Karlstadt), and perhaps Philip Melancthon, his grandnephew. Luther was also schooled in the *via moderna* that is Nominalism, which has its roots with William of Occam. He also was a devotee of Nicholas of Lyra. Although these influences may have shaped Luther's thinking, they did not turn him into a Jeromist. He was too independent for that. Instead, Luther's own theology would dictate his views on the canon, although St. Jerome did provide him with a prestigious authority to bolster his rejection of the deuterocanon.

521 Martin Luther, vol. 1 of *Resolutiones Disputationum de Indulgentiarum Virtute.* (*D. Martin Luthers Werke*), (Weimar: Hermann Böhlaus Nachfolger, 1883), 522–628.

522 See Martin Brecht, *Martin Luther: His Road to Reformation, 1483–1521* (Minneapolis: Fortress Press, 1985), 219.

523 Bernard Lohse, *Martin Luther: An Introduction to His Life and Work* (Philadelphia: Fortress Press, 1980), 125.

524 Martin Luther, vol. 1 of *Luthers Werk*, (Weimar), 529.

525 Ibid., 559.

526 Ibid., 591.

527 Martin Luther, vol. 1 of *Ad Dialogum Silvestri Prieratis de Potestate Papae Responsio. Luthers Werke*, (Weimar), 644–686.

528 Martin Luther, in vol. 1 of *In Praesumpturas Martini Lutheri conclusiones de potestate Papae Dialogus.*

529 Martin Luther, vol. 1 of *Luthers Werk*, (Weimar), 647.

530 Howorth, *Bible*, 12.

531 Martin Luther, *Luther's Works, Vol. 31: Career of the Reformer I*, eds. Jaroslav Jan Pelikan, Hilton C. Oswald, and Helmut T. Lehmann (Philadelphia: Fortress Press, 1999), 47.

532 Martin Luther, vol. 1 of *Luthers Werke*, (Weimar), 358. Emphasis added.

533 As quoted in *Luther's Works*, 31, 47, FN 7.

534 For example, the first line of the very next thesis (thesis 10) translates the Latin *Scriptura* as Scripture. Compare "This I prove in the following way: *Scripture* does not speak of dead things" (emphasis added) with the Latin *Probo: Quia scriptura non habet istum de mortius loquendi modum.*

535 Luther's *protestatio* in his *Reply to Prierias* comes close to proclaiming *sola scriptura.* Later, Luther makes a similar statement at the Diet of Worms (1521).

536 Martin Luther, as quoted in Breen, *Introduction*, 516. Luther's words seem to echo those of Robert Helot. Emphasis added.

537 See Henry Howorth, "The Bible Canon of the Reformation," *IJA*, 20, Series VI (1910), 8–10.

538 Luther knew that Eck's interpretation of Maccabees was unassailable and the Church's acceptance of Maccabees could not be ignored. Luther, in what Sundberg called "an argument of desperation," first appealed to Jerome and then posited that the Church is not competent to determine the canon. (Also see Albert Sundberg, Jr., "The Protestant Canon: Should It Be Re-Examined?" *CBQ* 28 (1966), 195).

539 Howorth, *Bible*, 14.

540 The First Vatican Council stated, "But the Church holds these books as sacred and canonical, not because . . . *they were approved by its authority* . . . but because, having been written by the inspiration of the Holy Spirit, they have God as their author and, as such, they have been handed down to the Church itself" (*DS-H* 3006). Emphasis added.

541 Or as Johann Eck replied, *Cum doctissimi fuerint in eo consilio viri, malo credere*

concilio quod a spiritu sancto regitur quam domino Luthero, non quod concilium faciat aliquid de scriptura quod non sit, sed quod credam concilium melius habere sen sum et intelligentiam scriptu rarum decernendo hoc esse de scriptura quod in scriptura reperitur.

542 This thesis is further explored and demonstrated in *The Case for the Deuterocanon.*

543 See *Works of Martin Luther,* United Lutheran Church in America, trans. C.M. Jacobs (Philadelphia: Muhlenberg Press, 1932), 6.363ff. Also see Reuss, *History,* 321.

544 See Robert C. Dentan, *The Apocrypha, Bridge of the Testaments* (Greenwich, Connecticut: Seabury, 1954), 18–19. Also Metzger, *Introduction,* 181.

545 Luther's evaluation of these books is explained in detail in the prefaces to this German translation. For example, Luther believed that the Epistle of James was "not the writing of an apostle" because it was "Flatly against St. Paul and the rest of Scripture" by ascribing "righteousness to works." He, therefore, could not put James "among the chief books" (Preface to the Epistles of James and Jude, 1522).

546 See Henry Howorth, "The Bible Canon Among Later Reformers," *JTS* 10 (1909), 207–08.

547 Luther is, quite literally, guilty of the charge commonly launched against Catholicism by Protestants today. He has, to paraphrase Scripture, made void the word of God by his own tradition.

548 For a detailed summary of the early Christian "canonical" use of the deuterocanon, see *The Case for the Deuterocanon,* 106–238.

549 This phenomenon can be seen in the earliest Christian editions of the Old Testament (e.g., the great Codices, the Old Latin, and various codices of the *Latin Vulgate*).

550 Dentan, *The Apocrypha,* 18–19.

551 Luther's German Bible (1545), as quoted in Metzger, *Introduction,* 183.

552 A few words ought to be said about the term *apocrypha.* Daubney follows Lightfoot in distinguishing three particular stages of development of this term: "*Firstly,* it was taken to designate those books which were 'held in reserve and studied privately' but not read in church (orig. Ep. Ad Afric. 9). *Secondly,* it came to denote books affected by heretics, and carried with it the ideas of 'spurious' and 'heretical' (Iren. I. xx. 1); and *Thirdly,* it was applied to non-canonical books whether genuine or spurious (Jer. Prol. Gal. 1)" (Daubney, 3). Emphasis his. Later, Jeromists distorted this term in an attempt to reconcile Jerome with the Church (e.g., Alcuin, *Against Elipandus,* Book 1, 18; Peter Comestor, *Preface to the Book of Joshua;* and possibly Hugh of St. Cher, *Postillea in Joshua,* prologue). By Luther's time, the term had been so distorted as to render it practically useless. For example, even some fathers of the Council of Trent, who argue for the

full canonicity and inspiration of the deuterocanon, call them apocrypha. The Evangelical Lutheran Church recognizes this broad medieval definition in its joint statement on the canon of Scripture. See *Lutheran-Orthodox Dialogue: Agreed Statements 1985–1989* (Geneva: Lutheran World Federation, 1992), 22 and footnote.

553 Indeed, Luther's *German Translation* was not considered a complete Bible until the "Apocrypha" section was completed. See vol. 1 of *The Cambridge History of the Bible: The West from the Reformation to the Present Day*, ed. S.L. Greenslade (Cambridge: Cambridge University Press, 1963), 96.

554 The New Testament deuterocanon consists of the epistle to the Hebrews, James, Jude, and Revelation.

555 The Protestant theologian Wilhelm H. Neuser notes that Luther's new arrangement of the Old Testament "broke radically with previous Church tradition" ("The Reformed Churches and the Old Testament Apocrypha" in *The Apocrypha In Ecumenical Perspective*, UBSMS 6 (United Bible Societies, 1991), 89).

556 Howorth, *Bible*, 25. Emphasis added.

557 See Westcott, *History*, 270. Emphasis his. Oecolampadius's list omits the deuterocanonical sections of Esther and the book of Hebrews. Howorth, *Bible*, 27.

558 Neuser, *Apocrypha*, 90.

559 *Preface to the 1531 Zurich Bible* as quoted in Neuser, *Apocrypha*, 91.

560 As quoted in Neuser, *Apocrypha*, 91. Emphasis added.

561 The public reading of a book in church attests to the belief that a given book is Scripture since the ancient liturgy, like the synagogue before it, held a special station for the reading of Sacred Scripture.

562 Scholars believe this first preface is not the work of John Calvin, but his cousin Olivetan.

563 As quoted in Neuser, *Apocrypha*, 93.

564 As quoted in Neuser, *Apocrypha*, 95–96.

565 Cholinus in the 1542 *Latin Bible* stated that Sirach was written in Hebrew. See Neuser, *Apocrypha*, 96.

566 The decree of the fourth session addressed the authority of apostolic Tradition, the canon of the Old and New Testaments, and the *Latin Vulgate* as the authoritative translation for theological debate.

567 John Calvin, *Antidote to the Council of Trent, Session Four*, trans. Henry Beveridge (Edinburgh, 1851), 69.

568 Ibid., 68. Emphasis added.

569 Ibid., 70–71.

570 John Calvin, *The Institutes of the Christian Religion*, book 1, ch. 8, section 10, 80; the Beveridge translation erroneously has Calvin discussing 1

Maccabees 12:43; 2 Maccabees 12:43 is the correct citation. The quotation from Augustine comes from *Contra Gaudentium*, 31, 38.

571 We have already discussed this point earlier in our treatment of Augustine. Augustine's comments about Maccabees being profitable if read or heard with soberness is true for any book of the Bible.

572 Calvin, *Institutes*, book 3, 5, section 8.

573 Ibid., 441 (book 4, 9, section 14).

574 Neusner, *Apocrypha*, 101. Calvin has it backward. It's from Scripture that we learn true doctrine, not from doctrine that we determine which books are Scripture.

575 Ibid., 102–103.

576 This is a gross generalization. Neither the protocanonical nor deuterocanonical books of Scripture were immune from questions or doubts by individuals. What matters is whether these doubts reflected the Church as a whole or the theological speculations of the individual.

577 *Belgic Confession*, article 5 as quoted in Philip Schaff's vol. 3 of *The Creeds of Christendom: The Evangelical Protestant Creeds with Translations* (New York: Harper & Brothers, 1919), 386–387.

578 Ibid.

579 *Gallican Confession*, IV, as quoted in Schaff, *Creeds*, vol. 3, 361–362. Here, the confession was apparently applying the following text from Calvin's *Institutes* to the canon: "But although we may maintain the sacred word of God against gainsayers, it does not follow that we shall forthwith implant the certainty which faith requires in their hearts. Profane men think that religion rests only on opinion, and, therefore that they may not believe foolishly, or on slight grounds desire and insist to have it proved by reason that Moses and the prophets were divinely inspired. But I answer that the testimony of the Spirit is superior to reason. For as God alone can properly bear witness to his own words, so these words will not obtain full credit in the hearts of men, until they are sealed by the inward testimony of the Spirit (*Institutes of the Christian Religion*, book 1, chapter 7, 72).

580 See Neuser, *Apocrypha*, 106.

581 From the ninth and tenth sessions as quoted in Howorth, "The Bible Canon Among the Later Reformers," *JTS* 10 (1909), 224–225.

582 *The Epigones: A Study of the Theology of the Genevant Academy at the Time of Wiliam McComish* (Eugene, OR: Pickwick Publications, 1989), 57. Remonstrants were the Armenian party in the Dutch Reformed Church.

583 Metzger, *Introduction*, 185–186.

584 Bruce, *Canon*, 102–103. Bruce and others point out that the book order of Tyndale's New Testament follows closely that of Luther's German Bible and suggest that he would have followed Luther in the Old Testament.

585 Bruce, *Canon,* 103.
586 Reuss, *History*, 339–340. Translator's note.
587 *Hagiographa* is the Greek title of the third section of the Hebrew Scripture known as the Writings. Its use here implies that the deuterocanon is part of the third division of the Old Testament.
588 Reuss, *History*, 340. Emphasis added.
589 Episcopalians also hold these articles to be authoritative.
590 *The Thirty-Nine Articles of the Church of England Illustrated by Copious Extracts from the Liturgy, Homilies, Nowell's Catechism, and Jewell's Apology and Confirmed by Numerous Passages of Scripture*, ed. William Wilson (Oxford: W. Baxter, 1821), 29–30.
591 Ibid., 189. Article 35. Emphasis added.
592 Daubney, *Use of the Apocrypha*, 67–68.
593 Ibid., 69.
594 The Greek means literally "every Scripture."
595 For example, Catholics may find purgatory taught both in the protocanon and deuterocanon. Daubney's solution would prescribe that the deuterocanon can only be used to confirm doctrine that is found in the New Testament *as explicated* by the *Articles.* In effect, this solution places the *Articles* as the determiner of Scripture.
596 *Westminster Confession*, 1, 3.
597 As quoted in Goodspeed, *Apocrypha*, 6.
598 John Strype, *The Life and Acts of John Whitgift*, Vol. 1 (Oxford, 1718), 80 as quoted in Daubney, *Use of the Apocrypha,* 72.
599 John Strype, *The Life and Acts of John Whitgift*, 1, 590 (1722 edition) as quoted in Metzger, *Introduction*, 196.
600 Goodspeed, *Apocrypha*, 6. If Goodspeed's assessment is correct, it is frightening to imagine what the Puritans must have thought about certain portions of the protocanon that appear even more sensational and/or of a lower "moral level" than the deuterocanon.
601 The use of "Authorized Version" is misleading since there were two "authorized" texts prior to the Kings James Version.
602 Metzger notes that there were 113 references to the disputed books in the King James Version (1611), with 102 found in the Old Testament and 11 in the New Testament. These 11 New Testament references are listed in Metzger, *Introduction*, 188 FN 6. Emphasis added.
603 Daubney, *Use of the Apocrypha*, 21.
604 Ibid.
605 The Apocrypha-less Bibles were styled as "the new cut" and slowly grew in vogue as something of a new fashion among English Protestants.
606 Edward Arber, *A Transcript of the Registers of the Company of Stationers of London*,

Volume 5 (Birmingham, 1894). Violators were given a year in prison.

607 These were the 1626, 1629, 1630, and 1633 editions.

608 Goodspeed, *Apocrypha*, 7.

609 Out of the 227 printings of the Bible (between 1632 and 1826), only 40 percent included the deuterocanon. See Wilhelm Gundert, "The Bible Societies and the Deuterocanonical Writings" in *The Apocrypha in Ecumenical Perspective* (United Bible Societies, 1991), 135.

610 Anonymous author, *Essay on the Books Commonly Called Apocrypha* (1740).

611 Wilhem Gundert, in "The Bible Societies and the Deuterocanonical Writings" *The Apocrypha in Ecumenical Perspective, UBS Monograph Series* (New York: United Bible Societies), 135.

612 Biased footnotes and skewed prefaces had long been tools for proselytizing. Unsuspecting Bible readers unwittingly use these footnotes to interpret Scripture in line with the particular sect that published the Bible. The British and Foreign Bible Society in London tried to avoid this type of sectarianism by printing bibles without footnotes or commentaries. See *The Third Statement of the Committee of the Edinburgh Bible Society, Being a Statement Respecting Their Conference, on April 4, 1826, With a Deputation From the Committee of the British and Foreign Bible Society, relative to the Circulation of the Apocrypha* (Edinburgh: W. Whyte & Co.), 4.

613 Haldane was a supporter of the British and Foreign Bible Society when he learned, almost by accident, that the Society had committed funds to print bibles with the deuterocanon.

614 Gundert, *Bible Societies*, 137.

615 "We conceive that the very terms in which the designs and character of the Society are declared, in the body of rules and regulations, do fully admit of the circulation of the Scriptures, as they are received by different established churches throughout the world; and we wish it to be considered whether the whole spirit of the Society, as breathing love to mankind, and a desire for the salvation of the world, be not contravened by the resolution in question" (London Bible Society, March 21, 1825).

616 This can be seen in an article quoted from *The Eclectic Reviewers* without title or author in *The Third Statement*, 108–109.

617 "[T]he Apocrypha is no part of the word of God. We are aware that it may be quite lawful for us to propagate many things, which are not inspired. But to these . . . we should make the same objection, and hold it good; because when we send them interspersed with the Bible, or in company with it, so as to arrogate the same authority which it possesses, and claim the same submission which it demands, we corrupt the holy communication of heaven—we put the wisdom, or it may be the folly, of man on a level with the unerring counsels of God—and we so far endeavor

to counteract the effect, as well as degrade the character, of divine revelation. This maxim applies to the ablest and the purest of mere human productions; and to say that least of it, we see nothing in the Apocrypha which for us to know that it is not the word of God, to satisfy us that we do wrong, and commit sin, when we give it to any of our fellow creatures, under the designation, or wearing on it appearance, of the word of God" (*Second Statement*, 15).

618 Edinburgh Bible Society, *Second Statement*, 16.

619 The "fundamental teachings" that the deuterocanon is said to strike against was not the protocanon, but the society's interpretation of the protocanon. Catholicism has no difficulty harmonizing the teachings of the deuterocanon with the protocanon.

620 Edinburgh Bible Society, *Second Statement*, 16–17, paragraph 3. Emphasis added.

621 The traditional format being the deuterocanon intermixed with the protocanon. This is the format of the most ancient Christian codices and canonical lists.

622 Edinburgh Bible Society, *Second Statement*, 17–18, paragraph 3. Emphasis added.

623 Ibid., 17–18. Emphasis added.

624 Ibid., *Second Statement*, 51–52. Emphasis added.

625 This "purification" was to be total. All references to the deuterocanon in the table of contents, footnotes, and even the cross-references were to be entirely omitted: "But, besides notes and comments in the contents, and marginal references to the parts of holy Scripture, there are many marginal references to the Apocrypha, also. *This we hold to be a recognition of the Apocrypha as an inspired record. It is employed to prove and illustrate divine truth dogmatically, which presupposes it to be a part of the divine revelation.* And though the Apocrypha is excluded from the volume that is circulated, this reference to it, in common with the accompanying references to passages of Holy Writ, must give the reader an impression of both being on a level in point of origin and authority. And this being done, Apocryphas [sic] are to be had in abundance for consultation by those who are thus prepossessed with reference for them as part of God's word. [e.g., 1 Corinthians 10:25–Baruch 6:28; 1 Timothy 1:18–Sirach 46:1; 2 Corinthians 9:7–Sirach 35:9]" (*Second Statement*, 135–136). Emphasis added. No trace of the deuterocanon was left behind. This omission was so complete that, as Goodspeed laments, "Very few people nowadays know that the Apocrypha are, much less what they have to say" (Goodspeed, *Apocrypha*, 11).

626 *Westminster Confession*, Chapter 1, Section 6.

627 Edinburgh Bible Society, *Second Statement*, 50.

628 Ibid., 17, paragraph 3. Emphasis added.

629 Ibid., 50. Emphases theirs and mine.

630 From "Twenty-One Reasons for Not Contributing to the Circulation of the Apocrypha Among the Churches Which Deem It Canonical," Edinburgh Bible Society, *Second Statement*, 4. Emphasis added.

631 Edinburgh Bible Society, *Second Statement, 39.*

632 Ibid., 108. Emphasis added.

633 Opposition came from both moderate and liberal Protestants in the Church of England as well as Bible societies on the continent of Europe.

634 Edinburgh Bible Society, *Second Statement*, 54. Emphasis added.

635 Bruce, *Bible*, 112. Emphasis added.

636 Metzger, *Introduction*, 102.

637 Howorth, "The Bible Canon Among the Later Reformers," *JTS* 10 (1909), 215.

638 Ray Allen Billington, *The Protestant Crusade 1800–1860*, (Gloucester: Peter Smith, 1963), 42–43.

639 Few Americans are aware how deeply rooted anti-Catholicism is in American culture and that these anti-Catholic movements spawned violent assaults against Catholics and Church property. For further reading, I recommend Ray Billington's *The Protestant Crusade* (see FN 727); Mark J. Hurley's *The Unholy Ghost: Anti-Catholicism in the American Experience* (Our Sunday Visitor, 1992); and more recently Philip Jenkins, *The New Anti-Catholicism: The Last Acceptable Prejudice* (Oxford University Press: 2003).

640 "Notices," *IJA,* 12 (1916), 17.

641 Daubney, *Use of the Apocrypha*, 11 FN 1.

642 Goodspeed, *Apocrypha,* 10–11.

643 *The Case for the Deuterocanon: Evidence and Arguments* contains an extensive list of how the early Fathers of the first four centuries of the Church used these books both in regard to their inspiration and their ability to confirm doctrine, and their use alongside protocanonical quotations.

644 Metzger, *Introduction*, 181.

645 In the first edition, my comments on Luther suggested he denied the existence of purgatory. This was an unfortunate parochial choice of words. What I meant was that Luther denied the full Catholic understanding of purgatory (the Ninety-Five Theses include some brief descriptions of his own view). At this point in Luther's life and theological development, he still believed in a kind of purgatory but one that looked very different from what was given, for example, at the Council of Florence.

646 Luther's comment that Maccabees "is of weight with the faithful, but avails nothing with the obstinate" suggests a spectrum of authority. Likewise, Luther's later comments in the same debate that the Church cannot give

greater authority and strength to a book than it already possesses by its own virtue. Once again, the notion of greater or lesser authority and strength does not fit the modern binary of inspired/non-inspired or canonical/non-canonical, but it does fit Luther's "canon-within-a-canon" view.

647 Neuser, "The Reformed Churches and the Old Testament Apocrypha" in "The Apocrypha in Ecumenical Perspective," 88.

648 Ibid.

649 For a more detailed treatment on this question see *The Case for the Deuterocanon*, 245–249.

650 Emanuel Tov, "The Status of the Masoretic Text in Modern Text Editions of the Hebrew Bible" in *The Canon Debate* (Hendrickson Publishers, 2002), 241–242.

651 Ibid., 240. This squares very well with what we have seen concerning Akiva and the redefinition of Judaism under his auspices.

652 Albert C. Sundberg Jr., "The Protestant Canon: Should It Be Re-examined?" *CBQ* (1966), 28, 202–203.

653 *Preface to the 1531 Zurich Bible* as quoted in Neuser, *Apocrypha*, 91.

654 Luther's view of the deuterocanon was much higher than that of Protestantism a generation or two later. Calvin considered these writings holy and useful for Christians to read as well, although he notes that others had a different opinion.

655 John Hey, vol. 4 of *Lectures on Divinity Delivered in the University of Cambridge* (Cambridge: Parker, 1797), 490.

656 See *The Case for the Deuterocanon*, 92–93.

657 For example, anti-Catholics sometimes appeal to the Councils of Carthage and Hippo as authentic expressions of the ancient view of the New Testament canon, while ignoring that these very same councils also define the Old Testament canon with the deuterocanon.

658 The word *apostolic*, in Luther's theology, does not mean any historical connection to the apostles. It means only that it "preached Christ" like the apostles.

659 Charles A. Briggs, *General Introduction to the Study of Holy Scripture* (New York: Charles Scribner's Sons, 1899).

660 Metzger, *Introduction*, 199.

661 Francis De Sales, pt. 2, art. 1, c. 6 of *The Catholic Controversy, St. Francis De Sales's Defense of the Faith*, trans. H.B. Mackey (Rockford: TAN Books and Publishers, 1989), 112.

662 It would appear to violate Exodus 20:12; Deuteronomy 5:16; Matthew 5:14; 19:19; et al.

663 This method also violates the principle of *sola scriptura* since it places one's intellectual prowess and investigative abilities as the norm that sets the norm of Scripture. See Appendix 1.

664 Reuss, *History*, 361.

665 *DS-H* 186. (Latin, Esdras, *liberi duo.*)

666 See Oesterley, *Introduction*, 133.

667 Jerome, *Preface to the Book of Kings*. Emphasis added.

668 *Preface to the Book of Psalms* in Eusebius, *History*, 6, 25.

669 Both Cyril (*Catechetical Letters*, IV. 33) and Rufinus (*Commentary on the Apostles Creed*) speak of two books of Ezra, "which the Hebrews reckon one." This cannot be the books of Esdras and Ezra-Nehemiah since rabbinic Judaism never accepted the books of Esdras as canonical, nor did they combine the book of Esdras and Ezra-Nehemiah into one book.

670 John Betts composed an excellent treatment of this problem in his article "Esdras and the Early Church: A Response to William Webster," http://www.catholic-legate.com/articles/esdras.html.

671 T.C. Vrezen and A.S. van der Woude, *Ancient Israelite and Early Jewish Literature*, trans. Brian Doyle, (Boston: Brill, 2005), 517–518.

672 C. Souvay, "Esdras" in *The Catholic Encyclopedia* (New York: Robert Appleton Company, 1909. Retrieved May 15, 2017 from New Advent) http://www.newadvent.org/cathen/05535a.htm.

673 Metzger, *Introduction,* 11–12.

674 Beckwith, *Old Testament*, 174. Emphasis added.

675 Ibid., 186.

676 Ibid., 339–340. Emphasis added.

677 *Concilium Tredentinum: Diariorum, Actorum, Epistularum, Tractatuum* (Nova Collectio) edidit Societas Goerresiana, Tomus Quintus. Question four of the *Captia Dubitationum*, 41, lines 30–31.

678 Ibid., 52, lines 22–32.

INDEX

1 Clement, 83-84, 87
2 Esdras (Esdras B), 317
2QSir, 45
4Q197-200, 45
7Q2, 45
A Dialogue against Martin Luther's Presumptuous Theses Concerning the Power of Pope, 240
Abbott, George, 275
Acusilaus of Argos, 38
Adoptionism, 185
Aegidius, 198, 201
Aelia Capitolina, 81
African Code, 164-165
Against Apion, 34, 37-38, 183
Against Elipandus, 185-186
Against Peter of Bruys, 200
Akiva ben Joseph, 42, 74-82, 114
Alcuin, 184-186, 188
Aleppo, Codex, 28
Alexander of Alexandria, 112-113
Alexandrinus (A), Codex, 168, 235
Alfrick, 197
Alphonso de Zamora, 223
Alphonso of Alcala, 223
Alphonsus Tostatus, 219-221
Ambrose of Milan, 138, 154
Amiatinus (A), Codex, 186
Amphilochius of Iconium, 132, 181
Anastasius II, Pope, 164
Anastasius of Jerusalem, 180
Anastasius of Sinai, 179
Anna the Prophetess, 46
Antidote to the Council of Trent, 253
Antioch, Council of, 83, 109, 137, 145, 180
Antiochus IV, King, 55
Antoninus, 90, 114, 222
Aphraates, 111-113
Apollinaris, 145
Apology Against Faustus the Manichean, 156
Apostolic Canons, 164, 180, 190
Apostolic Fathers, 83, 88-90, 96
Aquila, 77, 82, 114
Archelaus, 109, 113
Armenian Scripture, 164
Artaxerxes I, King, 18, 34-38, 42
Athanasius, 117-125, 127, 130, 132, 140, 164
Athenagoras, 96, 113
Augustine of Hippo, 138, 153-160, 177, 179, 207-208, 225, 240-241, 244, 254-256, 318-319, 321
Avot of Rabbi Natan, 75
b. Baba Bathra 14b, 28
b. Baba Bathra 12b, 35, 38, 42
Baba Kamma 92b, 25
Babylonian Talmud, 40
Barmby D.D., James, 173
Barnabas, Epistle of 83, 85, 87
Basel, Council of, 212, 216
Basil the Great, 129-130
Becke, Edmund, 265
Beckwith, Roger, 320-323
Bede the Venerable, 181-184, 189, 191
Beleth, Jean, 203
Belgic Confession (1561, rev. 1619), 260, 262
Bertano, Pietro, 231
Biblical inerrancy, 311, 314
Billington, Ray Allen, 289

Bonaventure, 205
Boniface, Pope, 164
Bookends Argument, 26, 29-30
Book of Homilies, 268-270
Bosnians, 216
Bowman, John, 76
Breen, A.E., 9, 106, 111, 132, 152, 170, 182, 222, 231
Briggs, Charles, 307
British and Foreign Bible Society, 277, 279, 284, 286-289
Bruce, F.F., 161, 199, 268, 287
Bucer, Martin, 242
Bunyan, John, 271, 308-309
Burchard of Worms, 197
Cadmus of Miletus, 38
Callistus I, Pope, 99
Calvin, John, 251, 253-259
Calvinism, 235, 272, 280
canon within a canon, 245, 246, 296, 303, 305, 307
Cantata Domino, Bull, 218
Capita dubitationum, 322, 324
Cappadocian Fathers, 129-130
Carthage III, 138, 160-161, 163, 189, 228, 234, 294, 317-318
Carthage IV, 163
Cassiodorus, 110, 175-177
Catacombs, 97
Catechetical Lectures, 125
Cavensis, Codex, 190
Cessation of prophecy theory, 18, 33, 35, 37, 39, 43, 46
Chalcedon, Council of, 179
Chaldeans, 216, 349
Charlemagne Bible, 185
Charlemagne, Emperor, 184
Charles I, King, 235
Charles II, King, 275
Charles, R.H., 291
Cheltenham List, 138
Chrysostom, John, 137-138,
Church of England, 263, 266-267, 270-273
City of God, The, 159, 318
Claromontanus, Codex, 162
Clement of Alexandria, 99, 102, 113
Clement of Rome, 83, 89, 338
Clement VI, Pope, 210
Codex Canonum Ecclesiasticarum, 175
Comestor, Peter, 201, 206
Commentary on the Psalms, 103-105
Commentary on the Symbol of the Apostles, 139, 256
Complutensian Polyglot, 223
Concluding Discourses (1523), 250
Confession of the Catholic and Apostolic Eastern Church, 235
Constans, Emperor, 123
Constantine, Emperor, 110, 112
Constantinople IV, Council of, 190
Constantinople, Synod of, 184
Copts, 179
Costello, Charles J., 160
Council of Rome, see Decree of Damasus I
Coverdale Bible (1535), 263, 291
Cranmer, Thomas, 265-267, 271
creation *ex nihilo*, 87, 108
Cyprian, 95, 100, 113, 160, 256
Cyril Lucar, 234-235
Cyril of Jerusalem, 124, 132, 319
Damasus I, Pope St., 133, 145
Daubney, William H., 211, 268-270, 274
De Divinis Officiis, 200
De Virtutibus et Vitiis, 186
Dead Sea Scrolls, 146, 291, 298, 312
Decree of Damasus, 163
Decree of Pope Gelasius, 164, 195, 197, 208, 228, 231, 318
Decree on Reunion with the Greeks, 216

del Monte, Francesco, 232
Denis of Chartreux, 222
Dialogue Against Martin Luther's Presumptuous Theses Concerning the Power of the Pope, 240
Dialogue Between a Christian and a Jew, 95, 198
Dialogue with the Jew Trypho, 91
Didache, 83, 88
Dionysius Exiguus (the Little), 175
Dionysius the Great, 109, 113
Divine Office, 198, 200, 203
Dort, Synod of, 261-262, 300
Dutch Bible (1637), The, 262
East-West Schism, 190
Ebionites, 246
Ecclesiastical Books, 140-141, 143, 250, 254, 261
Ecclesiastical History of the English People, 182
Eck, Johann Maier von, 242-245, 254, 295
Edersheim, Alfred, 63
Edinburgh Bible Society, 279, 282-285, 299
Eichhorn, Johann, 29
English Revised Version (1895), 291
Ephesus, Council of, 91, 170, 179
Ephraemi Rescriptus (C), Codex, 168
Epiphanius of Salamis, 133-136, 184
Epistle of Polycarp, 87
Erasmus, 224-225
Essenes, 31, 71
Ethiopian canon, 164
Eugene IV, Pope, 216
Eugenius II (the younger), 179
Eusebius Pamphilus, 111
Exsuperius, 162, 165
Faustinus, 163
First Apology, 90
First Clement, 83-85, 87
First Jewish Revolt, 72-74
First Principles, 103-104, 140
Florence, Council of, 5, 212, 215-219, 222, 231-232, 234, 294, 310
Forty-Two Articles (1553), 267
Fourth Ezra, 323, 324
French (Gallican) Confession (1559), *The*, 261
Gates, Milo H., 290, 300
Geisler, Norman, 215, 217-218
Geneva Bible (1540), 251
Geneva Bible (1560), 265
Geneva Bible (1599), 273
George of Antioch, 180
German Translation, Luther's, 238, 246, 251, 277
Gigot, Francis E., 147, 196
Ginzberg, Louis, 79-81
Gislebert (Gilbert Crispin), 198
Glasgow Bible Society, 279
Glossia Ordinaria of Sacram Scripturam, 188-189, 196
Gnostics, 97, 246
Goodspeed, E. J., 273, 275
Grabbe, Lester, 37
Great Bible (1539), 265
Great Codices, 167-168, 170, 192
Gregory II, Pope, 187
Gregory of Nazianzus, 129-130, 132, 181
Gregory of Nyssa, 129
Gregory the Great, Pope St., 171, 187, 210
Grosseteste, Robert, 206
Guido de Bres, 260
Gundert, Wilhelm, 278
Hadrian, Emperor, 80-81, 90, 114
Haldane, Robert, 278
Hampton Court Conferences (1604), 147
Harding, Stephen, 197
Heidelberg Disputation, 241-242

Helmeted Prologue, 148, 174, 177, 187, 204, 211, 224, 227, 231, 296
Helot, Robert, 208
Henry VIII, King, 263, 265-267
Herodotus, 38
Hexapla, 102, 114, 298
Hey, John, 299
Hilary of Poitiers, 106, 128
Hillel the elder, 42
Hippo Regius, The council of, 110, 138, 160-161, 163, 181, 189, 195, 234
Hippolytus of Rome, 98-100, 113
Honorius of Autun, 198, 203
Horne, Andrew, 209-210
Howorth, Henry H., 133, 149, 241, 244-246, 288
Hugh of St. Cher, 206-207
Hugh of St. Victor, 198-200, 213
Iconoclasm, 184, 186-187
Ignatius of Antioch, 83
Ildephonsus, 179
Inclusion and Exclusion method, 76
Infallibility, papal, 172-174, 215-216, 233, 243-244
inner witness approach, 283, 303, 306-307
Innocent I, Pope, 162-163, 165, 189, 195, 228, 231, 298, 318
Institutes of the Christian Religion (1536), 258
Institutes of the Christian Religion (1539), 258
Institutes of the Christian Religion (1559), 256, 261
Irenaeus of Lyon, 86, 96
Isidore of Seville, 177, 188
Islam, 179, 195
Ivo of Chartres, 197
J. Ta'anith, 36
Jacobites, 179, 216, 218, 222
Jamnia, City of, 73-74, 78, 81
Jerome, 5, 8, 110-111, 134, 139, 141-142, 145-153, 156, 161-163, 165, 167, 172, 174-177, 183, 185, 187, 189, 195-197, 199-200, 202-205, 207, 209-213, 215, 220-222, 224-228, 231, 233, 238, 240, 244-245, 248, 250-258, 262, 267, 283, 294, 296-298, 303, 318-319, 322
Jerusalem, Synod of, 235
John Cassian, 164
John Damascene, St., 184
John of Ragusa, 212
John of Salisbury, 203-204, 213
John the Baptist, 30, 46
John XXII, Pope, 210
Josephus, Titus Flavius, 34-38, 42, 111, 182-183, 321
Jud, Leo, 249-250
Julius Africanus, 100, 113, 117, 137, 147, 149, 161, 175, 294
Junilius Africanus, 175
Justin Martyr, 90, 102, 114
Karlstadt, Andreas, 243
Kenyon, Sir. Frederic, 272
King James Bible (1611), 49-50, 273, 275, 289
Lactantius, 110, 113
Laetenur coeli, Bull, 218
Laodicea, Council of, 126, 180, 190, 310
Lateran IV, Council of, 204
Latin Vulgate, 161, 230, 317, 323
Leningrad [St. Petersburg] Codex, 28
Leo X, Pope, 224, 240
Leontius of Byzantium, 170
Letter to Diognetus, 83
Lightfoot, J. B., 60, 88-89
Lohse, Bernard, 239
Luther, Martin, 103, 210-211, 215-218, 224, 226, 237-251, 254, 262,

264, 271, 273, 277, 288, 290, 295-296, 300, 303, 305-308
Maccoloni, Silvester, 240
Magna Moralia, 171, 173
Manes, 109
Marcionites, 246
Maronites of Cyprus, 216
Mary, Queen, 267
Mas1h, 45
Masoretic Text, 57, 77, 146-147, 223-224, 320
Masada, 45, 73
MasSir, 45
Matthew Bible, 264-265
McGriffith, A.C., 95
Melito of Sardis, 92-95, 111, 114
Methodius of Tyre, 110
Metrophanes Critopulus, 235
Metzger, Bruce M., 56, 62, 64-65, 274, 287, 295, 320
Modalism, 112
Mommsen Catalogue, 138
Mommsen, Theodor, 138
Monophysites, 179
Montanists, 98
MT, see Masoretic Text
Muratorian Fragment, 97, 113
Myles Coverdale Bible, 263
Nativist movement, 290
Nestorians, 179
Netter, Thomas, 208
Neuser,William H., 258, 261, 296-297
Neusner, Jacob, 40
New American Standard Bible, 327
Nicaea, Council of, 110-112, 122, 200, 218
Nicaea II, Council of, 184-187
Nicephorus, 187-188
Nicholas I, Pope St., 189-190, 195, 212
Nicholas of Lyra, 209, 213
Nicodemus, 47
Ninety-Five Theses, 237-240
Nominalism, 210
North African councils, see African Code
Notker Balbulus, 191
Oecolampadius, 249
Old Latin translation, 146, 167
Olivetan Bible (1535), 251, 264
On Christian Doctrine, 154, 177, 208, 254-256
On the Unification of the Jacobites, 216
Onesimus, 93-95, 114
Origen of Alexandria, 95, 101-109, 111, 113-115, 117, 121-122, 127, 135, 138-141, 149, 151-152, 155, 294, 298, 319
Osiander, Joseias, 248, 296
Osterley, W.O.E., 181
Parthenius, Patriarch, 235
Paul Coronel of Salamanca, 223
Paul of Constantinople, 180
Paul of Tella, 179
Paulinus (Carolinus), Codex, 185
Peels, H.G., 30
Pelagius II, Pope, 171
Pentry, John, 272
Percival, Henry, 163-165, 181
Peter of Alexandria, 180
Peter of Blois, 204
Peter of Bruys, 200
Peter of Cluny, 200
Peter of Riga, 201
Pharisees, 32, 46, 71, 73, 152
Philistinian Syria, 81
Philo of Alexandria, 23-24
Photius, 189-190
Pilgrim's Progress, 271, 308
Plumptre, E.H., 62
Polycarp of Smyrna, 83, 86-87, 89, 96

Pontian, Pope, 99
Primasius, 174-175, 183
Prologue on the Psalms, 128
Prologue to the Book of Psalms, 106
prophets, *post facto*, 20-21, 34
prophets, public, 20-21, 33
Pseudo-Dionysius Areopagita, 164
Psychopannychia (1542), 258-259
Ptolemy II Philadelphus, 135
Puritans, 271-273, 280
Purvey, John, 211
Quinisext, see Trullo, Council of
Qumran, 23, 45, 73, 297-298, 320
Rabbis Eliezer, 42
Resolutions [or Explanations] of the Disputation Concerning the Power of Indulgences, 239
Resolutions to the Leipzig Disputation, 296
Response to Prierias, 241
Reuss, Edward, 25, 107, 314
Rewritten Scripture, 320, 323
Rhabanus Maurus, 188-189
Rome, Council of, 133, 163
Rudolf of Flavigny, 201
Rufinus of Aquileia, 139-143, 145, 150-152, 155, 250, 254, 256, 319
Rupert of Deutz, 199
Sadducees, 31, 71-73, 119
Samaritans, 31, 71, 74
Samuel the Little, 42
Sardica, Council of, 123
Schaff, Philip, 180
Second Clement, 88
Second Great Awakening, 289
Second Jewish Revolt, 74-75, 78, 80, 82, 90, 92, 114
Second Leipzig Disputation, 243, 246, 295
Seder Olam Rabbah, 35, 39, 42
self-attestation, 303, 308
semi-Pelagianism, 154, 157-160
Sens, Synod of, 228
Septuagint, 56-57, 62, 68, 77, 79-80, 85, 91-92, 114, 135, 146-147, 150, 157-158, 186, 223, 317-318, 321
Seripando, Girolamo, 231
Shepherd of Hermas, 83, 87
Simeon, 46, 78, 81
Simon bar Kokhba, 74-75, 79
Sinaiticus (Aleph), Codex, 168
Sippo MD, Arthur, 172-173, 181
Sixtus V, Pope, 187
Sixty Books, The, 179-180
Statinus (Vallicellianus), Codex, 185
Sundberg, A.C., 298
Symbolum Fidei, 230
Symmachus, 82
Synopsis of Sacred Scripture, 164
Syrians, 216
Syro-Hexaplar, 179
Targum Onkelos, 223
Ten Articles (1536), *The*, 266
Tertullian, 97-98, 100, 102, 113
The Great Bible (1539), 265
The Necessary Doctrine and Erudition of Any Christian Man, 267
The Plea for Christians, 96
Theodore of Mopsuestia, 136, 145
Theodoret of Cyrus, 164
Theodulf of Orleans, 186
Third Maccabees, 265, 323
Thirty-Nine Articles (1562), 267, 270-271 275, 296
Thirty-Ninth Festal Letter, 119, 123, 164
Thomas Aquinas, 205, 207, 222, 226-227
Thomas de Vio (Cajetan), 226-228, 233
Thucydides, 38
Toletanus (T), Codex, 190

Tosefta Sotah, 35, 41-42
Tov, Emmanuel, 297
Treatise on the Resurrection, 96
Trent, Council of, 9, 15, 192, 212, 215-218, 229-235, 237, 253-255, 259, 284, 293-294, 299-300, 317-318, 322-323
Trullo, Council of, 164, 180-181, 190, 195
Tyndale, William, 264
Unigentius Dei Filius, 210
Urban I, Pope, 99
Urim and Thummim, 33, 36, 40
Usha, City of, 81
Vatican I, Council, 11, 174, 234-236
Vaticanus (B), Codex, 168-169, 291
Vincent of Lerins, St., 164
Von Canstein Bible Society, 277
Vulgate, 146-147, 152, 161, 165, 167, 177, 185-186, 196, 198, 215, 223-224, 229-230, 235, 241-242, 248, 253, 317-318, 323
Walafrid Strabo, 188-189
Westcott, B.F., 210
Westminster Confession (1646), 270-271, 283
Whitgift, John, 272
William of Occam, 210, 213
Wycliffe, John, 208, 210-212, 247, 254
Ximenes de Cisneros, Franciscus, 223-224
Y. Taanith, 40
Yadayim, 77
Yahanan ben Zakkai, Rabban, 72-73
Yavne, see Jamnia
Zealots, 72-73
Zechariah the son of Jehoiada, 27-28
Zechariah the son of Barachiah, 26
Zephyrinus I, Pope St., 98-99
Zurich Bible (1531), 249, 299
Zurich Bible (1543), 250
Zwingli, Huldrych, 249-250, 264, 266, 271